Infographics

**Designing
and visualizing
data**

G000045259

promopress

INFOGRAPHICS
Designing and Visualizing Data

Editor: Wang Shaoqiang
English texts revised by: Gwenydd Jones

Copyright © 2014 by Sandu Publishing Co., Ltd.
Copyright © 2014 English language edition by
Promopress for sale in Europe and America.

ISBN: 978-84-16504-92-3

Promopress is a brand of:
Promotora de Prensa Internacional S.A.
C/ Ausias March, 124
08013 Barcelona, Spain
Phone: 0034 93 245 14 64
Fax: 0034 93 265 48 83
info@promopress.es
www.promopresseditions.com
Facebook: Promopress Editions
Twitter: Promopress Editions @PromopressEd

Sponsored by Design 360°
-Concept and Design Magazine
Edited and produced by
Sandu Publishing Co., Ltd.
Book design, concepts & art direction by
Sandu Publishing Co., Ltd.
info@sandupublishing.com

Cover design :
Mot: Graphic Design & Art Direction

First published in English: 2014
Reprinted 2015
Reprinted 2017

Printed in Bosnia and Herzegovina

CONTENTS

Future perspectives in data visualisation

BY FOREIGN POLICY DESIGN

Foreign Policy Design is a team of idea makers and story tellers who help clients develop their brands through the creative and strategic deployment of traditional terrestrial and digital media channels.

Helmed by creative directors Yah-Leng Yu and Arthur Chin, the group works on a smorgasbord of projects, ranging from creative/art direction and design, branding, brand strategy, digital strategy and strategic research to marketing campaign services for fashion and lifestyle brands, fast-moving consumer brands, arts and cultural institutions and think-tank consultancies.

www.foreignpolicydesign.com

PREFACE

We are deep in the digital age. But far from being at its zenith, the age of technology has just started. The connectedness and multiple input/output possibilities of digital devices that provide the option of near-constant information updates have created new standards for exploring the world in novel, dynamic ways. Many companies have also realized the potential behind beautiful infographics, giving designers opportunities to contextualize information in the most creative ways.

What is data visualization? And how is it different from information graphics? To put it simply, data visualization involves the creation and study of the visual representation of data. In the words of Edward Tufte: "The world is complex, dynamic, multidimensional; the paper is static, flat. How are we to represent the rich visual world of experience and measurement on mere flatland?" This is not something new: geometric diagrams and navigational maps dating from the sixteenth century are considered the predecessors of what we call infographics today. As time passed, human population and economic statistics began to be collated for governing purposes, and the subject of data visualization began to be recognized as a field in its own right.

The face of infographics has changed in the last few years, with help from the Internet. The World Wide Web has seen a wave of websites dedicated to data visualization, the most famous of which is *Visual.ly*. In the face of increasing web saturation however, some have come to tire of and question the fate of infographics. So what comes next? Where do we move on from here? Do we really need to quantify everything through visuals? A new challenge has been laid out: to display complex concepts and create fresh and interesting content of incredible quality and utility. Going beyond a vague notion of aesthetics, the information presented needs to be understood not only by the aesthetically inclined, but by the average person as well.

In this book we showcase the innovative techniques used in the latest and freshest infographics, drawn from a wide range of fields of interest. Our intention is simple: to introduce advanced data-related works that push the boundaries of visual imagery. The designers of these infographics show us the world from different perspectives, and as you will see, data visualization has no fixed approach or form of expression. Huge possibilities are left in this field, and it is my hope that the projects presented in this book will inspire many excellent works of data visualization in the future.

FOREIGN POLICY
DESIGN

CATEGORY

BLOCKS

The rectangle, like the square, is one of the most commonly recognized shapes. We see them applied in our everyday lives ‒ From building shapes to our television sets. From bars to squares to cubes, the upcoming pages redefine the rectangle, a celebration of all its four-cornered glory.

CURVES

Fascinations with curves began long before they were the focus of mathematicians — The simple curve is appreciated for its decorative use in art and commonplace objects, such as the colloquial "Stop" sign and Yayoi Kusama's polka-dotted masterpieces.

NETS

There is a complex network of connections running through the chaos of the universe surrounding us. English mathematician Ada Lovelace understood this thoroughly and her studies had a profound influence on Charles Babbage's *Analytical Engine.* Complicated networks, structures and complex organizations are all around us — from a city's transportation network, Facebook (The ultimate social network) and Wall Street's financial markets, it is inevitable that we are part of an interwoven net of data.

CIRCLES

The circle of life — Known since before the beginning of recorded history, the simple circle is the basis of the wheel, which makes up the backbone of gears and modern machinery. Much more than just being used for pie charts, the circle's perfect rotundity establishes it as the most unique and fascinating geometric shape.

→ PROCESS

Process is defined as a series of actions or steps taken in order to achieve a particular end. It is the cornerstone of complex workflows, functions and sequences — Breaking down individual steps as boxes of various kinds, highlighting the important and cutting out the dispensable, ultimately clearing away the fog and seeing things in a new light.

☐ MAPS

Maps, a symbolic representation of physical space. The most amazing fact? Our three-dimensional world is broken down into a two-dimensional piece of paper. With intricate lifework and abstract symbols, maps also help us make sense of the space around us. They lead us down untrodden paths and open doors to new, exciting territories.

▦ DATAGRAM

Bridging the unknown and the familiar — Rather than bombarding us with cold figures, the information is placed within direct context of its intended topic. This makes it easier for readers to draw their own interpretations of the theme in question, at the same time transporting them into a living, breathing scenario which the designer had intended at the start.

▨ DATAPHORIC

Pablo Picasso once said "Everything you can imagine is real" — In this chapter, information as art is explored. Data is used as a means to express personal feelings and to create pieces of art that reach out to our senses and emotions.

DEREK KIM

Network Osaka is the design moniker for Derek Kim, an artist and designer who lives and works in San Francisco, CA. His portfolio includes work for world-class brands, such as Nike, Wieden+Kennedy, Target, Dodge, Nokia, Stanford University, Google and Microsoft, among others.

Q | Please introduce yourself.

A | I am an artist and designer, and currently live in San Francisco, CA. I have a broad range of interests within art and design, including non-traditional art, illustration, typography, poster art, editorial and identity design, and environmental art.

Q | Can you tell us a little about your background and how you came to work in infographic design and data visualization?

A | My first data visualization project was my university thesis, entitled Extinct (http://www.artistascitizen.org/projects/9/extinct). The goal of this project was to raise awareness about the millions of species on the verge of extinction. I created 26 different cards, depicting various endangered species in an abstract form, alluding to the vanishing beauty of the animal kingdom resulting from extinction. This entire project was driven purely by data analytics and infographics, to bring to light the alarming rate of extinction, using tangible evidence and facts.

Q | How did you get started with data visualization and infographic design?

A | For some reason, I have always loved charts; maybe because of my fascination with aircraft interfaces, which are all about data and information.

Q | Which designers do you most admire?

A | Harold Edgerton is a photographer known for his time-lapse photographs. There is something truly graceful and elegant about the way he treats photography, as a visualization tool. The way a golfer swings, a person runs and a ballet dancer performs are perfectly explained in a single image. In the same way, I try to create concise visual images that explain complex information.

Q | Please describe your design process. Do you adhere to any specific routines or techniques?

A | Research always comes first. Once I have gathered the appropriate data, I then map it out using a software program, like Excel. The final phase involves adjusting the visual aspects of the data (type, colours, layout).

TIMES SQUARE

D | Designer: Derek Kim

A data visualization of leading companies, presented through neon signage in Times Square (New York City).

The visual image is divided into six different business sectors: Business/Finance, Media/Entertainment, Food/Dining, Retail/Shopping, Hotel/Accommodation and Consumer Electronics.

Global Warning is a personal project I took up when my family was facing financial difficulties, following the recent economic crisis. Its aim is to educate and create awareness about a topic that most people tend to overlook, until it is too late. Therefore, I created a visual survey of events and statistics summarizing the economic crisis of 2007–2008, and its remnants in the current economy.

This poster was created as a public service, to inform the masses of the missteps that led us to this major global economic collapse and the lessons that have been drawn, for the world to take notice.

GLOBAL WARNING

(D) Designer: Derek Kim

(Q) A lot of infographics might be attractive to look at, but may not make much sense to the average viewer. How do you take a complex chunk of information and make sense out of it?

(A) Trimming the fat is a very common strategy in my approach. I always tend to strip the data down to the essentials, to make it easy to understand. Once I have done that, it is just a matter of slight stylistic visual tweaks.

(Q) What is the most rewarding part of the whole experience?

(A) Being able to disseminate knowledge and educate people.

(Q) Visualization courses are being taught in higher education. What do you make of this? Is formal education necessary for information design?

(A) I have always been self-driven to learn new things, and infographics were no different. I believe creating online resources for everyone to share would be more valuable than formal education. The key is to provide everyone with access to this type of knowledge, not just those who can afford formal education.

(Q) Do you have any advice for aspiring designers who are starting to dip their toes into information design?

(A) Learn how to use Excel. It is a really helpful tool when you are just getting started.

(Q) Do you think it is beneficial for your work to have a signature style?

(A) With infographics, style becomes secondary. The most important thing is to be able to communicate complex pieces of information in a digestible format.

(Q) Myriad topics have been the subject of data visualization. Are there any topics you feel have yet to be approached succinctly?

(A) I have always wondered about the differences in walking patterns between males and females inside a shopping mall, and the areas each gender frequents the most. A random topic, I know, but I have always been curious.

(Q) What excites you most about the future of information design?

(A) The way data is being represented through code is very exciting. The possibilities of being able to map real-time data is especially fascinating to me.

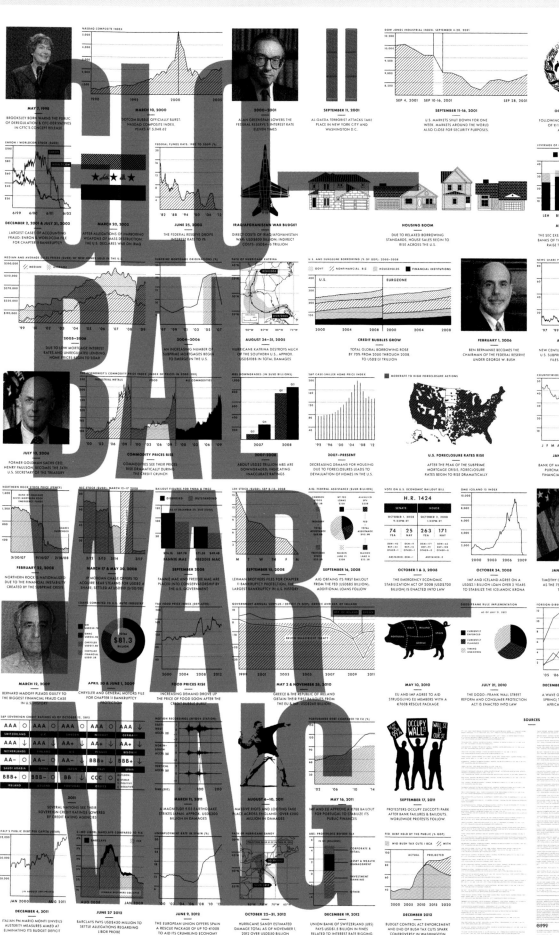

GLOBAL WARNING / DEREK KIM

RELAJAELCOCO

Relajaelcoco is a laid-back graphic design studio, based in Madrid. Their purpose is to spread graphic design all over the world, and improve talent and knowledge.

Q How did you get started with data visualization and infographic design?

A Our passion for synthesis and illustration. For us, this was the most interesting area of graphic design: making powerful use of storytelling and composition, and analyzing how to enrich data and distribute it, so the final user can read it in layers, through a step-by-step composition.

Q Please introduce yourself.

A ¡Hola! We are Pablo Galeano and Francesco Furno, and together we created Relajaelcoco—Spanish for 'Relax your mind'—a fun graphic design studio, based in Madrid. We work in all the different graphic design specializations, like infographics, editorial design, branding, 3D and lettering.

Our process is based on a fresh methodology, which involves mixing rationality and emotions as we try to find the best customized solution for each client.

Q Can you tell us a little about your background and how you came to work in infographic design and data visualization?

A Pablo studied art, and Francesco, economics. We met in Barcelona on a three-year graphic design course, at the IED (Istituto Europeo di Design). Three months later, we decided to form Relajaelcoco.

It was by chance that we started working with infographics, about three years ago. A client of ours asked if we could condense a huge amount of data into an A3 document. We accepted the challenge and came up with our first major project: *The Unbelievable Happiness Process*. Since then, we have received numerous offers from companies asking us to do the same.

HOW TO BE AN INFOGRAPHICS EXPERT

CD Content and Design: Relajaelcoco
C Client: Kartz (Japan)

Produced in five different languages, this infographic was made for Kartz Media Works, Japan, to guide readers on how to be experts in infographics. It also informs readers about the role of a graphic designer.

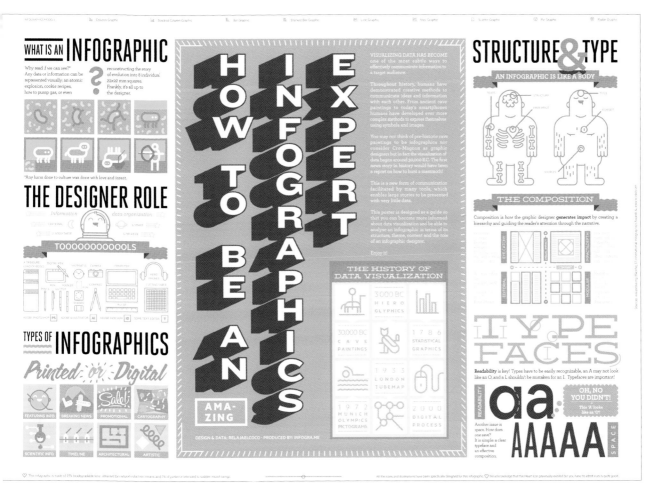

Q Which designers do you most admire?

A We love Francesco Franchi's work, especially his work for IL (*Intelligence in Lifestyle*) magazine. Also, we really like Muti, South Africa; Stefan Sagmeister; Vincent Mahé, France, and numerous others.

Q Please describe your design process. Do you adhere to any specific routines or techniques?

A We usually produce each project while having a lot of fun. Playing is the first step to achieving a high level of enthusiasm, and we use all our energy to do the best we can. Our relationship with the client is the most important aspect for ensuring an effective process. Every project we do is based on a rational procedure, where we try to mix rationality with emotions.

Q A lot of infographics might be attractive to look at, but may not make much sense to the average viewer. How do you take a complex chunk of information and make sense out of it?

A We always consider the final user and reader. The content must be easy to read, but this does not mean it has to be for dummies. The final user is smarter than people think, and the idea is to create a complex structure with a lot of details and hidden references. These enrich the infographic and give the user the opportunity to read it in a minute or an hour, depending on how interested they are in the content.

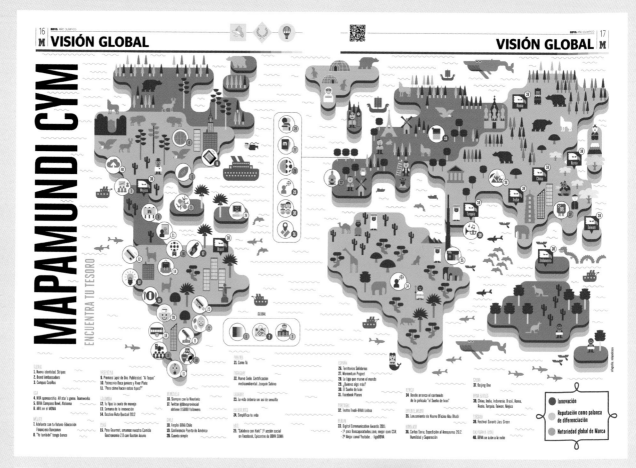

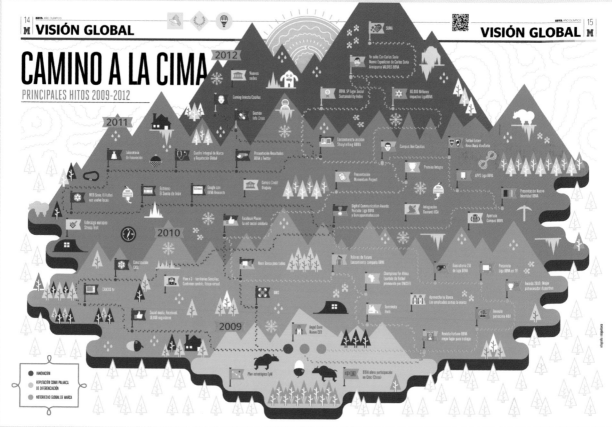

Q What is the most rewarding part of the whole experience?

A The greatest reward is when our customers are satisfied, and the relationship is one of synthesis and respect; when we all enjoy ourselves in the process of producing a complex artwork. When this happens, it also means we were working for a sensitive client, with great respect for the content they want to communicate intelligently.

Q Visualization courses are being taught in higher education. What do you make of this? Is formal education necessary for information design?

BBVA INFOGRAPHICS

AD Art Director: Relajaelcoco
A Agency: Brands & Roses
E Editor: Gregorio Panadero
D Director: Ignacio Villoch
C Coordinator: Mario Tascón (Prodigioso Volcán)

An infographic, based on BBVA data, which documents the biggest milestones of the last few years.

A Actually, we teach infographics at six different educational establishments in Spain. We think data visualization and infographics are essential in the education process. They represent a summary of everything the students have learned: synthesis, composition, typography, branding, colour theory and visual hierarchy.

We live in complex times. The world of information is changing so quickly that more infographics are needed, to let readers take in as much information as they can, in the shortest possible time.

Q Do you have any advice for aspiring designers who are dipping their toes into information design?

A Please remember we are not artists: we work to convey a clear message through each infographic, to let people learn about and understand a specific subject. The data is very important, and the graphic design has to outline it as effectively as possible.

Q Do you think it is beneficial for your work to have a signature style?

A Clients are always looking for something that works. They feel comfortable if another company has worked with us before. As graphic designers, we are trying to reach a kind of visual freedom that allows us to express ourselves the best we can. We usually try to break away from the idea of style, and explain to clients that each project is unique and different.

Q Myriad topics have been the subject of data visualization. Are there any topics you feel have yet to be approached succinctly?

A It would be great to have a website about the globalization of organized crime. There must be a huge amount knowledge, which could be spread worldwide.

Q What excites you most about the future of information design?

A Change is the most exciting part—we are referring to products like Oculus Rif and Google Glass—because augmented reality needs information design more than many other sectors.

FRANCESCO FRANCHI

Francesco Franchi is Art Director at IL, the monthly magazine issued by Il Sole 24 ORE. He is also a journalist, lecturer at IUAV (University of Venice), and visiting lecturer at Domus Academy, IED Milan, IED Barcelona, UCSC (Catholic University of Milan) and the Polytechnic University of Milan, not to mention the author of Designing News.

I think I was lucky because I started working while I was still studying.

I worked at a graphic design studio in Milan, called Leftloft, for 5 years, where I was involved in different projects, based on a range of topics, related to culture, fashion, publishing and brand identity.

As a result of the editorial projects we started at the studio, I was able to get to know the workflow of different newsrooms in Italy (including leading ones, like Corriere della Sera). When I went to *Il Sole 24 Ore*, to develop *IL Magazine*, in May 2008, we tried to apply this paradigm to our newsroom. We attempted to promote the design and infographics aspect (a process I call 'infographic thinking') throughout the whole magazine.

Q Please introduce yourself.

A I am an editorial and information visual designer, a journalist, a lecturer and the author of *Designing News: Changing the World of Editorial Design and Information Graphics* (Gestalten, 2013).

Since 2008, I have been the Art Director at *IL*, the monthly magazine issued by *Il Sole 24 ORE* (the leading Italian finance and economics newspaper). Before that, I worked for five years as a senior designer at *Leftloft*, a Milan-based design studio, dealing with communication design, editorial projects and infographics. I have been a professional journalist since 2010, and am currently a visiting lecturer at Università IUAV di Venezia, Domus Academy, IED Milan and the Polytechnic University of Milan.

Last but not least, I am a member of The Society of Publication Designers, New York, and a professional member of AIAP (Italian Association of Visual Communication Design).

Q Can you tell us a little about your background and how you came to work in infographic design and data visualization?

A I studied graphic design at the Polytechnic University of Milan for 5 years, from 2002 to 2007. I also had an Erasmus year in London, in 2005.

V&A MEMORY PALACE

D Designer: Francesco Franchi

What we decided to do was focus the content on how the reader can be an expert at recognizing the main parts of an infographic artwork, and learn what the role of a graphic designer is.

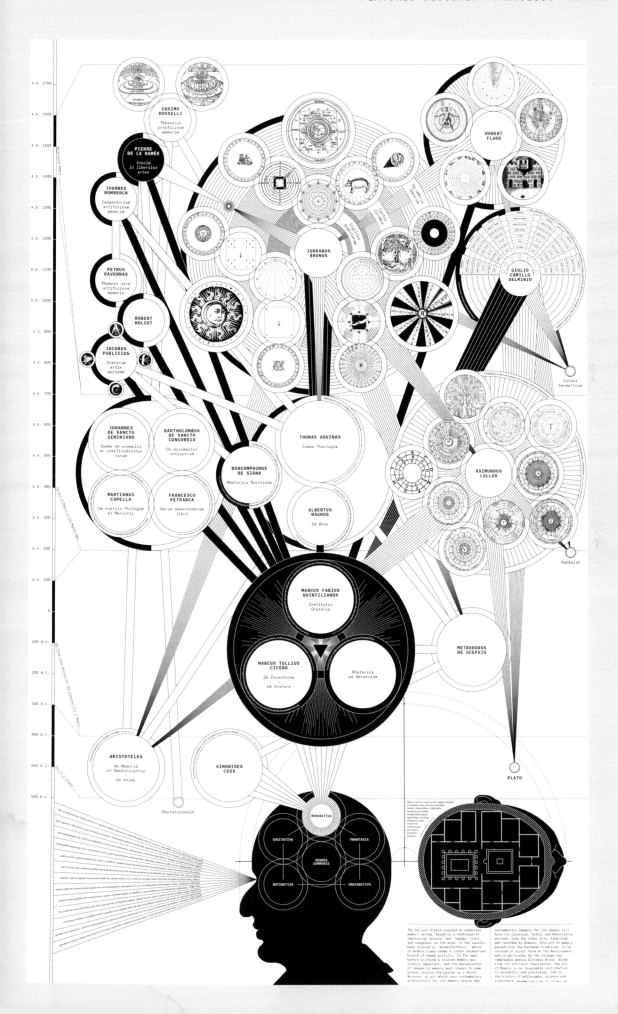

Q How did you get started with data visualization and infographic design?

A Even as a child, I would avoid writing if I could get away with a diagram or drawing. At secondary school, I used to do schematic diagrams of the contents of textbooks, using colours, arrows and infoboxes. I found I learnt quickest that way, and actually enjoyed it.

Q Which designers do you most admire?

A Bruno Munari, Le Corbusier, Otto Neurath, Max Bill, Herb Lubalin, Oliver Reichenstein, Steve Duenes, Khoi Vinh and Nicholas Felton.

Q Please describe your design process. Do you adhere to any specific routines or techniques?

A Firstly, it is very important to sketch a project by hand.

I usually try to create dense, structured pages. I am used to working with type, grid and a limited colour palette, to create distinctive layouts and signal a certain association to the reader: applying the identity of the publication, creating appeal, aesthetics, and emotional and contextual considerations. Simplicity, above all, is key. The best way to achieve simplicity is by intelligently reducing the elements and objects that distract us from the message. Careful editing is crucial as well: it is important to delete surplus portions of the design, while ensuring the intrinsic value of the message is not lost.

By creating reading layers, we give the reader the chance to explore the page in depth, and discover curious details and signs. Since I communicate using graphs, charts, maps and schemes, I try to be rational and concise, by using widely understood conventions.

Q A lot of infographics might be attractive to look at, but may not make much sense to the average viewer. How do you take a complex chunk of information and make sense out of it?

A I see it as a spectrum: on one side you have the illustration, on the other, information. Designs that are too close to either end of the spectrum (too arty or too utilitarian) are rarely interesting. Another important issue has to do with the audience. You have to know where you need to be on that spectrum for the audience you are trying to reach. While you may say that infographics are at the mercy of a data designer's imagination, they should not be works of art. Applying a graphic style to the information is not nearly as important as giving a graphic form to the actual content, with a clear understanding of how that content will be perceived and processed by an audience.

Q What is the most rewarding part of the whole experience?

A The effort involved in an infographic spread is to combine and organize data, to select and choose how to display it, in order to tell a story that is an alternative to an

AMERICA IN AFRICA GUARDIE E LADRI

D Designer: Francesco Franchi
and Matteo Cellerino
I Illustrator: Giacomo Gambineri
E Editor: Alessandro Giberti

The feature, *America in Africa: guardie e ladri (America in Africa: cops and robbers)*, details the United States military presence in Africa. It was developed collaboratively, between *IL* Art Director, Francesco Franchi, and the participants in Franchi's Infographic Thinking workshop, held at Gestalten Space in July.

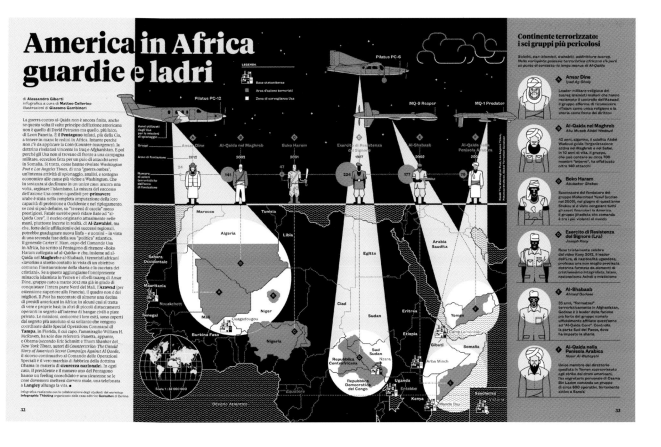

article of ten thousand words or more. An infographic is both design and narrative. This means finding a union between graphics and journalism, because it is not only a representation, but also a critical interpretation of reality. Visual language adds one more variable to the reading experience: non-linearity. Readers can choose a route, like in a palimpsest, where uprightness is a resource. I believe in the intelligence of our readers, and their ability to explore new and unusual graphical forms that can expand their visual vocabulary.

Q Do you have any advice for aspiring designers who are dipping their toes into information design?

A Always start from a strong journalistic idea.

Q What excites you most about the future of information design?

A The fact that we can now derive data sets from objects around us, or things we use, in addition to recording our day-to-day activities.

PIÙ VELOCE DELL'AEREO ⇄

D Designer: Francesco Franchi

Più veloce dell'aereo is a carefully detailed map of high-speed railway lines worldwide, developed by Francesco Franchi, for *IL* magazine.

FEATURED DESIGNER / FRANCESCO FRANCHI

IL | **GLOBAL REPORT** – ANALISI GRAFICA

LA FACCIA DELLA RAPIDITÀ

Alcuni esempi di treni ad alta velocità attualmente operativi. Per ciascuno è indicato il Paese, il nome, l'anno di entrata in servizio e la velocità massima

acela
STATI UNITI
Acela Express
2000
250 km/h

ITALIA
Frecciarossa - Etr 500
2008
300 km/h

Più veloce dell'aereo

Il Giappone progettava le prime linee rapide già negli anni Cinquanta. Oggi i binari jet nel mondo sono quasi 10 mila km. Ma nel 2025 saranno il triplo e ruberanno i passeggeri al cielo

– di **Francesco Franchi**

LINEE VELOCI NEL MONDO

La mappa mostra i collegamenti ferroviari mondiali ad alta velocità (≥250 km/h). Le corone circolari indicano, per ogni Stato, la **lunghezza totale** e la **velocità media** delle tratte in questione. Più l'arco è spesso, maggiore è la velocità; più l'arco è ampio, maggiore è la lunghezza.

- Chilometri operativi
- Chilometri in costruzione
- Chilometri in progetto
- Tratte operative
- Tratte in costruzione e in progetto
- Aggiornamento linee tradizionali

| **1956** | Il Giappone progetta una linea veloce (250 km/h) tra Tokyo e Osaka. Viene inaugurata nel 1964 | **1970** | Iniziano i lavori per la Direttissima tra Roma e Firenze. L'intera tratta è ultimata nel 1992 | **1976** | La Sncf francese lancia il progetto di linea veloce Parigi-Lione. Entra in funzione nel 1981 | **1991** | Primi InterCityExpress in Germania: Hannover-Würzburg e Mannheim-Stoccarda |

38 % è l'aumento degli investimenti cinesi per l'alta velocità nel primo semestre 2008

IL

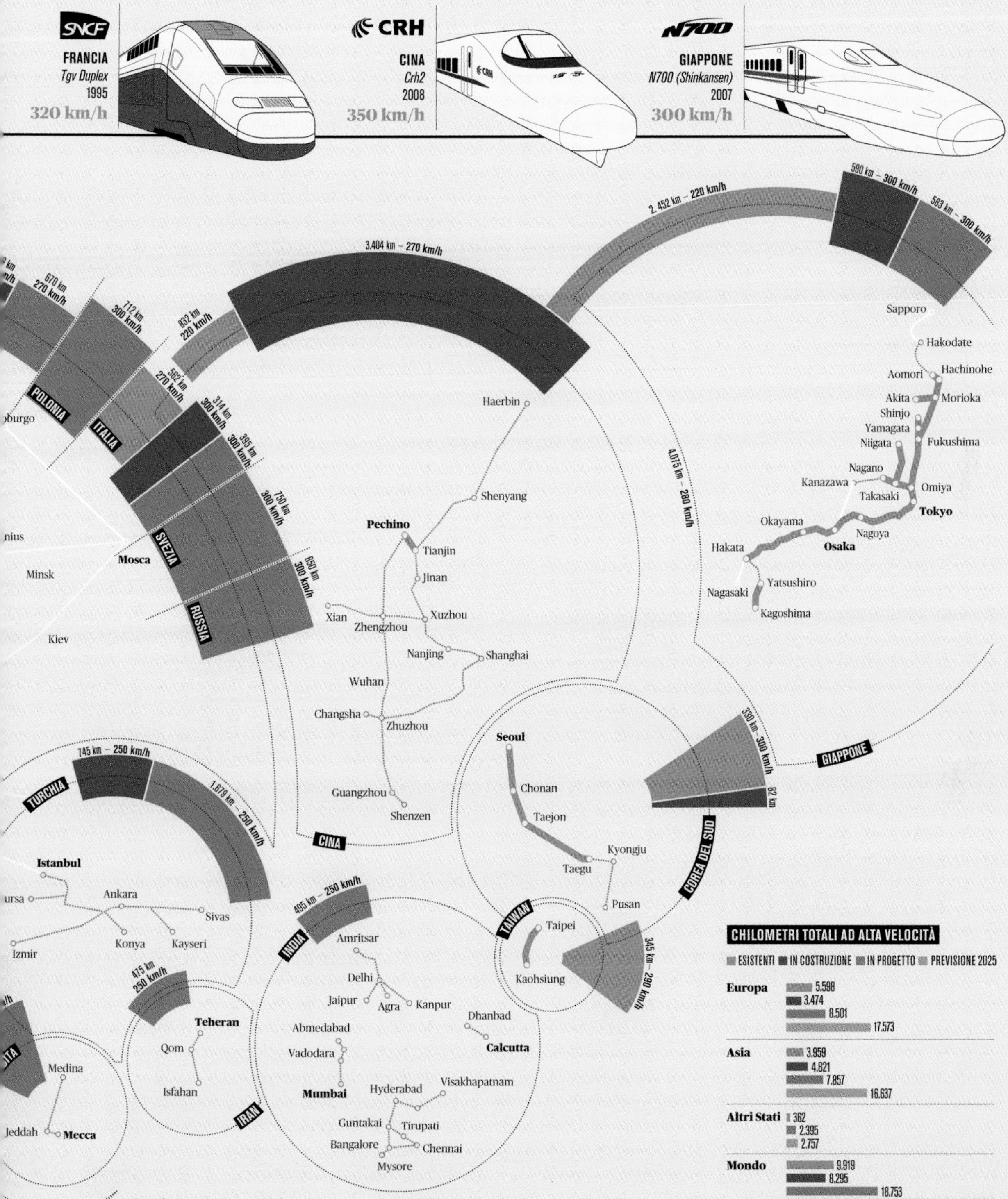
SNCF
FRANCIA
Tgv Duplex
1995
320 km/h
CRH
CINA
Crh2
2008
350 km/h
N700
GIAPPONE
N700 (Shinkansen)
2007
300 km/h
670 km 270 km/h
712 km 300 km/h
832 km 220 km/h
3.404 km – 270 km/h
2.452 km – 220 km/h
590 km – 300 km/h
583 km – 300 km/h
562 km 270 km/h
314 km 300 km/h
395 km 300 km/h
750 km 300 km/h
650 km 300 km/h
POLONIA
ITALIA
SVEZIA
RUSSIA
burgo
nius
Minsk
Mosca
Kiev
Haerbin
Shenyang
Pechino
Tianjin
Jinan
Xian
Zhengzhou
Xuzhou
Nanjing
Shanghai
Wuhan
Changsha
Zhuzhou
Guangzhou
Shenzen
CINA
4.075 km – 280 km/h
Sapporo
Hakodate
Aomori
Hachinohe
Akita
Morioka
Shinjo
Yamagata
Niigata
Fukushima
Nagano
Kanazawa
Takasaki
Omiya
Tokyo
Okayama
Nagoya
Osaka
Hakata
Nagasaki
Yatsushiro
Kagoshima
330 km – 300 km/h
82 km
GIAPPONE
COREA DEL SUD
Seoul
Chonan
Taejon
Kyongju
Taegu
Pusan
TAIWAN
Taipei
Kaohsiung
345 km – 290 km/h
745 km – 250 km/h
1.679 km – 250 km/h
TURCHIA
Istanbul
ursa
Ankara
Sivas
Izmir
Konya
Kayseri
495 km – 250 km/h
INDIA
Amritsar
Delhi
Jaipur
Agra
Kanpur
Dhanbad
Abmedabad
Vadodara
Calcutta
Mumbai
Hyderabad
Visakhapatnam
Guntakai
Tirupati
Bangalore
Chennai
Mysore
475 km 250 km/h
IRAN
Teheran
Qom
Isfahan
Medina
Jeddah
Mecca
CHILOMETRI TOTALI AD ALTA VELOCITÀ
ESISTENTI
IN COSTRUZIONE
IN PROGETTO
PREVISIONE 2025
Europa
5.598
3.474
8.501
17.573
Asia
3.959
4.821
7.857
16.637
Altri Stati
362
2.395
2.757
Mondo
9.919
8.295
18.753
36.967

FONTE: Uic (Union international chemin de fer)

1992 Diventa operativa la linea tra Madrid e Siviglia: prima tratta dell'alta velocità in Spagna

1999 In Giappone il treno Maglev (a levitazione magnetica) tocca in un test la velocità record di 552 km/h

2000 Negli Usa inizia a funzionare il collegamento veloce tra New York, Washington e Boston

2008 La Cina inaugura la linea Pechino-Tianjin: 120 km in 29 minuti. In Italia apre la Tav Milano-Bologna

PETER ØRNTOFT

Peter Ørntoft is a Danish designer. He works in the field of visual communication. He takes a contextual and research-based approach to traditional fields of design.

Ⓠ Please introduce yourself.

Ⓐ I am a Danish designer, based in Copenhagen. I work in the field of visual communication. I am currently working as the creative director for a tech startup in Copenhagen, where I am in charge of its visual identity and digital design strategy.

Ⓠ Can you tell us a little about your background and how you came to work in infographic design and data visualization?

Ⓐ I was born and raised in Copenhagen, and spent my childhood and youth there. In 2004, I moved to London, where I spent three years getting my bachelor degree in graphic design, at the London College of Communication. Since then, I have obtained a master's degree in visual communication, from the Danish Design School, and have worked for a Danish political and social think tank; the Danish Design Centre; and a digital design studio called 1508, all based in Copenhagen.

Ⓠ How did you get started with data visualization and infographic design?

Ⓐ While studying in London I became interested in structuring and analyzing things, in relation to my design work. Later on, I was attracted by data visualization and infographics, and found it to be a great field for me to work in, in view of my interests. I am not interested only in data visualizations and infographics, but in anything related to structuring and analyzing research and objects.

Ⓠ Which designers do you most admire?

Ⓐ I generally admire designers who are able to mirror the context they are dealing with, through their design projects. An example would be Sarah Illenberger.

Ⓠ Please describe your design process. Do you adhere to any specific routines or techniques?

Ⓐ My design process varies from project to project, but research is generally an unavoidable and essential part of my process. I never begin a project without a research phase. To me, this is the source of all the answers for the final design. I think the perfect project is one where the final outcome is a design that documents the research.

Ⓠ A lot of infographics might be attractive to look at, but may not make much sense to the average viewer. How do you take a complex chunk of information and make sense out of it?

Ⓐ With infographics, specifically, it is all about making things clear to the audience. Whether the final outcome is photographic, typographic or something else, the visual communication has to be clear, to avoid distorting the data. I often meet clients who want me to work with photographic infographics, but I often have to disappoint them because the information they want to communicate is unsuited to that style. Photographic visualizations can be great, to make a powerful statement with data, but if the data is powerful enough by itself, it should stand alone.

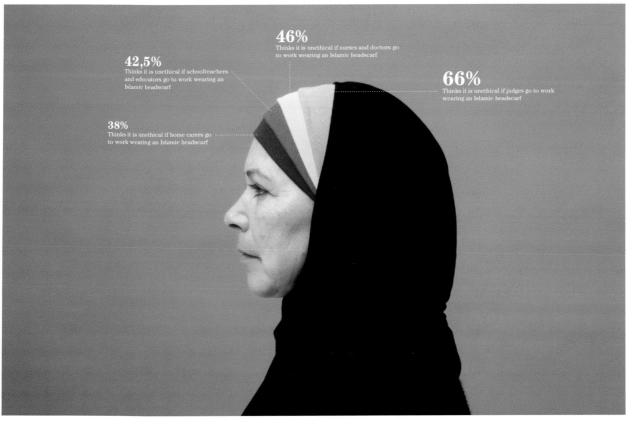

46%
Thinks it is unethical if nurses and doctors go
to work wearing an Islamic headscarf

42,5%
Thinks it is unethical if schoolteachers
and educators go to work wearing an
Islamic headscarf

66%
Thinks it is unethical if judges go to work
wearing an Islamic headscarf

38%
Thinks it is unethical if home carers go
to work wearing an Islamic headscarf

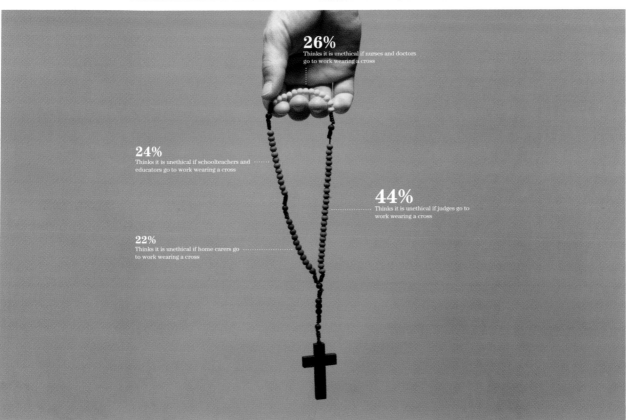

26%
Thinks it is unethical if nurses and doctors
go to work wearing a cross

24%
Thinks it is unethical if schoolteachers and
educators go to work wearing a cross

44%
Thinks it is unethical if judges go to
work wearing a cross

22%
Thinks it is unethical if home carers go
to work wearing a cross

INFOGRAPHICS IN CONTEXT / PETER ØRNTOFT

FEATURED DESIGNER / PETER ØRNTOFT

18%
Have changed their behaviour a lot because of gang related crime

26%
Have changed their behaviour because of gang related crime

55%
Have not changed behaviour because of the gang related crime

57%
Are very afraid of being in specific places because of gang related crime

26%
Are somewhat afraid of being in specific places because of gang related crime

16%
Are not afraid of being in any specific places in spite of gang related crime

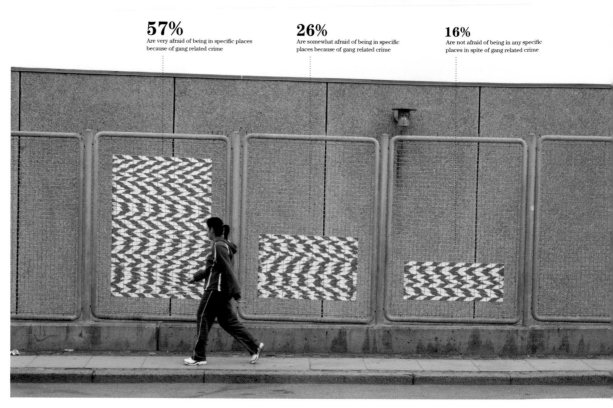

This project has investigative and conceptual characteristics. Peter wanted to explore data visualization, because it seemed to him an area within visual communication that still had a lot of possible directions to be taken. Besides this area, he also has a fascination for arranging and structuring numbers, texts, forms and colours, and looking for patterns in structures.

This project deals with data from a list of the socially related interests of the Danish public. The list is the result of an opinion poll run by a major consultancy company, in Denmark. Peter has used the context of specific opinion polls within each interest area, to shape and design diagrams. As a result of this, the receiver understands more layers of information in relation to the data.

INFOGRAPHICS IN CONTEXT

Ⓓ Designer: Peter Ørntoft
Ⓒ Concept: Peter Ørntoft
Ⓟ Photographer: Peter Ørntoft

Ⓠ What is the most rewarding part of the whole experience?

Ⓐ The most rewarding part of any design project is when the research makes all the pieces of the puzzle come together: when you can visualize the final outcome, even without having started on the design.

Ⓠ Visualization courses are being taught in higher education. What do you make of this? Is formal education necessary for information design?

Ⓐ If students want to work with visualizing data, I think it is more important that they understand the importance of data. That is essential learning for anyone who wants to work in this field.

Ⓠ Do you have any advice for aspiring designers who are dipping their toes into information design?

Ⓐ Learn to understand the importance of data and information in general.

Ⓠ Do you think it is beneficial for your work to have a signature style?

Ⓐ I think it is beneficial to find your own preferred way of working with design. I do not think you need to look for a recognizable style. I have never aimed to find one. I have, however, tried to find a process I feel comfortable with. That automatically led to a recognizable style.

Ⓠ Myriad topics have been the subject of data visualization. Are there any topics you feel have yet to be approached succinctly?

Ⓐ Not any specific ones. Eventually, every topic will have been communicated through data visualization. I think it is part of our natural urge to make things transparent.

MGMT. DESIGN

MGMT. design is a graphic design studio, based in Brooklyn, New York. Their clients include Al Gore, *The New York Times*, and the Thai royal family. Their data visualization projects have been inspired by their own ideas, but have also covered the death toll in Iraq, different methods of time travel and how to kill a wild pig.

Q Please introduce yourself.

A Alicia Cheng and Sarah Gephart, partners, MGMT. design.

Q Can you tell us a little about your background and how you came to work in infographic design and data visualization?

A We met while getting our MFAs in graphic design, at Yale University. We had an overlapping interest in information design and diagrammatic visual languages: Sarah and I were attracted to forms that were both beautiful and content bearing.

Q How did you get started with data visualization and infographic design?

A It was always an intrinsic area of interest for both of us, and was the primary focus of our thesis work at university. After MGMT was established in 2001, we received commissions for information design, and sought out ways of applying an infographic approach to our projects.

Q Which designers do you most admire?

A Ladislav Sutnar, Erik Nitche and Barbara Glauber.

Q Please describe your design process. Do you adhere to any specific routines or techniques?

A Our studio is very egalitarian. When starting any project, we open it up to everyone, and pin up sketches for discussion. We all provide feedback and determine which direction has the most potential to develop.

Q A lot of infographics might be attractive to look at, but may not make much sense to the average viewer. How do you take a complex chunk of information and make sense out of it?

A Much of what makes an effective infographic is successfully communicating complex information within an appealing visual form. All infographics should, in principle, make sense to the average viewer. A good infographic is one that also has built-in layers of interpretation, to provide the viewer with multiple levels of reading. So, it offers an overall big picture, while still giving them the opportunity to read more granular data.

UFOLOGY

D Designer: MGMT. design

A lunchtime discussion started the idea of an infographic about UFOs. This chart shows a lexicon of categories for each sighting, in addition to a tally of incidents that took place between 1962 and 2012.

UFOLOGY

Studies have established that the majority of UFO observations are misidentified conventional objects or natural phenomena. Most common of which are: aircraft, balloons, noctilucent and nacreous clouds, or astronomical objects such as meteors or bright planets. It is acknowledged that between 5% and 20% of reported sightings remain unexplained, and as such can be classified as 'unidentified.' Many reports have been made by trained observers such as pilots, police, and the military; some involve radar traces, so not all reports are visual. Proponents of the extraterrestrial hypothesis believe that these unidentified reports are of alien spacecraft, though various other hypotheses have been proposed. Shown below is a tally of sightings taking place between 1962 and 2012.

LIGHT
14,368

TRIANGLE
7,123

CIRCLE
6,305

DISK
5,358

OTHER
5,286

UNKNOWN
5,255

SPHERE
4,377

FIREBALL
4,359

OVAL
3,404

UNSPECIFIED
2,726

FORMATION
2,086

CIGAR
1,989

CHANGING
1,775

FLASH
1,173

RECTANGLE
1162

CYLINDER
1,127

DIAMOND
1,069

CHEVRON
866

EGG
734

TEARDROP
700

CONE
304

CROSS
206

DELTA
8

ROUND
2

CRESCENT
2

PYRAMID
1

FLARE
1

HEXAGON
1

DOME
1

COMMON APPEARANCES

Black Triangle
An enormous, silent, black triangular object, slowly cruising at low altitudes over cities and highways, usually at night. Often described as having either bright white lights or pulsing colored lights.

Fastwalkers
A term created by the North American Aerospace Defense Command to classify UFOs that enter or leave the atmosphere at a great velocity.

Green Fireballs
A classic UFO type first established in the 1940s. Early sightings primarily occurred in the southwestern United States, particularly in New Mexico.

Ghost Rockets
The first report in 1946 by Finnish observers, about 2,000 sightings were logged between May and December of that year, with peaks on August 9 and 11. Two hundred sightings were verified with radar, and authorities recovered physical fragments that were attributed to ghost rockets.

Flying Saucer
Disc-shaped flying objects have been sporadically recorded since the Middle Ages. The first highly publicized sighting was in 1947 and resulted in the creation of the term "flying saucer" by U.S. newspapers. The observer was quoted as saying the shape of the objects he saw was like a "saucer," "disc," or "pie-plate."

Mystery Airships
Best known from a series of U.S. newspaper reports in 1896 and 1897. It was popularly believed that the mystery airships were the product of some genius inventor not ready to make knowledge of his creation public. Thomas Edison was so widely speculated to be the mind behind the alleged airships that in 1897 he "was forced to issue a strongly worded statement" denying his responsibility.

HYNEK'S SCALE

Astronomer and UFO researcher J. Allen Hynek first suggested a system of classification for UFOs, identifying the first three kinds of encounters. Additional subcategories of encounters were later added by others, but these additional categories (i.e., abductions, close contact, communication efforts) are not universally accepted by UFO researchers.

First
Visual sightings of an unidentified flying object.

Second
Visual sightings plus physical effects on animate and inanimate objects.

Third
Sightings of "occupants" in and around the UFO.

REPORTS BY STATE

California	8,788
Texas	3,501
Florida	3,476
New York	2,909
Illinois	2,458
Unspecified/international	6,678
Busiest Month: July 2010	824

Q What is the most rewarding part of the whole experience?

A Finishing a project!

Q Visualization courses are being taught in higher education. What do you make of this? Is formal education necessary for information design?

A We have taught this topic at several universities. By definition, graphic designers are all information designers. We teach students to approach all content (be it branding or dataset) with the same visual problem-solving abilities. We encourage them to think as communicators, rather than imparting a set of explicit, 'how-to' rules on how to generate infographics.

Q Do you have any advice for aspiring designers who are dipping their toes into information design?

A Make it interesting for yourself, as well as others. Do not be afraid of numbers. Find solid, substantive data.

Q Do you think it is beneficial for your work to have a signature style?

A We are always open to, and inspired by, the talents of our designers and what they bring to the table. Ultimately, our 'style' is more about our approach to content. Our process always responds to the content provided, but hopefully, each outcome involves a solution that is both intelligent and elegant.

Q Myriad topics have been the subject of data visualization. Are there any topics you feel have yet to be approached succinctly?

A We are attracted to all types of content, and constantly trawl for items we would someday like to make into a visual image. Many of our self-initiated data visualization projects stem from lively lunchtime conversations at the studio. Topics range from a lexicon of UFOs and a timeline of manned space travel, to how to ride an ostrich.

Q What excites you most about the future of information design?

A The harnessing of big data and how effective it can be, if that data is communicated successfully.

RE: FLAGS

D Designer: MGMT. design

MGMT was commissioned by SFMOMA to 'rebrand America' for an online exhibition. The designers asked themselves the question, is there anything more American than the American flag? Using the American flag as the formal foundation, MGMT created 50 new flags, which are based on the current conditions of a changing nation.

These new standards utilize data visualization in a heraldic form, to reveal facts about the USA, from the obvious to the sublime. While sometimes superficial, these new metrics reveal aspects of America that go deeper than traditional patriotic symbols.

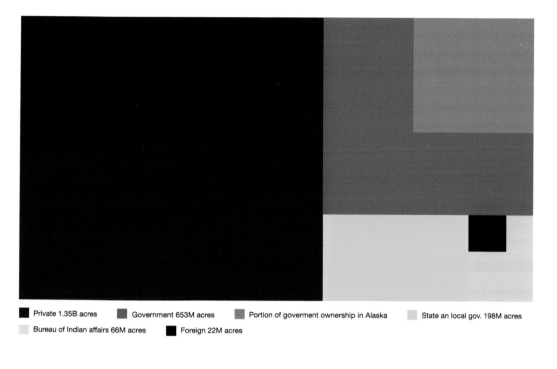

■ Private 1.35B acres   ■ Government 653M acres   ■ Portion of goverment ownership in Alaska   ■ State an local gov. 198M acres

■ Bureau of Indian affairs 66M acres   ■ Foreign 22M acres

Land Grab
The majority of American land is privately owned. Over a third of federal government-owned land is in Alaska.

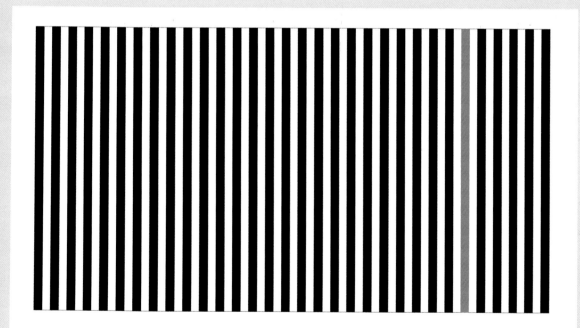

The Big House
One out of every 32 Americans in the U.S. is either in prison or on parole from prison.

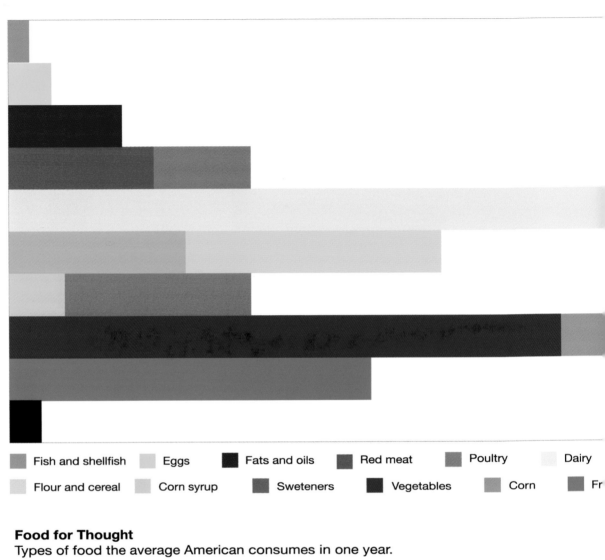

Legend:
- Fish and shellfish
- Eggs
- Fats and oils
- Red meat
- Poultry
- Dairy
- Flour and cereal
- Corn syrup
- Sweteners
- Vegetables
- Corn
- Fr

Food for Thought
Types of food the average American consumes in one year.

Wheat

Coffee, cocoa, and nuts

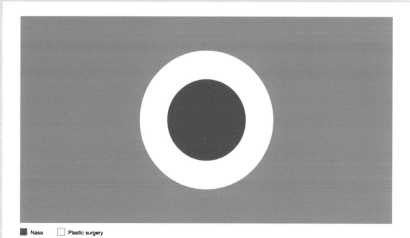

■ Nasa   ☐ Plastic surgery

Face Race
Last year, Americans spent over 10 billion dollars on plastic surgery. The federal budget for NASA's space operations was 3.5 billion dollars.

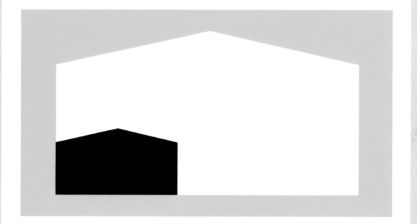

Room Boom
The average American hou se size is 2,349 square feet, more than double what it was in the 1950s.

Joy

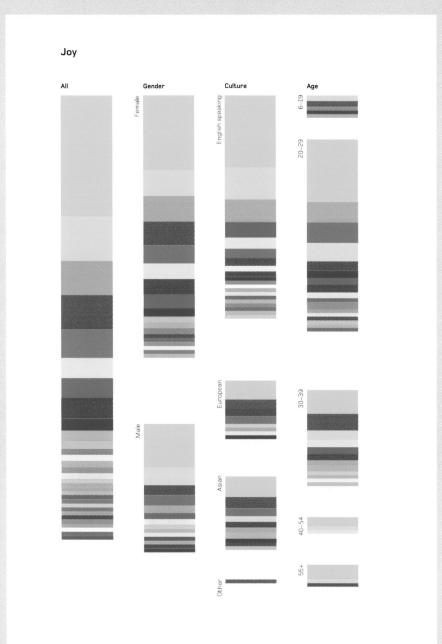

Anger

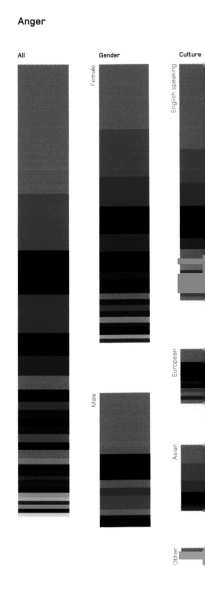

Love

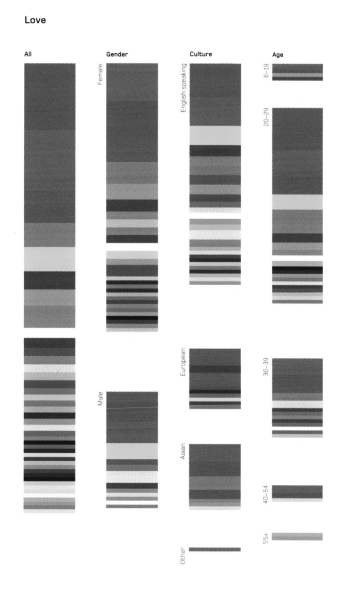

All

Gender

Female

Male

Other

Culture

English speaking

European

Asian

Age

6–19

20–29

30–39

40–54

55+

EMOTIONALLY]VAGUE COLOR RESEARCH

Ⓓ Designer: Orlagh O'Brien

A chart of 162 colours was developed, based on 250 people of different ages and from different cultures. They were asked, 'What colour do you associate with anger, joy, fear, sadness and love?' Using a mySQL database, queries were written to obtain age, nationality and gender breakdowns. The larger areas reflect how more people selected a colour. Fear is mostly grey and black, while sadness is a wide-ranging palette of cool colours. Anger is bloody and dark. Joy appears like the sun and sky, while love is a typical Valentine's Day card, of pinks and reds.

EUROPEAN DEBT CRISIS

ⒹDesigner: Severino Ribecca

This graphic was originally a runner-up in one of the monthly *Information is Beautiful* Awards competitions. Focusing on the current debt crisis in Europe, the infographic looks at the relationship between each country's GDP and the amount of government debt it has.

NATIONAL COLORS

ⒹDesigner: Tom Davie
ⒾIllustrator: Tom Davie

This data visualization project depicts significant global colour systems. The countries included in this visualization have been arranged alphabetically, and represent 74 of the world's most occupied nations. National colours are typically those contained on a country's flag, and those used during national ceremonies and events, including national and international sporting events.

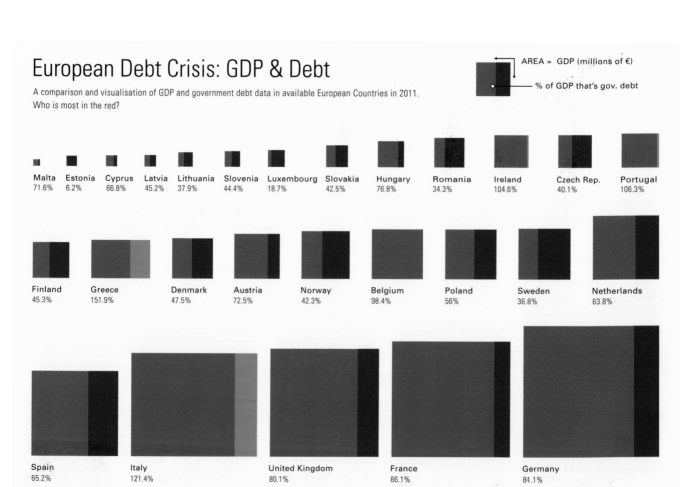

European Debt Crisis: GDP & Debt

A comparison and visualisation of GDP and government debt data in available European Countries in 2011. Who is most in the red?

AREA = GDP (millions of €)

% of GDP that's gov. debt

Malta 71.6%
Estonia 6.2%
Cyprus 66.8%
Latvia 45.2%
Lithuania 37.9%
Slovenia 44.4%
Luxembourg 18.7%
Slovakia 42.5%
Hungary 76.8%
Romania 34.3%
Ireland 104.6%
Czech Rep. 40.1%
Portugal 106.3%

Finland 45.3%
Greece 151.9%
Denmark 47.5%
Austria 72.5%
Norway 42.3%
Belgium 98.4%
Poland 56%
Sweden 36.8%
Netherlands 63.8%

Spain 65.2%
Italy 121.4%
United Kingdom 80.1%
France 86.1%
Germany 81.1%

SOURCE: http://epp.eurostat.ec.europa.eu

Severino Ribecca   www.rinodesign.co.uk

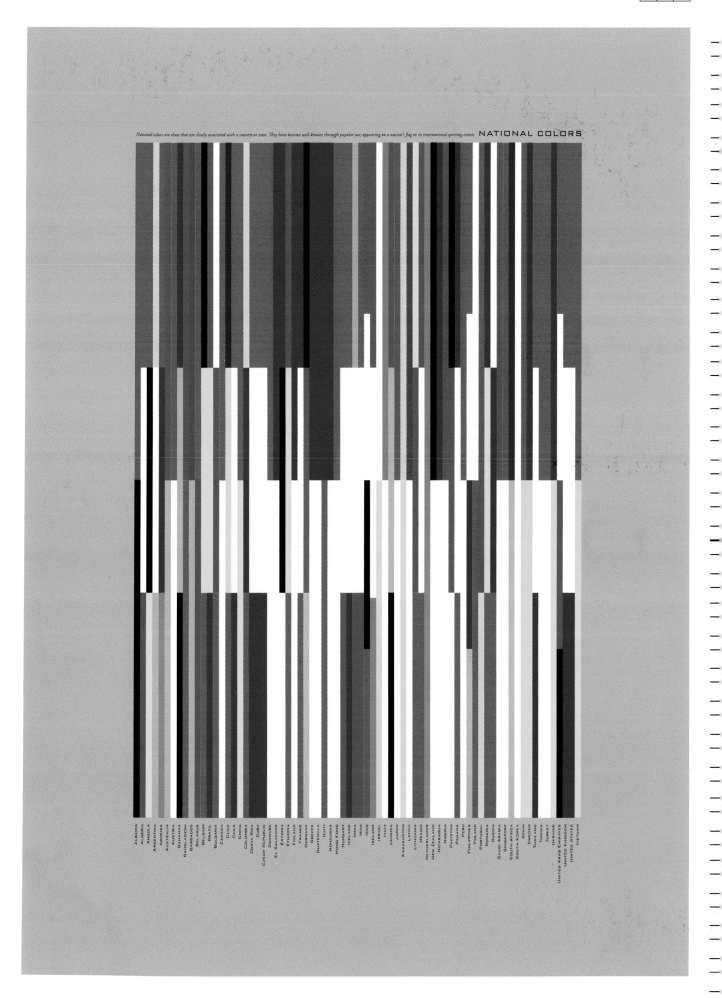

NATIONAL COLORS

National colors are those that are closely associated with a country or state. They have become well-known through popular use; appearing on a nation's flag or in international sporting events.

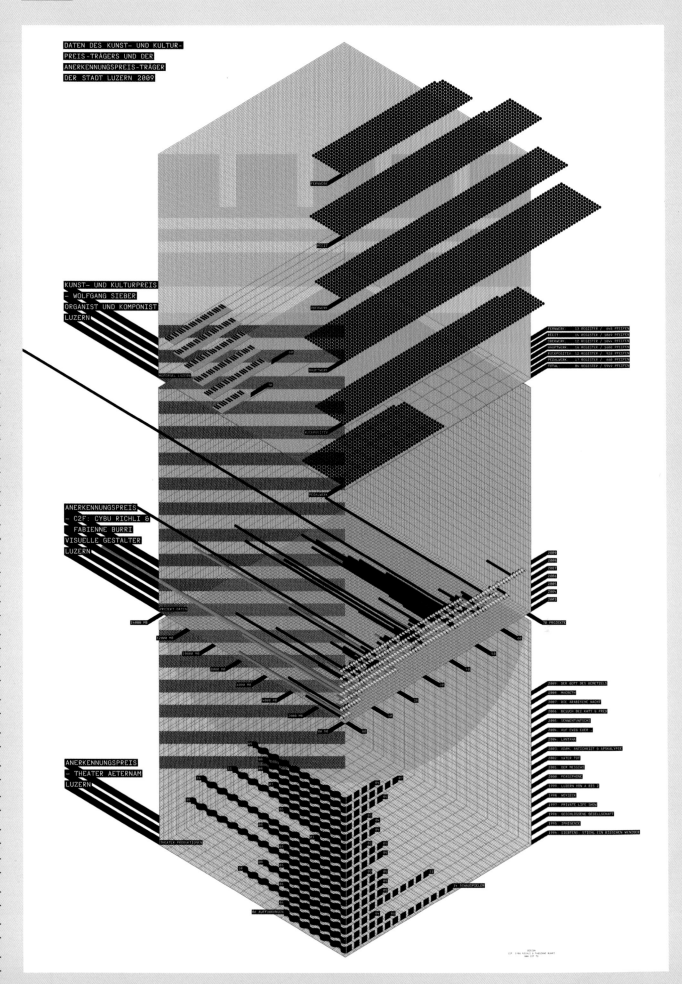

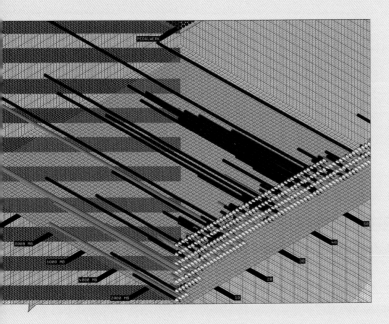

KUNST- UND KULTURPREIS CITY OF LUCERNE

Ⓓ Designer: C2f

Data visualization about the winners of the *Art and Culture* Award of the City of Lucerne.

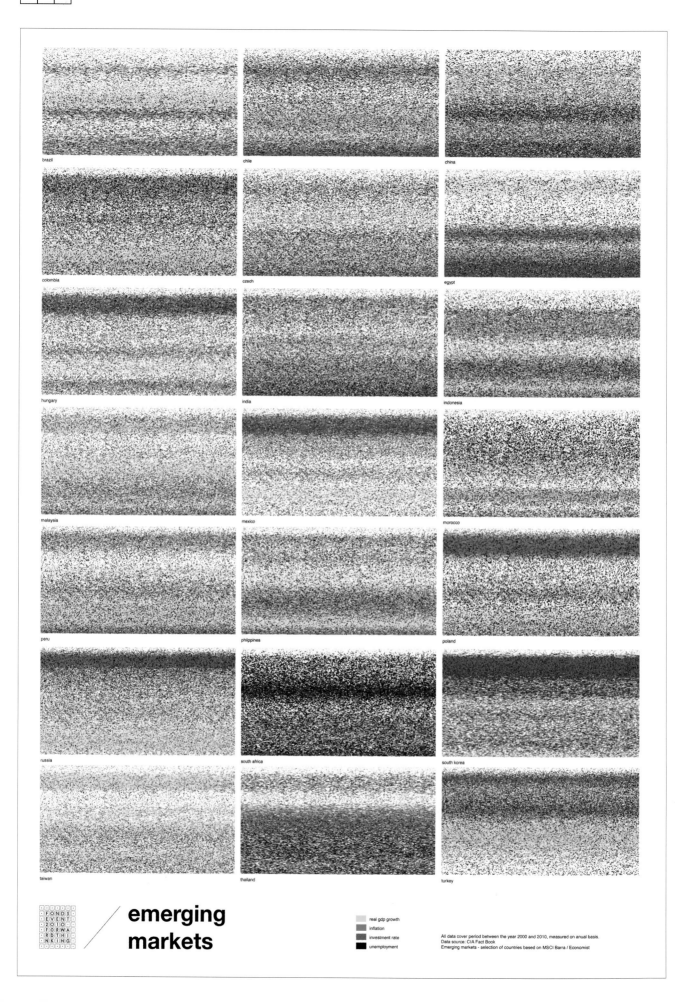

brazil

chile

china

colombia

czech

egypt

hungary

india

indonesia

malaysia

mexico

morocco

peru

philippines

poland

russia

south africa

south korea

taiwan

thailand

turkey

/ emerging
markets

real gdp growth
inflation
investment rate
unemployment

All data cover period between the year 2000 and 2010, measured on anual basis.
Data source: CIA Fact Book
Emerging markets - selection of countries based on MSCI Barra / Economist

FONDS
EVENT
2010
FORWA
RD THI
NKING

MARCH MADNESS BY THE COLORS

EMERGING MARKETS

Ⓓ Designer: Jan Franciszek Cieślak

This silkscreen poster consists of 21 'charts', each representing a developing economy, as recognized by MSCI Barra / *The Economist*. In each chart, data from four crucial economic measurements (such as unemployment and GDP growth rate), from the past 10 years, translates into a noise density pattern. Each of the four patterns have one of the CMYK colours assigned to it: when laid over each other, they create colourful 'flags'. These are nonsensical infographics for economic measurements.

MARCH MADNESS

Ⓓ Designer: MGMT. design

Each year, millions of Americans participate in March Madness office pools, and every one of them has a different winning strategy. Various reasons come into play when selecting tournament winners: selective seed picking, a sibling's travel history, a personal childhood memory, or just because.

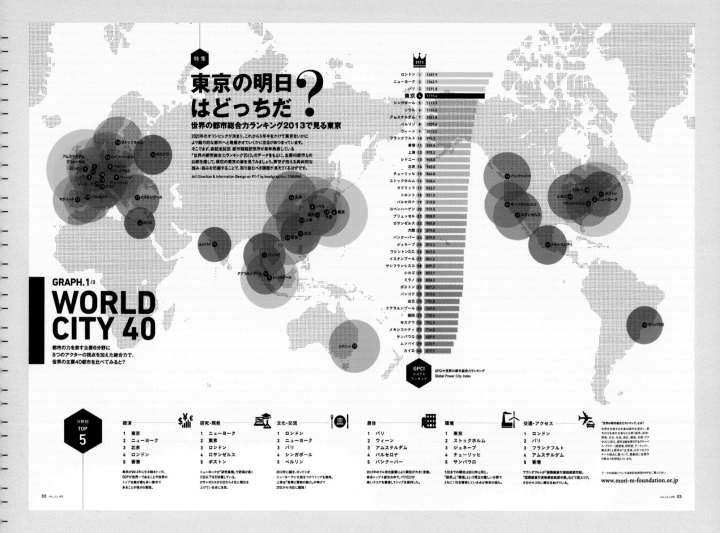

HILLSLIFE#64

Ⓓ Designer: bowlgraphics
Ⓘ Illustrator: bowlgraphics
Ⓜ Map: Inforab. (Ryoko Yamasaki)
ⒶⒹ Art Director: Plug-in Graphic (Nobuo Sekiguchi)
Ⓟ Publisher: SWITCH

A booklet showing data from Global Power City Index 2013. The target of the infographics is to consider the future of Tokyo, as a host city for the 2020 Olympic Games.

THE FAT PATH

Ⓓ Designer: Marcelo Duhalde

Based on WHO data, the visualization is constructed using worldwide obesity rates. The idea here was not to give each precise number by country, but instead, to use colours that change in accordance with percentage, and provide more information, country names and even a gender layer.

38 Hi WEEKLY GRAPHICS VOL 07 ISSUE 25 / SEPTEMBER 27, 2013

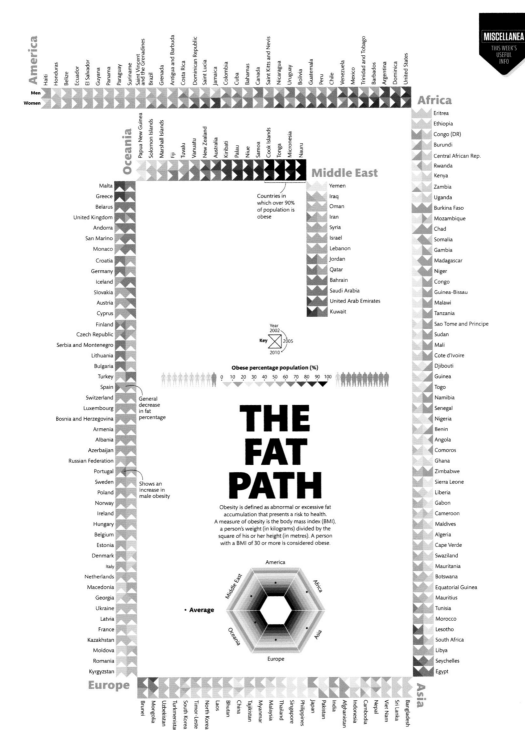

THE FAT PATH

Obesity is defined as abnormal or excessive fat accumulation that presents a risk to health. A measure of obesity is the body mass index (BMI), a person's weight (in kilograms) divided by the square of his or her height (in metres). A person with a BMI of 30 or more is considered obese.

Obese percentage population (%)

Countries in which over 90% of population is obese

General decrease in fat percentage

Shows an increase in male obesity

Key
Year 2002 / 2005 / 2010

• Average

SOURCE: THE WORLD HEALTH ORGANISATION DATABASE

GRAPHIC: MARCELO DUHALDE

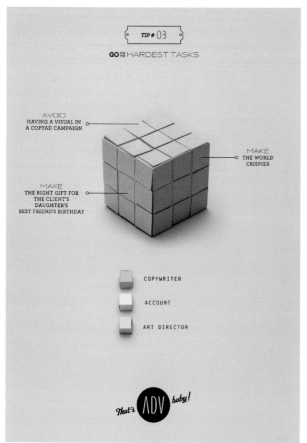

TIP # 03
GO FOR THE HARDEST TASKS

AVOID
HAVING A VISUAL IN
A COPYAD CAMPAIGN

MAKE
THE WORLD
CRISPIER

MAKE
THE RIGHT GIFT FOR
THE CLIENT'S
DAUGHTER'S
BEST FRIEND'S BIRTHDAY

COPYWRITER
ACCOUNT
ART DIRECTOR

That's ADV baby!

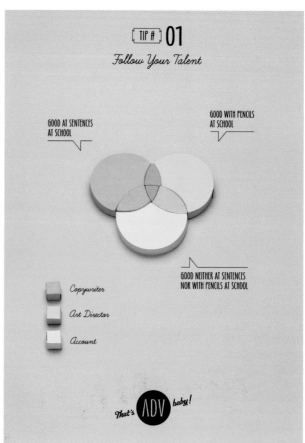

TIP # 01
Follow Your Talent

GOOD AT SENTENCES
AT SCHOOL

GOOD WITH PENCILS
AT SCHOOL

GOOD NEITHER AT SENTENCES
NOR WITH PENCILS AT SCHOOL

Copywriter
Art Director
Account

That's ADV baby!

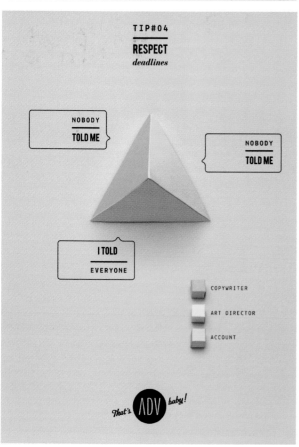

TIP#04
RESPECT
deadlines

NOBODY
TOLD ME

NOBODY
TOLD ME

I TOLD
EVERYONE

COPYWRITER
ART DIRECTOR
ACCOUNT

That's ADV baby!

THAT'S ADV, BABY!

© Copywriter: Fabrizio Tarussio
AD Art Director: Letizia Bozzolini
P Photographer: Photocirasa

A self-promoting manifesto made using a
papercraft infographic, which uses irony
to convey the average insider perspective
on the world of advertising.

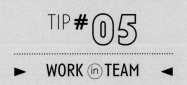

TIP #05

► WORK (in) TEAM ◄

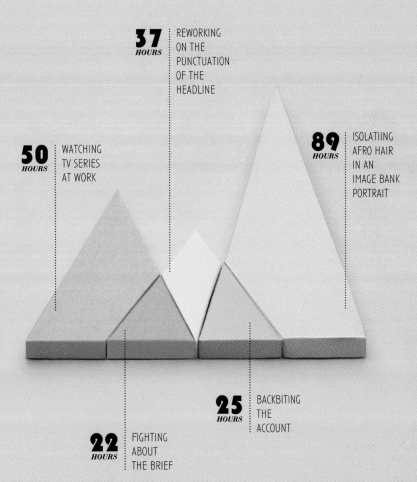

37 *HOURS* REWORKING ON THE PUNCTUATION OF THE HEADLINE

50 *HOURS* WATCHING TV SERIES AT WORK

89 *HOURS* ISOLATIING AFRO HAIR IN AN IMAGE BANK PORTRAIT

25 *HOURS* BACKBITING THE ACCOUNT

22 *HOURS* FIGHTING ABOUT THE BRIEF

ACCOUNT

COPYWRITER

ART DIRECTOR

That's ADV *baby!*

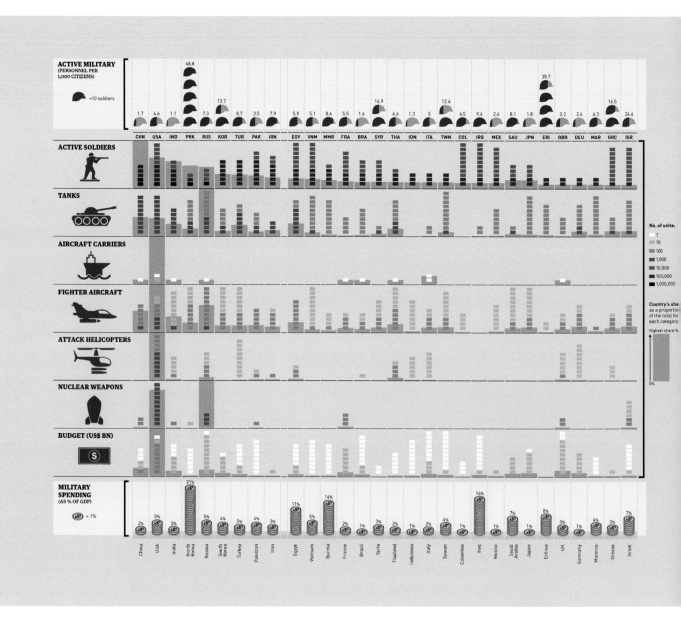

WHO IS LEADING THE ARMS RACE?

(D) Designer: Valentina D'Efilippo
(J) Data Journalist: James Ball

This infographic visualizes the relative size of the armies of different countries, taking into account personnel, weaponry and budget.

The artwork was created for *The Infographic History of the World*, and later published on *The Guardian G2* (online and offline).

SHELF LIFE

(D) Designer: Marcelo Duhalde

Some electronic products are made to last just a few years, and some for a very short period—shorter even than that of certain types of food. This comparison is shown in the visualization. The visual is a bar chart, but with perspective, set within a square. It grows towards the centre, using simple icons.

SHELF LIFE

Do you know that a pack of instant oats can outlive any electronic device? Here, we survey and compare how long a product could last before they are deemed unconsumable, or considered phased out or outmoded (i.e., a new model is introduced).

YEAR OF RELEASE — Atari Pong (1975) · Atari 2600 (1977) · Casio Database (1982) · Super Nintendo (1982) · Playstation (1994) · Nintendo 64 (1996) · Clippy (1997) · Windows 98 (1998) · iMac (1998) · iBook (1999)

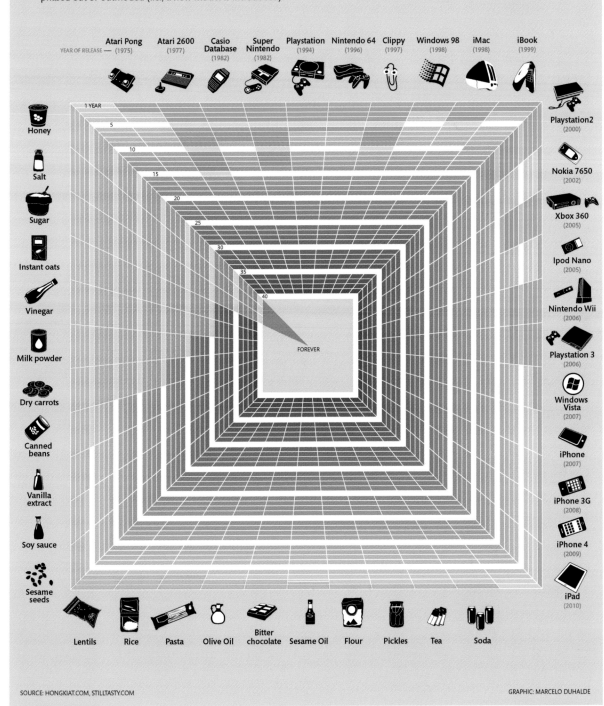

Honey · Salt · Sugar · Instant oats · Vinegar · Milk powder · Dry carrots · Canned beans · Vanilla extract · Soy sauce · Sesame seeds

Lentils · Rice · Pasta · Olive Oil · Bitter chocolate · Sesame Oil · Flour · Pickles · Tea · Soda

Playstation2 (2000) · Nokia 7650 (2002) · Xbox 360 (2005) · Ipod Nano (2005) · Nintendo Wii (2006) · Playstation 3 (2006) · Windows Vista (2007) · iPhone (2007) · iPhone 3G (2008) · iPhone 4 (2009) · iPad (2010)

1 YEAR · 5 · 10 · 15 · 20 · 25 · 30 · 35 · 40 · FOREVER

SOURCE: HONGKIAT.COM, STILLTASTY.COM

GRAPHIC: MARCELO DUHALDE

44 DAYS OF SLEEP

Ⓓ Designer: Adam Griffiths

A project based on the designer's own personal
sleeping pattern, from 3 August to 15 September
2011. The data and findings were displayed on a king-
size screen-printed bed sheet.

44 DAYS O...

FROM 3RD AUGUST TO 15TH SEPTEMBER 2011

TOTAL HOURS OF SLEEP

431 HOURS

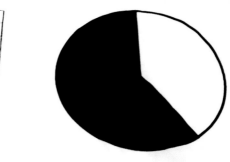

ASLEEP
AWAKE

THE EQUIVALENT OF BEING ASLEEP FOR

17 DAYS + 23 HOURS

AND AWAKE FOR

25 DAYS + 19 HOURS

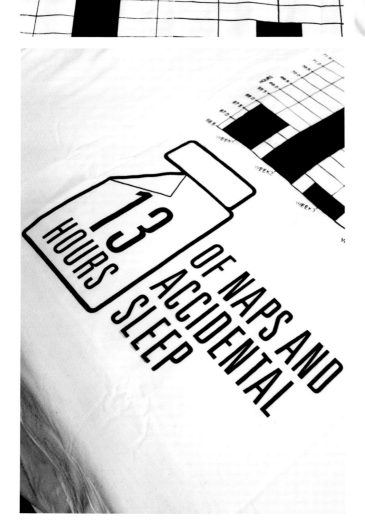

13 HOURS OF NAPS AND ACCIDENTAL SLEEP

STATISTICS STRIP

Ⓓ Designer: ART+COM
Ⓛ Location: Deutsches Hygiene-Museum, Dresden, 2009
Ⓒ Credits: Curated by Praxis für Ausstellungen und Theorie [Hürlimann | Lepp | Tyradellis]
Ⓢ Scenography: Chezweitz & Roseapple
Ⓒ Client: Deutsches Hygiene-Museum, Dresden

For a temporary exhibition, called *Work. Meaning and Worry*, ART+COM developed the *Statistics Strip*, a visualization of large volumes of data and facts. It runs along the walls and ceilings of the exhibition rooms, in the form of a two- and three-dimensional ribbon, measuring 150 m, with embedded time-based and interactive elements. The statistical strip wound and weaved its way through the exhibition rooms, widening occasionally into various types of graphs and charts: three-dimensional graphs that unfolded into the room, two-dimensional histograms, and large-scale scatter plots, which jutted out of the walls, presenting information in a highly readable way.

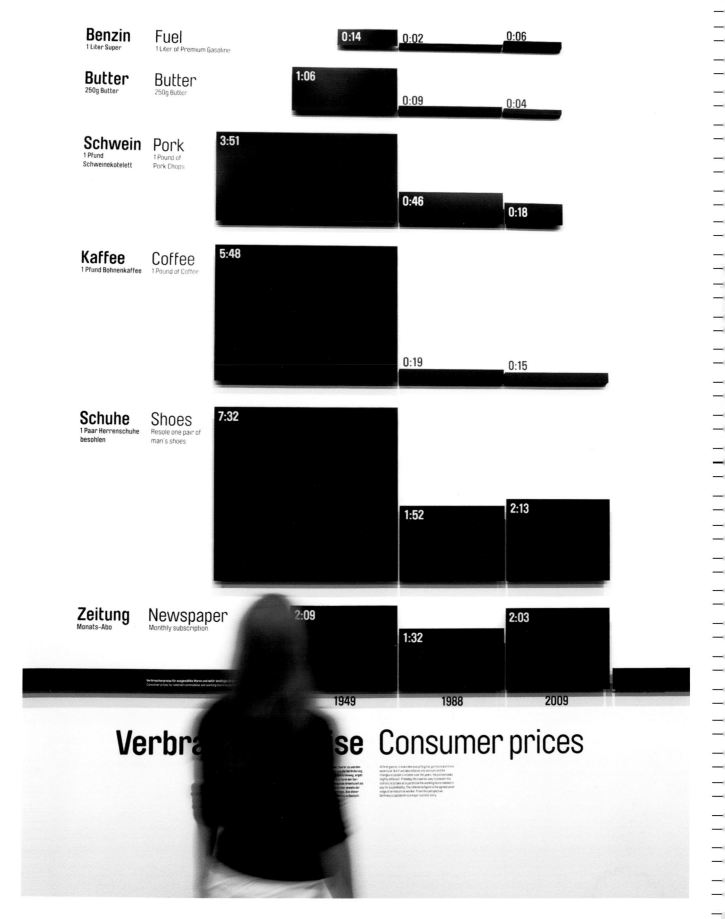

Benzin
1 Liter Super

Fuel
1 Liter of Premium Gasoline

0:14   0:02   0:06

Butter
250g Butter

Butter
250g Butter

1:06   0:09   0:04

Schwein
1 Pfund
Schweinekotelett

Pork
1 Pound of
Pork Chops

3:51   0:46   0:18

Kaffee
1 Pfund Bohnenkaffee

Coffee
1 Pound of Coffee

5:48   0:19   0:15

Schuhe
1 Paar Herrenschuhe
besohlen

Shoes
Resole one pair of
man's shoes

7:32   1:52   2:13

Zeitung
Monats-Abo

Newspaper
Monthly subscription

2:09   1:32   2:03

1949   1988   2009

Verbra... ...se Consumer prices

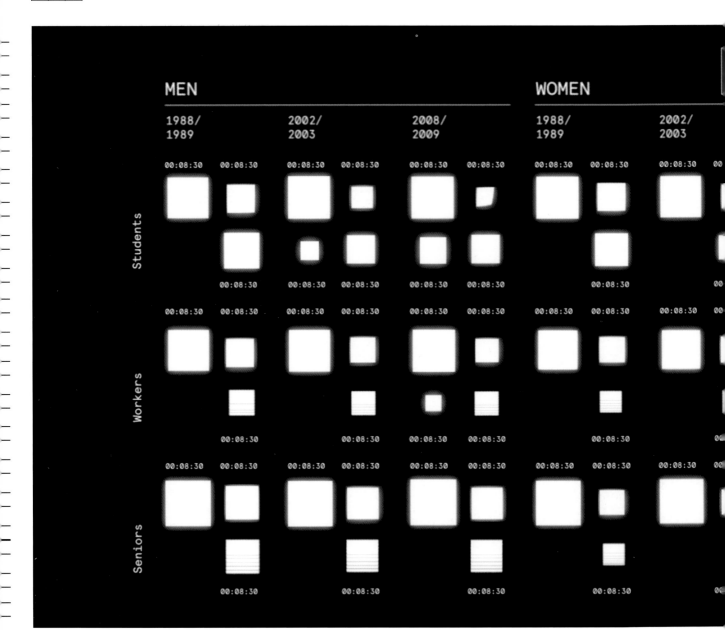

ITALIANS' LEISURE TIME ACTIVITIES

ⓓ Designer: Sofia Girelli

This infographic visualizes how Italians spend their leisure time. It focuses on four activities and compares the average time spent per day. The population is divided into three categories: students, workers and retired people. Each category is split into male and female. The visualization also compares three different periods of time, each lasting one year: 1988–89, 2002–03, 2008–09.

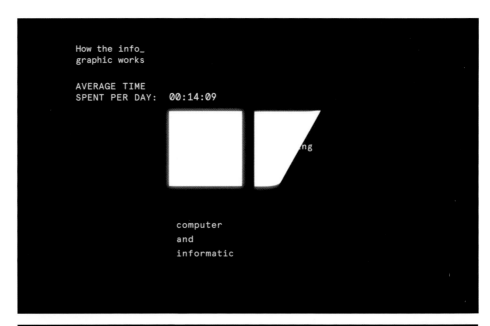

How the info_
graphic works

AVERAGE TIME
SPENT PER DAY: 00:14:09

ng

computer
and
informatic

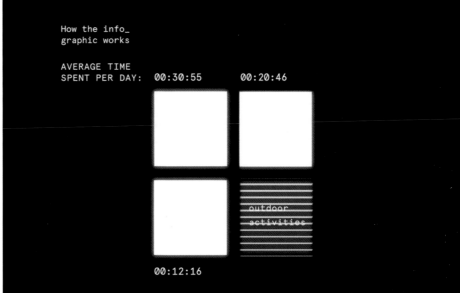

How the info_
graphic works

AVERAGE TIME
SPENT PER DAY: 00:30:55   00:20:46

outdoor
activities

00:12:16

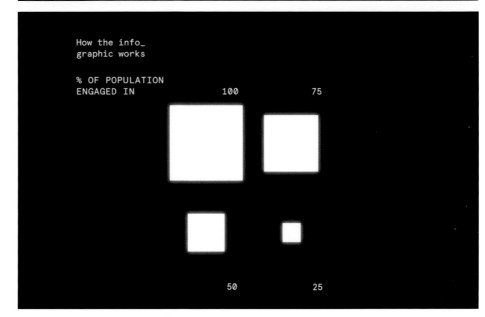

How the info_
graphic works

% OF POPULATION
ENGAGED IN   100   75

50   25

LIQUID STATISTICS

Ⓓ Designer: Domestic Data Streamers

A data collection system that allows comparison and
visualization of the academic journey each person chooses,
the level of certainty with which this decision is made,
and whether the student is from a creative background.
Produced in collaboration with IDEP Barcelona.

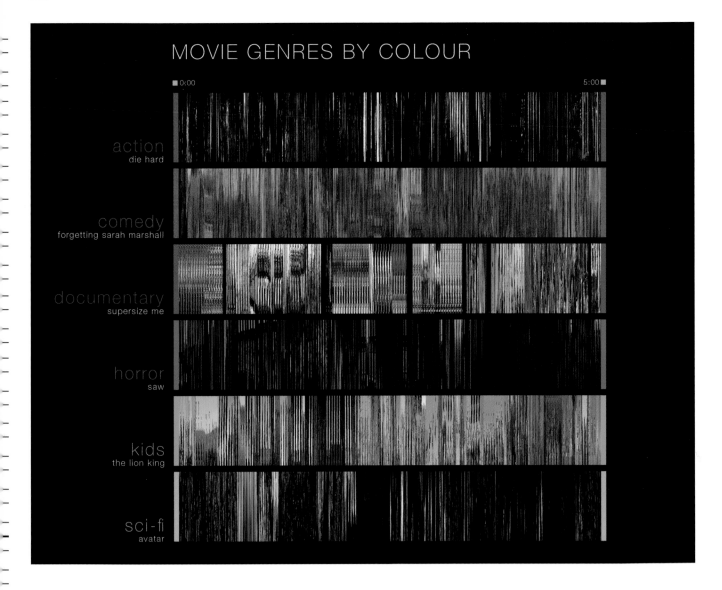

MOVIE GENRES BY COLOUR

Designer: Nicole Lyndal Smith

⇅

Movie Genres by Colour is a data visualization demonstrating colour use in film scenes, across varying genres. The artwork was created by exporting each frame in a five-minute sequence, using films from six different genres. These frames were then resized to 240 px x 1 px, and compiled together into a sequence using macros, to create colour patterns that represent the narrative progression of each film.

LIFE IN DATA

Designer: Ben Willers

⇄

The designer uses his own collection of self-monitoring data to visualize his eating, walking and sleeping patterns, in addition to fluctuations in his spending, television viewing and body weight.

MY VIEWING
ATTENTION
LEVEL

HIGH

LOW

18:00   21:00   00:00

TIME

TELEVISION VIEWING
12TH FEBRUARY - 11TH MARCH 2011

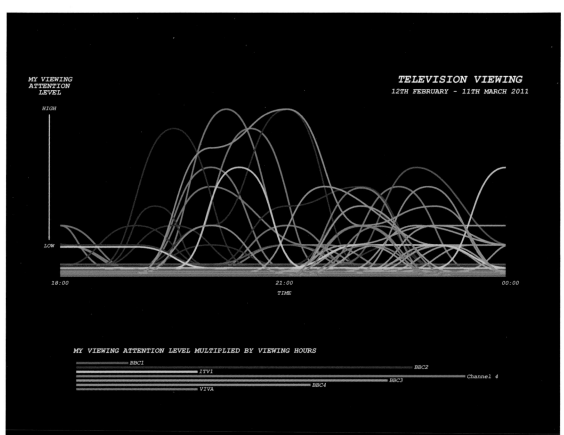

MY VIEWING ATTENTION LEVEL MULTIPLIED BY VIEWING HOURS

BBC1
BBC2
ITV1
Channel 4
BBC3
BBC4
VIVA

SPLIT BY WEEK DAY   SPLIT BY CHANNEL

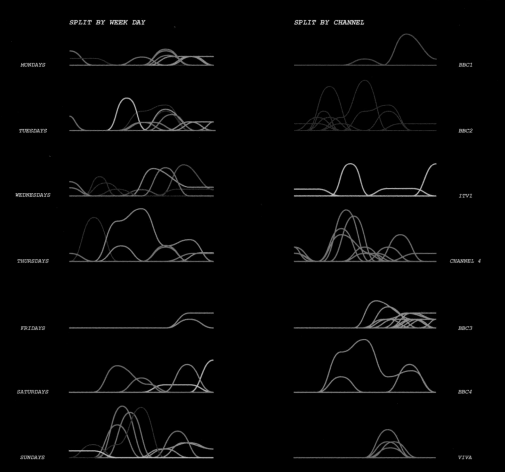

MONDAYS   BBC1

TUESDAYS   BBC2

WEDNESDAYS   ITV1

THURSDAYS   CHANNEL 4

FRIDAYS   BBC3

SATURDAYS   BBC4

SUNDAYS   VIVA

MARATHON COURSE ELEVATIONS

Ⓓ Designer: Tom Davie

This data visualization project compares the elevation profiles of the largest and most prestigious marathons in the world. Each dot represents 1/10 of a mile, and when combined, they depict the course elevation of the entire 26.2 miles of the race. The five marathon courses represented in this visualization are: Boston, New York City, Chicago, London and Berlin.

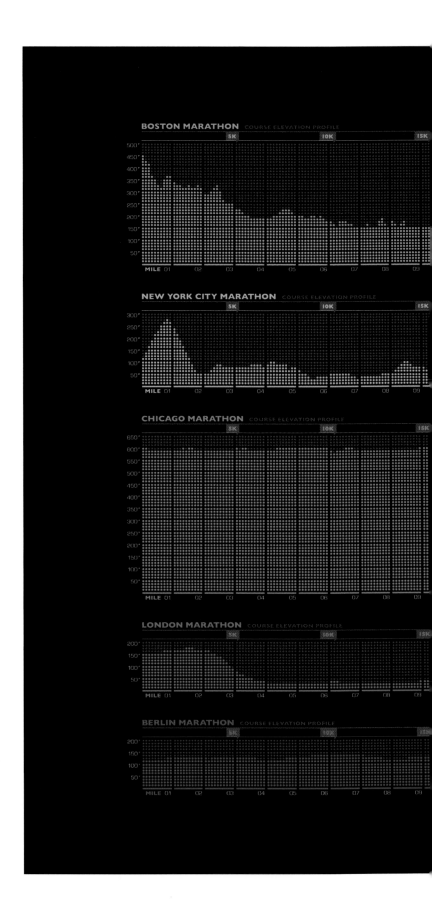

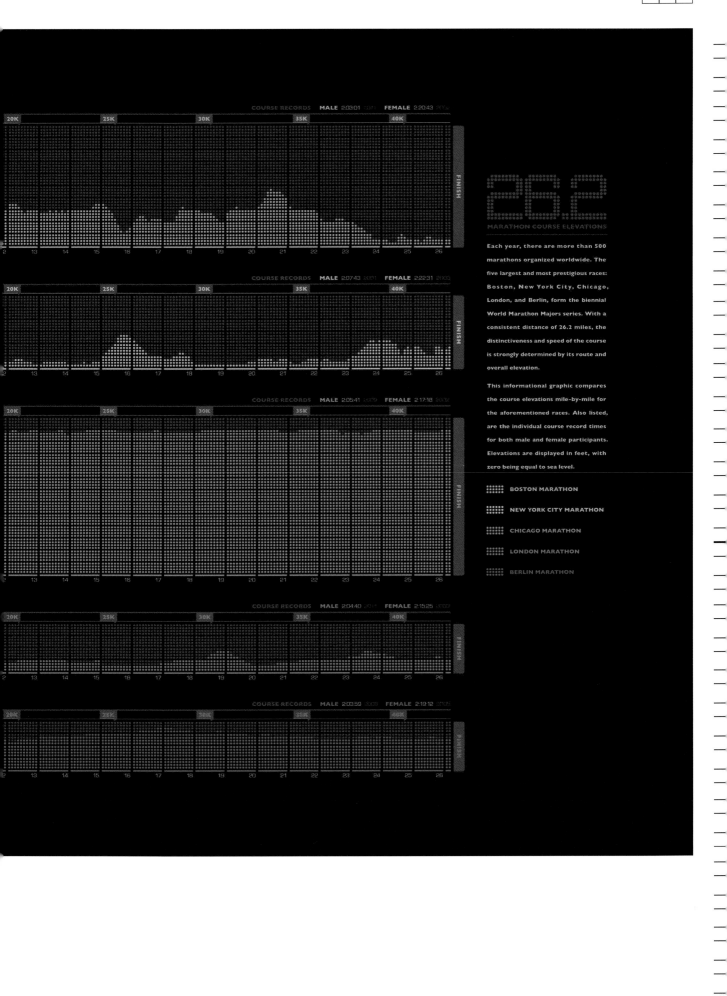

MARATHON COURSE ELEVATIONS

Each year, there are more than 500 marathons organized worldwide. The five largest and most prestigious races: Boston, New York City, Chicago, London, and Berlin, form the biennial World Marathon Majors series. With a consistent distance of 26.2 miles, the distinctiveness and speed of the course is strongly determined by its route and overall elevation.

This informational graphic compares the course elevations mile-by-mile for the aforementioned races. Also listed, are the individual course record times for both male and female participants. Elevations are displayed in feet, with zero being equal to sea level.

BOSTON MARATHON

NEW YORK CITY MARATHON

CHICAGO MARATHON

LONDON MARATHON

BERLIN MARATHON

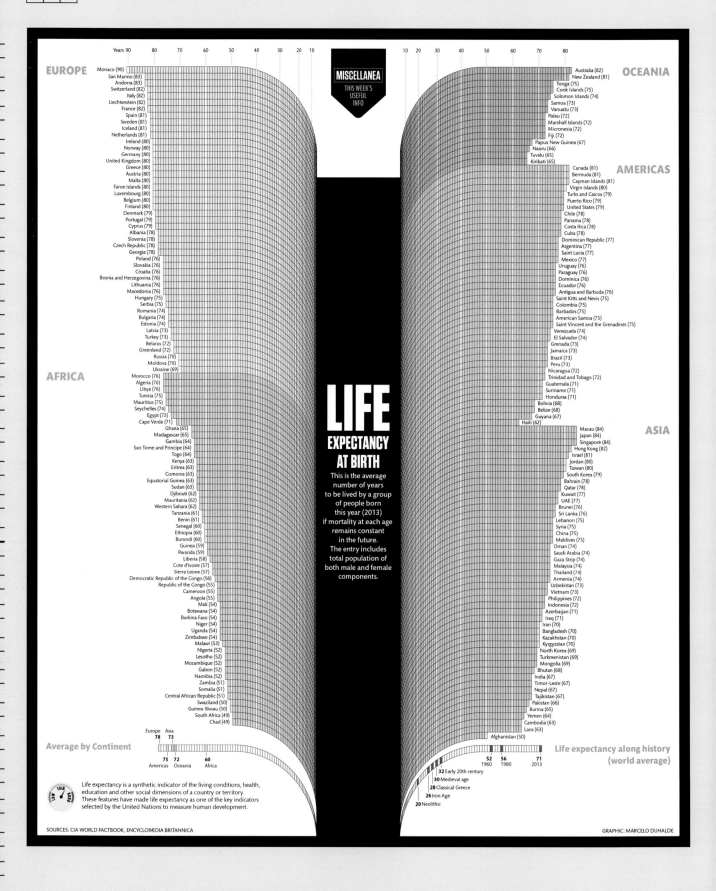

MISCELLANEA
THIS WEEK'S USEFUL INFO

LIFE
EXPECTANCY
AT BIRTH

This is the average number of years to be lived by a group of people born this year (2013) if mortality at each age remains constant in the future. The entry includes total population of both male and female components.

EUROPE

Monaco (90)
San Marino (83)
Andorra (83)
Switzerland (82)
Italy (82)
Liechtenstein (82)
France (82)
Spain (81)
Sweden (81)
Iceland (81)
Netherlands (81)
Ireland (80)
Norway (80)
Germany (80)
United Kingdom (80)
Greece (80)
Austria (80)
Malta (80)
Faroe Islands (80)
Luxembourg (80)
Belgium (80)
Finland (80)
Denmark (79)
Portugal (79)
Cyprus (79)
Albania (78)
Slovenia (78)
Czech Republic (78)
Georgia (78)
Poland (76)
Slovakia (76)
Croatia (76)
Bosnia and Herzegovina (76)
Lithuania (76)
Macedonia (76)
Hungary (75)
Serbia (75)
Romania (74)
Bulgaria (74)
Estonia (74)
Latvia (73)
Turkey (73)
Belarus (72)
Greenland (72)
Russia (70)
Moldova (70)
Ukraine (69)

AFRICA

Morocco (76)
Algeria (76)
Libya (76)
Tunisia (75)
Mauritius (75)
Seychelles (74)
Egypt (73)
Cape Verde (71)
Ghana (65)
Madagascar (65)
Gambia (64)
Sao Tome and Principe (64)
Togo (64)
Kenya (63)
Eritrea (63)
Comoros (63)
Equatorial Guinea (63)
Sudan (63)
Djibouti (62)
Mauritania (62)
Western Sahara (62)
Tanzania (61)
Benin (61)
Senegal (60)
Ethiopia (60)
Burundi (60)
Guinea (59)
Rwanda (59)
Liberia (58)
Cote d'Ivoire (57)
Sierra Leone (57)
Democratic Republic of the Congo (56)
Republic of the Congo (55)
Cameroon (55)
Angola (55)
Mali (54)
Botswana (54)
Burkina Faso (54)
Niger (54)
Uganda (54)
Zimbabwe (54)
Malawi (53)
Nigeria (52)
Lesotho (52)
Mozambique (52)
Gabon (52)
Namibia (52)
Zambia (51)
Somalia (51)
Central African Republic (51)
Swaziland (50)
Guinea-Bissau (50)
South Africa (49)
Chad (49)

OCEANIA

Australia (82)
New Zealand (81)
Tonga (75)
Cook Islands (75)
Solomon Islands (74)
Samoa (73)
Vanuatu (73)
Palau (72)
Marshall Islands (72)
Micronesia (72)
Fiji (72)
Papua New Guinea (67)
Nauru (66)
Tuvalu (65)
Kiribati (65)

AMERICAS

Canada (81)
Bermuda (81)
Cayman Islands (81)
Virgin Islands (80)
Turks and Caicos (79)
Puerto Rico (79)
United States (79)
Chile (78)
Panama (78)
Costa Rica (78)
Cuba (78)
Dominican Republic (77)
Argentina (77)
Saint Lucia (77)
Mexico (77)
Uruguay (76)
Paraguay (76)
Dominica (76)
Ecuador (76)
Antigua and Barbuda (76)
Saint Kitts and Nevis (75)
Colombia (75)
Barbados (75)
American Samoa (75)
Saint Vincent and the Grenadines (75)
Venezuela (74)
El Salvador (74)
Grenada (73)
Jamaica (73)
Brazil (73)
Peru (73)
Nicaragua (72)
Trinidad and Tobago (72)
Guatemala (71)
Suriname (71)
Honduras (71)
Bolivia (68)
Belize (68)
Guyana (67)
Haiti (62)

ASIA

Macau (84)
Japan (84)
Singapore (84)
Hong Kong (82)
Israel (81)
Jordan (80)
Taiwan (80)
South Korea (79)
Bahrain (78)
Qatar (78)
Kuwait (77)
UAE (77)
Brunei (76)
Sri Lanka (76)
Lebanon (75)
Syria (75)
China (75)
Maldives (75)
Oman (74)
Saudi Arabia (74)
Gaza Strip (74)
Malaysia (74)
Thailand (74)
Armenia (74)
Uzbekistan (73)
Vietnam (73)
Philippines (72)
Indonesia (72)
Azerbaijan (71)
Iraq (71)
Iran (70)
Bangladesh (70)
Kazakhstan (70)
Kyrgyzstan (70)
North Korea (69)
Turkmenistan (69)
Mongolia (69)
Bhutan (68)
India (67)
Timor-Leste (67)
Nepal (67)
Tajikistan (67)
Pakistan (66)
Burma (65)
Yemen (64)
Cambodia (63)
Laos (63)
Afghanistan (50)

Average by Continent

Europe	Asia
78	73

Americas 75 Oceania 72 Africa 60

Life expectancy along history (world average)

	52 1960	56 1980	71 2013

32 Early 20th century
30 Medieval age
28 Classical Greece
26 Iron Age
20 Neolithic

Life expectancy is a synthetic indicator of the living conditions, health, education and other social dimensions of a country or territory. These features have made life expectancy as one of the key indicators selected by the United Nations to measure human development.

SOURCES: CIA WORLD FACTBOOK, ENCYCLOPÆDIA BRITANNICA

GRAPHIC: MARCELO DUHALDE

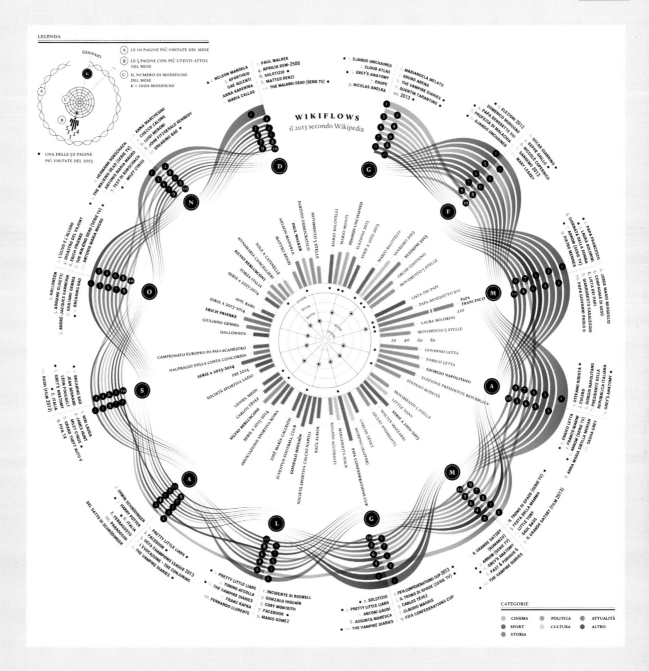

WIKIFLOWS
il 2013 secondo Wikipedia

LIFE EXPECTANCY ⇕

Ⓓ Designer: Marcelo Duhalde

A bar chart showing life expectancy, based on the latest data provided by the CIA report and Encyclopedia Britannica. The shape here is connected to the low-life-expectancy countries, and is similar to a sort of abyss, with the black square emulating a waterfall.

WIKIFLOWS ⇄

Ⓓ Designer: Michele Mauri, Valerio Pellegrini

Wikipedia, whether we like it or not, has become a leading source of information. Whenever something happens, such as when a particular book is quoted or a famous person dies (who we really know nothing about), we just google it, and, in most cases, end up on a Wikipedia page. Out of interest, it is possible to use Wikipedia as a device to obtain information about the past. Which were the most visited pages in 2013? Which were the most edited? What is the overall picture of one year of history, when viewed through Wikipedia?

WEATHER CHART

Ⓓ Designer: Clever°Franke

Clever°Franke focused on the relationship between the 2012 weather data provided by the KNMI (Royal Netherlands Meteorological Institute) and sentiments shared on social media about the weather during that year. Does the way people rate the weather on the Internet match meteorological facts? To analyze this, 714,843 messages about the weather were used in this chart. The messages were collected from a variety of websites, social media platforms and internet fora. The data was provided by Finchline, a company specializing in social media monitoring.

The 2012 weather chart provides several interesting observations. Sunshine is prominent in the way most people rate the weather. Overall, Dutch weather is predominantly rated negatively (58%). Only in April and March did people give mostly positive ratings of the weather.

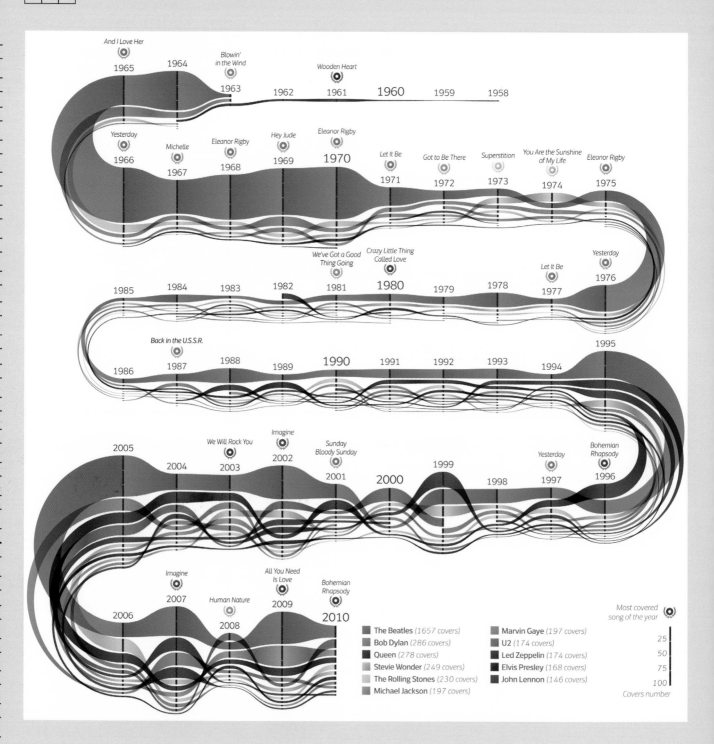

COVER-MANIA: BEATLES WIN

ⒹDesigner: Michele Mauri

This visualization shows the most-covered bands from 1958 to 2012. Each band is represented as a coloured ribbon. Ribbon height is proportional to the total numbers covered. The most-covered song each year is highlighted by a crest. This visualization won the *Information is Beautiful* prize, 2012.

ENERGY CONSUMPTION IN THE UNITED KINGDOM

Ⓓ Designer: Ben Willers

The United Kingdom, if you believe the tabloids, is currently on the brink of an energy crisis. Rising fuel costs and dwindling resources are forcing the country to look elsewhere, to satisfy its thirst for power. Much media attention has recently been focused on the uptake of renewable energy. But, how significant are these changes in the grand scheme of things?

Energy consumption in the United Kingdom
Million tonnes of oil equivalent, 1970 - 2010

Total energy consumption

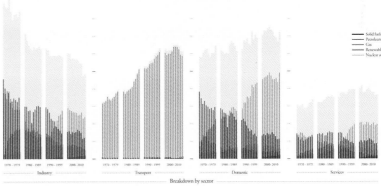

Breakdown by sector

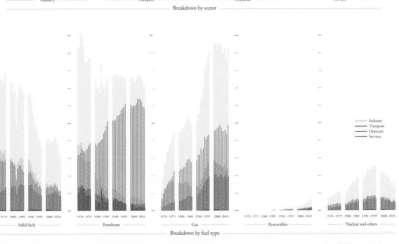

Breakdown by fuel type

Source: Department of Energy & Climate Change
bit.ly/uk_energy

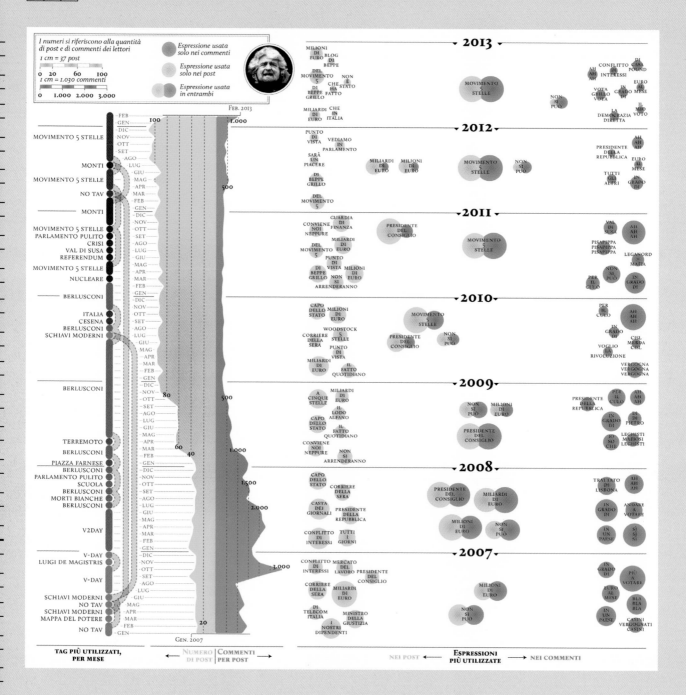

BEPPE GRILLO E IL LESSICO DELLA NEGAZIONE

Ⓓ Designer: Michele Mauri

Moimento 5 Stelle, one of the most influential political parties in Italy, is governed through an online blog, where, in theory, anyone can contribute. This visualization explores the evolution of the blog, which belongs to Beppe Grillo, the charismatic leader of the party, and analyzes the words the leader (in yellow) and commenters (in green) use most.

MOSQUITO-BORN DISEASE VISUALIZATION

Ⓓ Designer: Minsun Mini Kim, Beth Wernet and John Taikhyung Kim

Visualization of the number of mosquito-borne diseases reported around major cities in the United States, between August and October, 2012. The designers wanted to find out how temperature influences the number of mosquito-borne diseases reported.

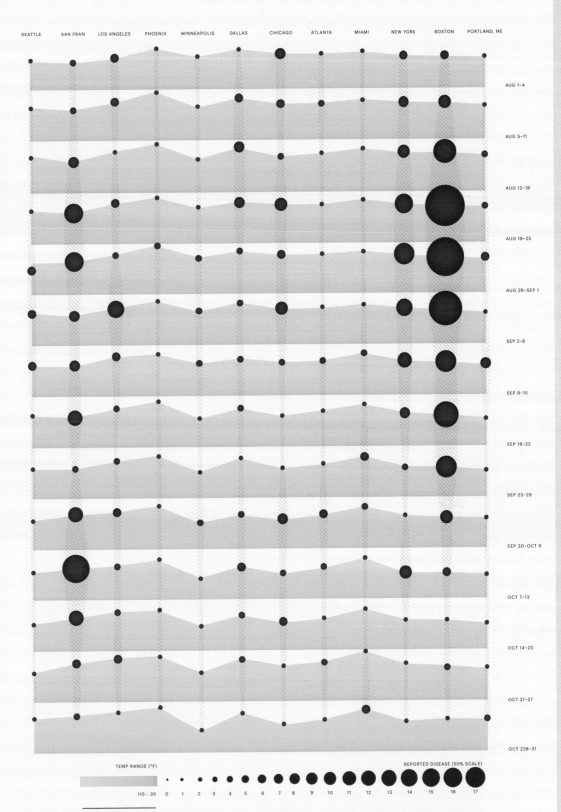

SEATTLE SAN FRAN LOS ANGELES PHOENIX MINNEAPOLIS DALLAS CHICAGO ATLANTA MIAMI NEW YORK BOSTON PORTLAND, ME

AUG 1-4
AUG 5-11
AUG 12-18
AUG 19-25
AUG 26-SEP 1
SEP 2-8
SEP 9-15
SEP 16-22
SEP 23-29
SEP 30-OCT 6
OCT 7-13
OCT 14-20
OCT 21-27
OCT 228-31

TEMP RANGE (°F)

115 - 35

REPORTED DISEASE (50% SCALE)

0 1 2 3 4 5 6 7 8 9 10 11 12 13 14 15 16 17

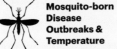

Mosquito-born Disease Outbreaks & Temperature

United States
August – October
2012

We visualized the number of mosquito-born diseases reported around major cities in the United States between August and October 2012. We wanted to find out how temperature and climate changes influences the number of mosquito-born diseases reported.

We focused on three most popular insect-born diseases: Easter Equine Encephalitis

(EEE), West Nile Virus and Dengue fever. There were total of 1137 reports related to these diseases in United States.

In the visualization you can see some relationship between temperature and reported diseases within 100 miles of each city. While there are also other factors such as population and humidity that affects the insect-born disease outbreaks,

this allows you to quickly scan for any patterns in temperature changes and disease.

It will be more beneficial to have more data points through out the year to identify better patterns. We also want to see how different types of diseases related to water, food and animals are affected by different temperatures.

We learned about analyzing data manually and thinking conceptually about the data, and enjoyed brainstorming many different story-telling possibilities with this data set.

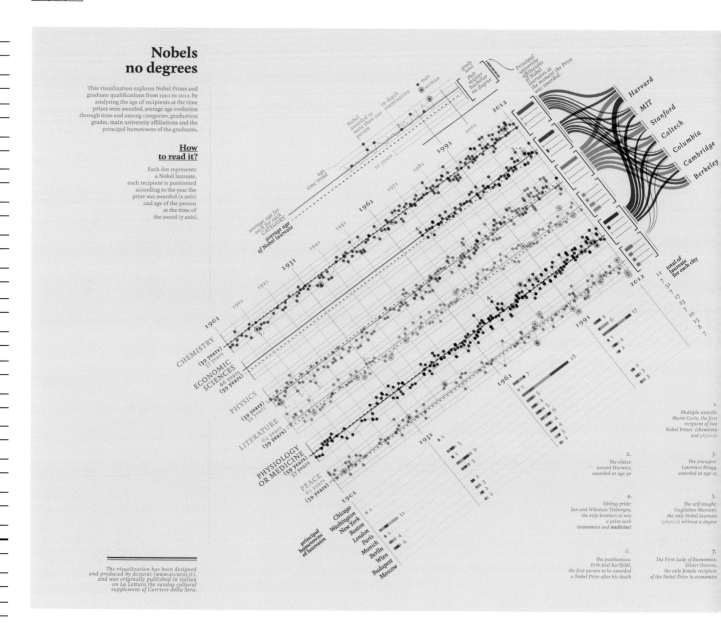

Nobels
no degrees

This visualization explores Nobel Prizes and graduate qualifications from 1901 to 2012, by analysing the age of recipients at the time prizes were awarded, average age evolution through time and among categories, graduation grades, main university affiliations and the principal hometowns of the graduates.

How
to read it?

Each dot represents a Nobel laureate, each recipient is positioned according to the year the prize was awarded (x axis) and age of the person at the time of the award (y axis).

The visualization has been designed and produced by Accurat (www.accurat.it), and was originally published in italian on La Lettura the sunday cultural supplement of Corriere della Sera.

1.
Multiple awards:
Marie Curie, the first recipient of two Nobel Prizes (chemistry and physics)

2.
The oldest:
Leonid Hurwicz,
awarded at age 90

3.
The youngest:
Lawrence Bragg,
awarded at age 25

4.
Sibling pride:
Jan and Nikolaas Tinbergen,
the only brothers to win a prize each
(economics and medicine)

5.
The self-taught:
Guglielmo Marconi,
the only Nobel laureate
(physics) without a degree

6.
The posthumous:
Erik Axel Karlfeldt,
the first person to be awarded a Nobel Prize after his death

7.
The First Lady of Economics:
Elinor Ostrom,
the only female recipient of the Nobel Prize in economics

LA LETTURA

Ⓐ Agency: Accurat Studio

La Lettura is a series of infographics that forms part of the Sunday cultural supplement of *Corriere della Sera*, the newspaper with the highest circulation in Italy.

Geniuses, visualized

The visualisation explores the one hundred geniuses of language identified in the book "Genius" by Harold Bloom. The composition of the individuals mirrors the structure of the chapters in the book, using the form of the Kabbalah Sephirot. Each individual is displayed by name, historical period of activity, main profession, continents of origin, number of pages dedicated in the book, visits to the relative pages on wikipedia.org, and relationships with other historical figures.

Harold Bloom, "Genius" italian edition
Rizzoli, 2002; britannica.com; toolserver.org

How to read it?

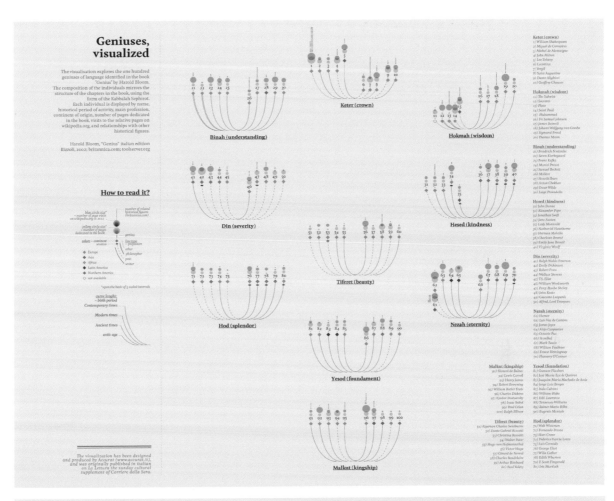

The visualization has been designed and produced by Accurat (www.accurat.it), and was originally published in italian on La Lettura the sunday cultural supplement of Corriere della Sera.

Brain drain

The phenomena of so-called «brain drain» is explored through a map showing incoming and outgoing flows of researchers in 16 countries.
Using a series of parameters, the map is an attempt to discover the motivations that move researchers from one country to another. Each country is visualized through the representation of GDP per capita, female employment rate, overall unemployment rate, university rankings, percentage of foreign researchers, percentage of foreign population, percentage of emigrant researchers, percentage of overall emigrant population, percentage of researchers returning to their country of origin, and the main countries researchers come from and move to.

How to read it?

The countries are positioned according to:
% of GDP invested in R&D (x axis)
n. of researchers per 1m people (y axis)
The analysis is based on the following data

(1) World Bank (2005-2010, worldbank.org)
(2) Foreign Born Scientists: Mobility Patterns for Sixteen Countries (2012 paper by Chiara Franzoni, Giuseppe Scellato and Paula Stephan, nber.org)
(3) Times Higher Education World University Rankings (2011-2012, timeshighereducation.co.uk)

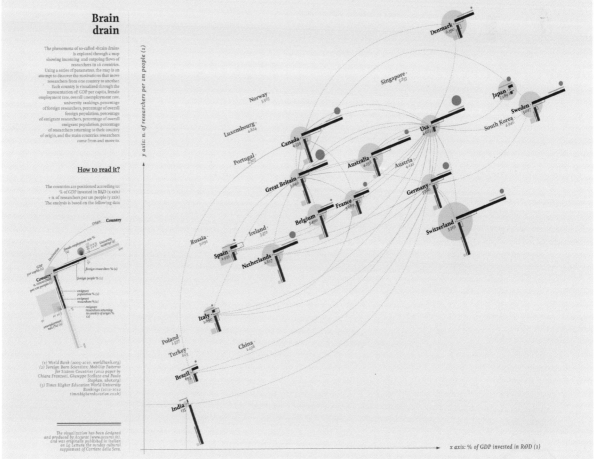

The visualization has been designed and produced by Accurat (www.accurat.it), and was originally published in italian on La Lettura the sunday cultural supplement of Corriere della Sera.

European banks and government debt

The visualisation compares the sovereign debt exposure of sixty-one European banks to the twenty-nine nations of the old continent. Each bank is positioned on the perpendicular according to the country of origin, and from the bottom upwards, based on the year of foundation (Monte dei Paschi being the oldest). The flow and quality of debt investment in the various states is displayed for each bank. The countries are arranged from left to right according to the internal relationship between public debt and GDP, and from the bottom upwards based on the growing number of inhabitants.

Sources: The Guardian, Eurostat (Ue), Business Week.
The data refers to the years 2011 and 2012

How to read it?

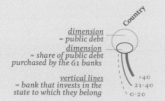

dimension
= public debt

dimension
= share of public debt purchased by the 61 banks

vertical lines
= bank that invests in the state to which they belong

>40
21-40
0-20

line type
= entity
of bank investment
(in billions of euro)
only if equal to or greater than
10% of total bank investment

colour
= Standard & Poor's rating

top notch
under observation
junk

number
of inhabitants
(in millions)

year of
bank foundation

2000

1900

1800

1700

1600

1500

1400

Estonia
Bulgaria
Luxemberg
Norway
Romania
Sweden
Czech rep.
Slovakia
Denm
Lithuania
Latvia
Slovenia

25

90
50
10

52
61
59
56
46
30
66
50
25
39
22
49

The visualization has been designed and produced by Accurat (www.accurat.it), and was originally published in italian on La Lettura the sunday cultural supplement of Corriere della Sera.

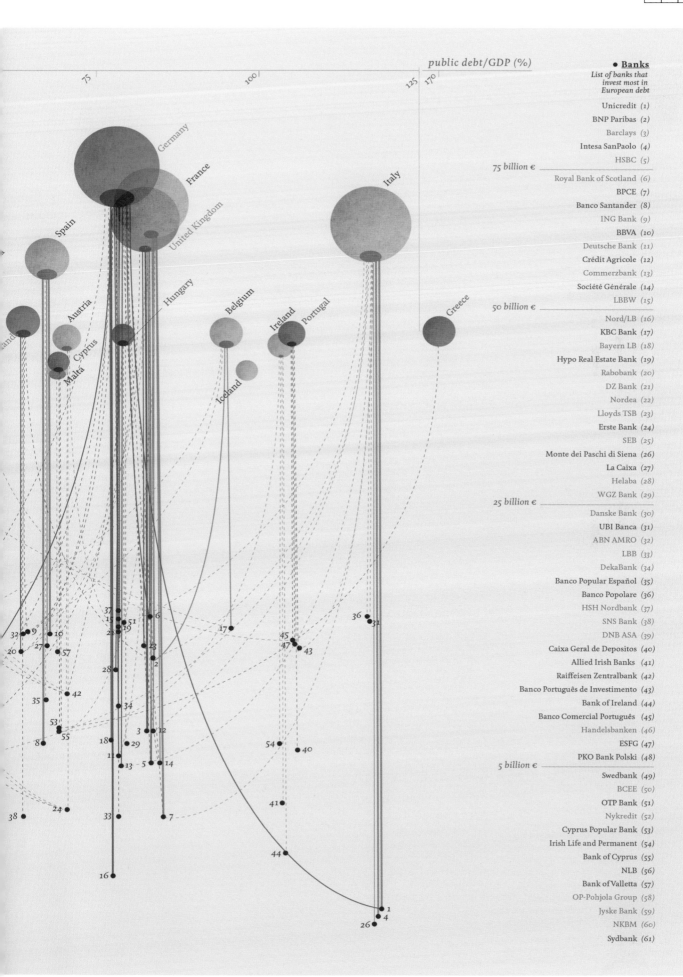

public debt/GDP (%)

75 | 100 | 125 170

● **Banks**
*List of banks that
invest most in
European debt*

Unicredit (1)
BNP Paribas (2)
Barclays (3)
Intesa SanPaolo (4)
HSBC (5)

75 billion €

Royal Bank of Scotland (6)
BPCE (7)
Banco Santander (8)
ING Bank (9)
BBVA (10)
Deutsche Bank (11)
Crédit Agricole (12)
Commerzbank (13)
Société Générale (14)
LBBW (15)

50 billion €

Nord/LB (16)
KBC Bank (17)
Bayern LB (18)
Hypo Real Estate Bank (19)
Rabobank (20)
DZ Bank (21)
Nordea (22)
Lloyds TSB (23)
Erste Bank (24)
SEB (25)
Monte dei Paschi di Siena (26)
La Caixa (27)
Helaba (28)
WGZ Bank (29)

25 billion €

Danske Bank (30)
UBI Banca (31)
ABN AMRO (32)
LBB (33)
DekaBank (34)
Banco Popular Español (35)
Banco Popolare (36)
HSH Nordbank (37)
SNS Bank (38)
DNB ASA (39)
Caixa Geral de Depositos (40)
Allied Irish Banks (41)
Raiffeisen Zentralbank (42)
Banco Português de Investimento (43)
Bank of Ireland (44)
Banco Comercial Português (45)
Handelsbanken (46)
ESFG (47)
PKO Bank Polski (48)

5 billion €

Swedbank (49)
BCEE (50)
OTP Bank (51)
Nykredit (52)
Cyprus Popular Bank (53)
Irish Life and Permanent (54)
Bank of Cyprus (55)
NLB (56)
Bank of Valletta (57)
OP-Pohjola Group (58)
Jyske Bank (59)
NKBM (60)
Sydbank (61)

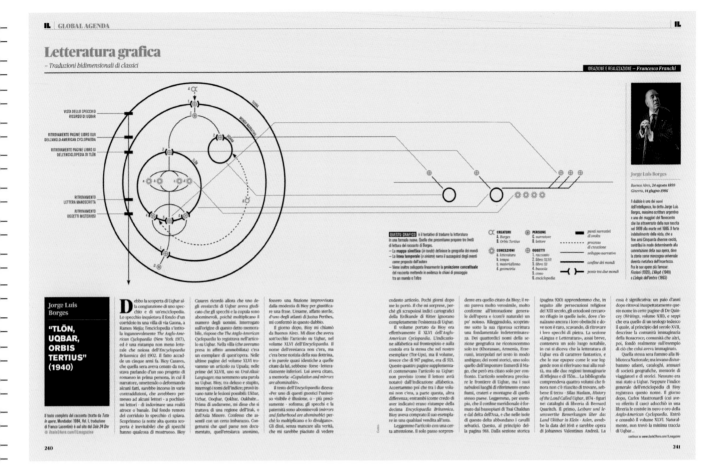

Letteratura grafica
– *Traduzioni bidimensionali di classici*

IDEAZIONE E REALIZZAZIONE – *Francesco Franchi*

Jorge Luis Borges

"TLÖN, UQBAR, ORBIS TERTIUS" (1940)

Il testo completo del racconto (tratto da Tutte le opere, *Mondadori 1984, Vol. I, traduzione di Franco Lucentini) è sul sito del* Sole 24 Ore *@ ilsole24ore/com/ILmagazine*

Debbo la scoperta di Uqbar alla congiunzione di uno specchio e di un'enciclopedia. Lo specchio inquietava il fondo d'un corridoio in una villa di via Gaona, a Ramos Mejía; l'enciclopedia s'intitolava ingannevolmente *The Anglo-American Cyclopaedia* (New York 1917), ed è una ristampa non meno letterale che noiosa dell'*Encyclopaedia Britannica* del 1902. Il fatto accadde un cinque anni fa. Bioy Casares, che quella sera aveva cenato da noi, stava parlando d'un suo progetto di romanzo in prima persona, in cui il narratore, omettendo o deformando alcuni fatti, sarebbe incorso in varie contraddizioni, che avrebbero permesso ad alcuni lettori – a pochissimi lettori – di indovinare una realtà atroce o banale. Dal fondo remoto del corridoio lo specchio ci spiava. Scoprimmo (a notte alta questa scoperta è inevitabile) che gli specchi hanno qualcosa di mostruoso. Bioy

Casares ricordò allora che uno degli eresiarchi di Uqbar aveva giudicato che gli specchi e la copula sono abominevoli, poiché moltiplicano il numero degli uomini. Interrogato sull'origine di questo detto memorabile, rispose che *The Anglo-American Cyclopaedia* la registrava nell'articolo su Uqbar. Nella villa (che avevamo presa in affitto ammobiliata) c'era un esemplare di quest'opera. Nelle ultime pagine del volume XLVI trovammo un articolo su Upsala; nelle prime del XLVII, uno su *Ural-Altaic Languages*; ma nemmeno una parola su Uqbar. Bioy, tra deluso e stupito, interrogò i tomi dell'indice; provò invano tutte le lezioni possibili: Ukbar, Ucbar, Ooqbar, Ookbar, Oukbahr... Prima di andarsene, mi disse che si trattava di una regione dell'Irak, o dell'Asia Minore. Confesso che assentii con un certo imbarazzo. Congetturai quel paese non documentato, quell'eresiarca anonimo,

fossero una finzione improvvisata dalla modestia di Bioy per giustificare una frase. L'esame, affatto sterile, d'uno degli atlanti di Justus Perthes, mi confermò in questo dubbio.

Il giorno dopo, Bioy mi chiamò da Buenos Aires. Mi disse che aveva sott'occhio l'articolo su Uqbar, nel volume XLVI dell'*Encyclopaedia*. Il nome dell'eresiarca non c'era, ma c'era bene notizia della sua dottrina, e in parole quasi identiche a quelle citate da lui, sebbene – forse – letterariamente inferiori. Lui aveva citato, a memoria: *«Copulation and mirrors are abominables»*.

Il testo dell'*Encyclopaedia* diceva: «Per uno di questi gnostici l'universo visibile è illusione, o – più precisamente – sofisma; gli specchi e la paternità sono abominevoli (*mirrors and fatherhood are abominables*) perché lo moltiplicano e lo divulgano». Gli dissi, senza mancare alla verità, che mi sarebbe piaciuto di vedere

codesto articolo. Pochi giorni dopo me lo portò. Il che mi sorprese, perché gli scrupolosi indici cartografici della Erdkunde di Ritter ignorano completamente l'esistenza di Uqbar.

Il volume portato da Bioy era effettivamente il XLVI dell'*Anglo-American Cyclopaedia*. L'indicazione alfabetica sul frontespizio e sulla costola era la stessa che nel nostro esemplare (Tor-Ups), ma il volume, invece che di 917 pagine, era di 921. Queste quattro pagine supplementari contenevano l'articolo su Uqbar: non previsto (come il lettore avrà notato) dall'indicazione alfabetica. Accertammo poi che tra i due volumi non c'era, a parte questa, altra differenza; entrambi (come credo di aver indicato) erano ristampe della decima *Encyclopaedia Britannica*. Bioy aveva comprato il suo esemplare in una qualsiasi vendita all'asta.

Leggemmo l'articolo con una certa attenzione. Il solo passo sorpren-

dente era quello citato da Bioy; il resto pareva molto verosimile, molto conforme all'intonazione generale dell'opera e (com'è naturale) un po' noioso. Rileggendolo, scoprimmo sotto la sua rigorosa scrittura una fondamentale indeterminatezza. Dei quattordici nomi della sezione geografica ne riconoscemmo solo tre (Khorassan, Armenia, Erzerum), interpolati nel testo in modo ambiguo; dei nomi storici, uno solo: quello dell'impostore Esmerdi il Mago, che però era citato solo per confronto. L'articolo sembrava precisare le frontiere di Uqbar, ma i suoi nebulosi luoghi di riferimento erano fiumi, crateri e montagne di quello stesso paese. Leggemmo, per esempio, che il confine meridionale è formato dal bassopiani di Tsai Chaldun e dal delta dell'Axa, e che nelle isole di questo delta abbondano i cavalli selvatici. Questo, al principio della pagina 918. Dalla sezione storica

(pagina 920) apprendemmo che, in seguito alle persecuzioni religiose del XIII secolo, gli ortodossi cercarono rifugio in quelle isole, dove s'innalzano ancora i loro obelischi e dove non è raro, scavando, di ritrovare i loro specchi di pietra. La sezione «Lingua e Letteratura», assai breve, conteneva un solo luogo notabile, in cui si diceva che la letteratura di Uqbar era di carattere fantastico, e che le sue epopee come le sue leggende non si riferivano mai alla realtà, ma alle due regioni immaginarie di Mlejnas e di Tlön... La bibliografia comprendeva quattro volumi che finora non c'è riuscito di trovare, sebbene il terzo – Silas Haslam, *History of the Lond Called Uqbar*, 1874 – figuri nei cataloghi di libreria di Bernard Quaritch. Il primo, *Lesbare und lesenswerthe Bemerkungen über das Land Ukkbar in Klein - Asien*, avrebbe la data del 1641 e sarebbe opera di Johannes Valentinus Andreä. La

cosa è significativa: un paio d'anni dopo ritrovai inaspettatamente questo nome in certe pagine di De Quincey (*Writings*, volume XIII), e seppi che era quello di un teologo tedesco il quale, al principio del secolo XVII, descrisse la comunità immaginaria della Rosacroce, comunità che altri, poi, fondò realmente sull'esempio di ciò che cohù aveva immaginato.

Quella stessa sera fummo alla Biblioteca Nazionale; ma invano disturbammo atlanti, cataloghi, annuari di società geografiche, memorie di viaggiatori e di storici. Nessuno era mai stato a Uqbar. Neppure l'indice generale dell'enciclopedia di Bioy registrava questo nome. Il giorno dopo, Carlos Mastronardi (cui avevo riferito il caso) adocchiò in una libreria le costole in nero e oro della *Anglo-American Cyclopaedia*. Entrò e consultò il volume XLVI. Naturalmente, non trovò la minima traccia di Uqbar...

continua su ilsole24ore.com/ILmagazine

Jorge Luis Borges
Buenos Aires, 24 agosto 1899
Ginevra, 14 giugno 1986

È dubbio è uno dei casi dell'intelligenza, ha detto Jorge Luis Borges, massimo scrittore argentino e uno dei maggiori del Novecento che ha attraversato dalla sua nascita nel 1899 alla morte nel 1986. Il forte indebolimento della vista, che a fine anni Cinquanta divenne cecità, contribuì in modo determinante alla connotazione della sua opera, dove la storia come menzogna universale diventa metafora dell'incertezza. Fra le sue opere più famose: *Ficciones* (1935), *L'Aleph* (1949) e *L'elogio dell'ombra* (1965).

Letteratura grafica

– *Traduzioni bidimensionali di classici*

DI – *Francesco Franchi*

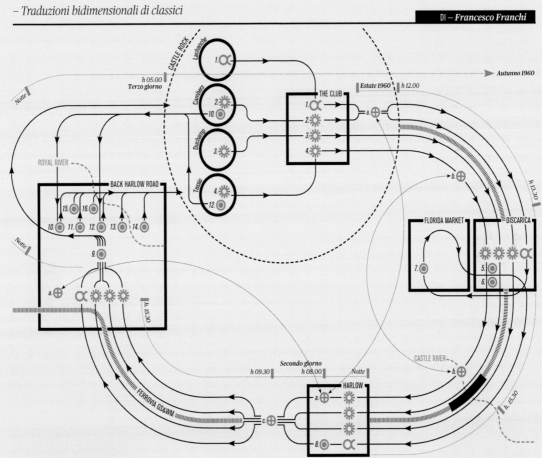

Stephen Edwin King

"IL CORPO - STAND BY ME" (1982)

Da questo racconto è tratto il film *Stand by me – Ricordo di un'estate* diretto da Rob Reiner (1986)

Narrato in prima persona da **Gordie Lachance** – *indicato nel grafico con il simbolo ∝* – è il racconto di un **viaggio** di due giorni che il protagonista compie nell'estate del 1960 con tre amici: Chris, Teddy e Vern – ☀ – attraverso i boschi che circondano la cittadina di Castle Rock, nel Maine. I ragazzi vogliono ritrovare il **corpo** di un coetaneo scomparso da tempo, sulla scia delle notizie che ne dà la radio. Sembra che Billy, il fratello di Vern, lo abbia scorto in una certa radura. Il loro cammino segue i binari della **ferrovia** che attraversa la contea. I quattro incontrano imprevisti e difficoltà che segneranno per sempre la loro vita. Alla fine, la missione avrà successo e vedere per la prima volta un **cadavere** – *9. ⊕* – li farà crescere.

∝ NARRATORE
1. *Gordon Lachance*

☀ PROTAGONISTI
2. *Chris Chambers*
3. *Teddy Duchamp*
4. *Vern Tessio*

◉ PERSONAGGI
5. *Milo Pressman*
6. *Chopper*
7. *George Dusset*
8. *femmina di daino*
9. *Ray Brower*
10. *Eyeball Chambers*
11. *Ace Merrill*
12. *Billy Tessio*

13. *Charlie Hogan*
14. *Jack Mudgett*
15. *Fuzzy Bracowicz*
16. *Vince Desjardins*

⊕ ALTRI ELEMENTI
a. *pistola*
b. *pettine*
c. *sanguisughe*

▬ *ponte*

→ *sviluppo narrativo*

▥▥▥ *ferrovia*

– – – *fiumi*

LE ALTRE INTERPRETAZIONI GRAFICHE

Nei numeri precedenti di *IL* abbiamo pubblicato le rielaborazioni grafiche di: *Tlön, Uqbar, Orbis Tertius* di **Jorge Luis Borges**; *Il lungo pranzo di Natale* di **Thornton Wilder** e *Il Piccolo Principe* di **Antoine de Saint-Exupéry**

Stephen Edwin King

Portland, Maine
21 settembre 1947

Stephen King, il re del brivido, vive e lavora nel Maine. Le sue storie sono bestseller in tutto il mondo e hanno ispirato film di successo, da *Shining* a *Misery non deve morire*

Corbis

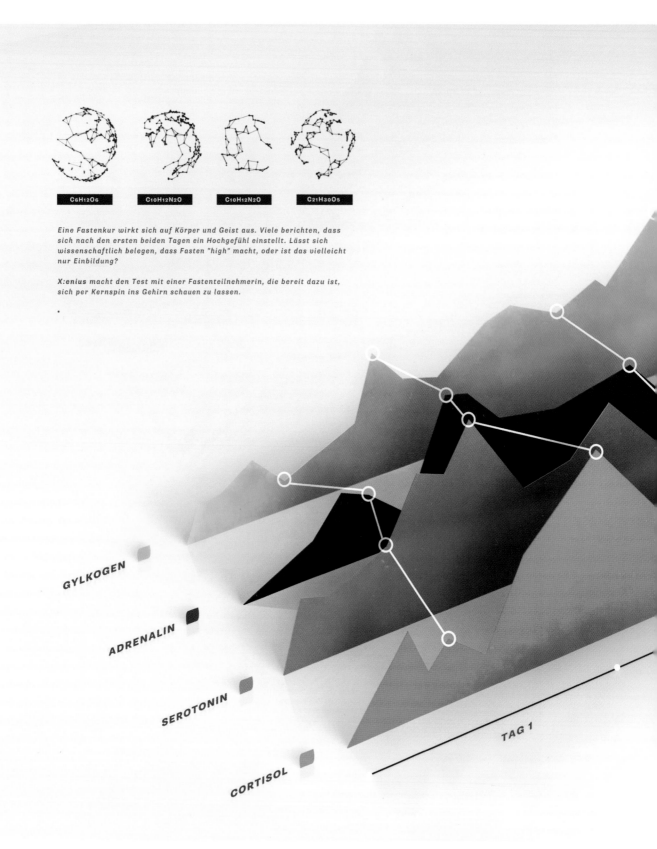

C6H12O6   C10H12N2O   C10H12N2O   C21H30O5

Eine Fastenkur wirkt sich auf Körper und Geist aus. Viele berichten, dass
sich nach den ersten beiden Tagen ein Hochgefühl einstellt. Lässt sich
wissenschaftlich belegen, dass Fasten "high" macht, oder ist das vielleicht
nur Einbildung?

X:enius macht den Test mit einer Fastenteilnehmerin, die bereit dazu ist,
sich per Kernspin ins Gehirn schauen zu lassen.

GYLKOGEN

ADRENALIN

SEROTONIN

CORTISOL

TAG 1

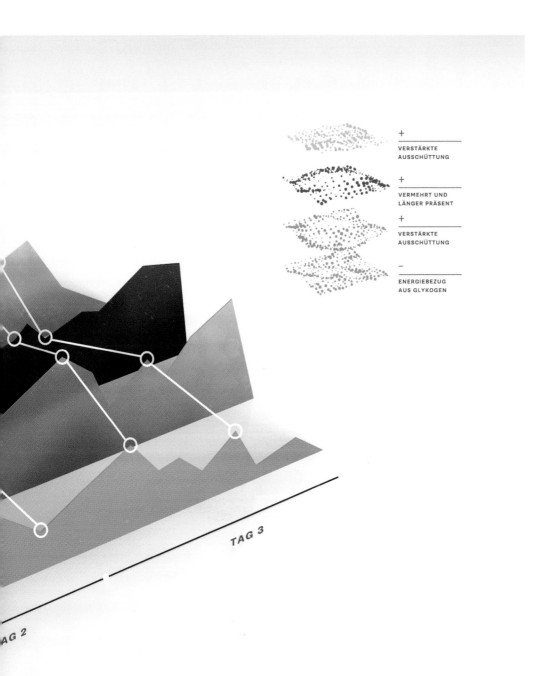

+
_____
**VERSTÄRKTE
AUSSCHÜTTUNG**

+
_____
**VERMEHRT UND
LÄNGER PRÄSENT**

+
_____
**VERSTÄRKTE
AUSSCHÜTTUNG**

–
_____
**ENERGIEBEZUG
AUS GLYKOGEN**

TAG 3

AG 2

X:ENIUS

Ⓓ Designer: Julian Hrankov

These infographics were developed as part of a
redesign study by arts TV program *X:enius*.

IDENTITÄT - THE GESTALT OF DIGITAL IDENTITY

ⓓ Designer: Studio NAND

Identität evaluates how 'digital identity' is generated by way of a series of digitally fabricated and readable data sculptures. More than 100,000 raw datasets from sources like Last.fm, delicious, Amazon and Twitter, were crawled from the web, to interrelate four different criteria: personal interests, communication behaviour, activities, and the age of the online participants. Based on the assumption that a digital identity is measurable and comparable, these datasets were then represented, using custom computational tools. The data was visually abstracted and interpreted, to give the disembodied digital identity a unique and characteristic *gestalt*, in the form of a data sculpture.

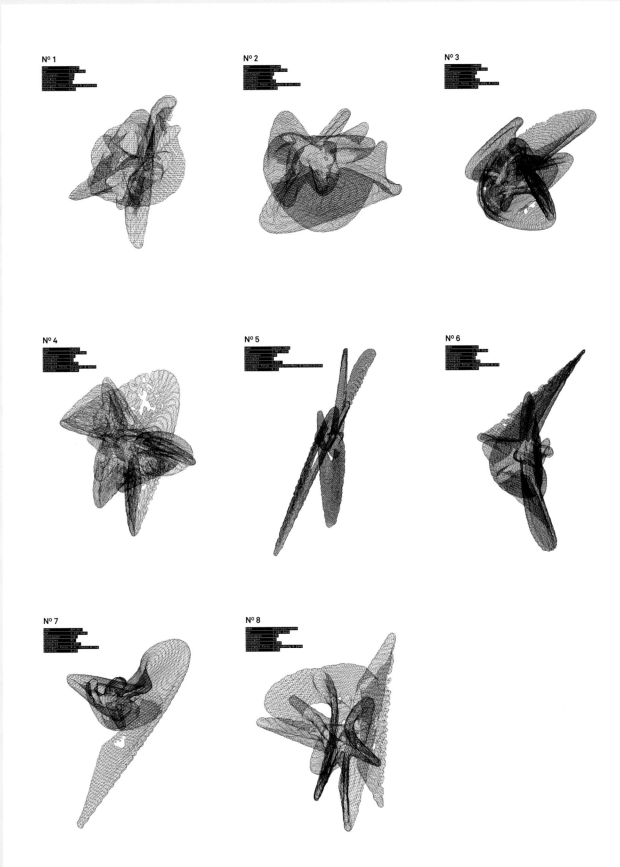

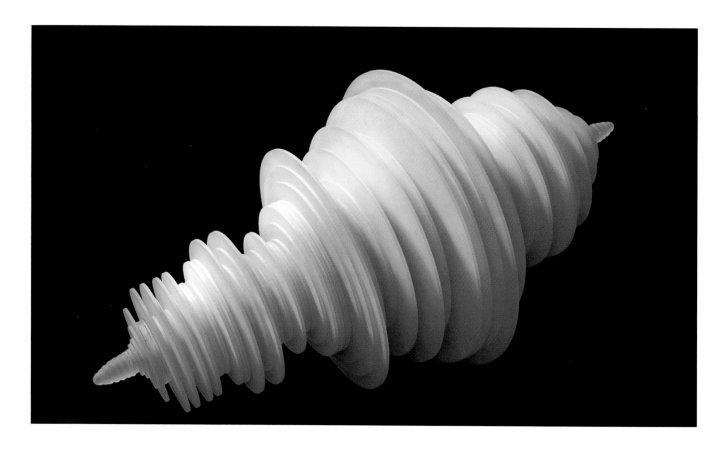

TŌHOKU JAPANESE EARTHQUAKE SCULPTURE

Ⓐ Artist: Luke Jerram

This sculpture was made to contemplate the 2011 Tōhoku earthquake and tsunami, in Japan. To create the sculpture, a seismogram of the earthquake was rotated, using computer-aided design, then printed in three dimensions, using rapid prototyping technology. The artwork measures 30 x 20 cm, and represents nine minutes of the earthquake.

DAY 5

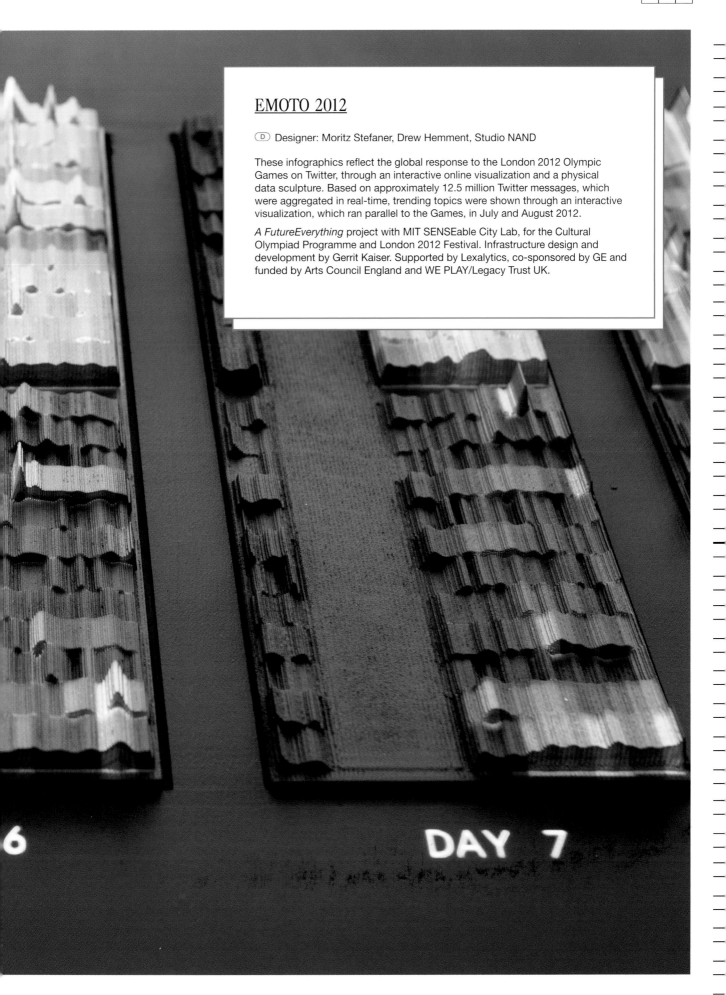

EMOTO 2012

Ⓓ Designer: Moritz Stefaner, Drew Hemment, Studio NAND

These infographics reflect the global response to the London 2012 Olympic Games on Twitter, through an interactive online visualization and a physical data sculpture. Based on approximately 12.5 million Twitter messages, which were aggregated in real-time, trending topics were shown through an interactive visualization, which ran parallel to the Games, in July and August 2012.

A FutureEverything project with MIT SENSEable City Lab, for the Cultural Olympiad Programme and London 2012 Festival. Infrastructure design and development by Gerrit Kaiser. Supported by Lexalytics, co-sponsored by GE and funded by Arts Council England and WE PLAY/Legacy Trust UK.

6   DAY 7

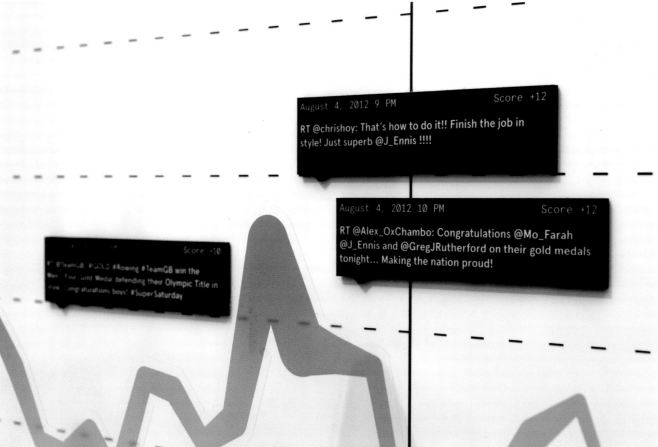

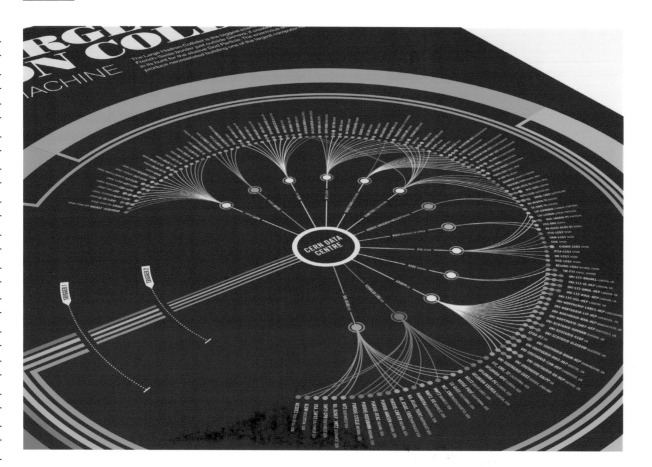

THE BIG BANG MACHINE

Ⓒ Copywriter: Josh Gowen
Ⓡ Researcher: Josh Gowen

This infographic was commissioned by Signal Noise, to produce a poster for *Less than a Second*, an exhibition based on how modern technology allows us to capture a huge amount of data in under a second. The designer studied the Large Hadron Collider, and the resulting A0 poster conveys the massive amounts of data these experiments produce, as they constantly exchange information over the specially created *Worldwide Computer Grid*.

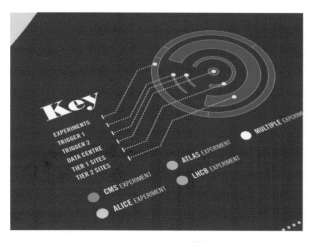

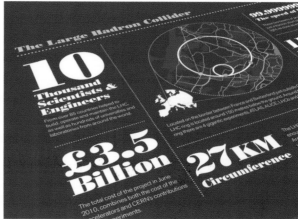

THE LARGE HADRON COLLIDER
THE BIG BANG MACHINE

The Large Hadron Collider is the biggest scientific experiment ever attempted. Spanning the French-Swiss border just outside Geneva, it creates millions of tiny Big Bangs every second in its hunt for the elusive God Particle. The enormous amount of data these experiments produce necessitated building one of the largest computer networks in the world.

CERN DATA CENTRE

Key

The Large Hadron Collider

10 Thousand Scientists & Engineers

£3.5 Billion

27 KM Circumference

99.999999% The speed of light

11,245 Times a Second

Higgs Boson The God Particle

Big Bang Conditions

The Data

600 Million

Trigger One 99.99% Data Discarded

1 PB Every Second

Trigger Two 99% Data Discarded

Data Centre 73 Thousand

Tier 1 11 Tier 1 Centres

Tier 2 140 Tier 2 Centres

The Grid 1.5 Million

10 GB A Second

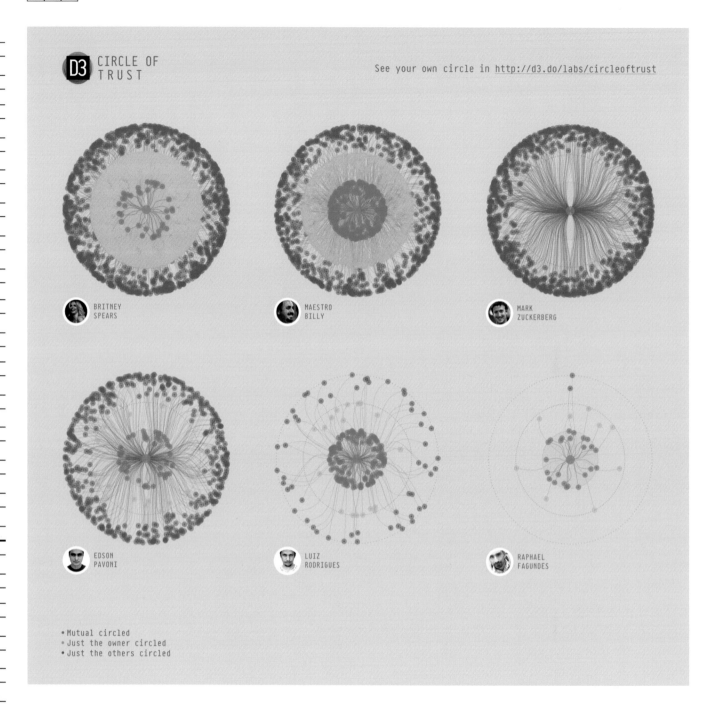

D3 CIRCLE OF TRUST

See your own circle in http://d3.do/labs/circleoftrust

BRITNEY SPEARS

MAESTRO BILLY

MARK ZUCKERBERG

EDSON PAVONI

LUIZ RODRIGUES

RAPHAEL FAGUNDES

- Mutual circled
- Just the owner circled
- Just the others circled

CIRCLE OF TRUST

ⓓ Designer: D3

How asymmetric is your relationship network at Google+? Is there a way to visualize how each person is using and constructing this social environment?

With these two questions in mind, D3 wanted to give viewers a quality, real example of how the new Google+ API can be used, in its early stages. The idea came from something that Jack Byrnes—a character in the film *Meet the Parents*—likes to call 'the circle of trust'. With free interpretation of Jack's theory, D3 made a simple algorithm to visualize the people inside this circle of trust and those outside it.

It all boils down to this: green represents mutual selection to be in each other's circle of trust, yellow represents the user's unreciprocated selection of people to be in their circle, and vice versa for red.

Circle of Trust is an interface data-visualization experiment using Google+ API and HTML5.

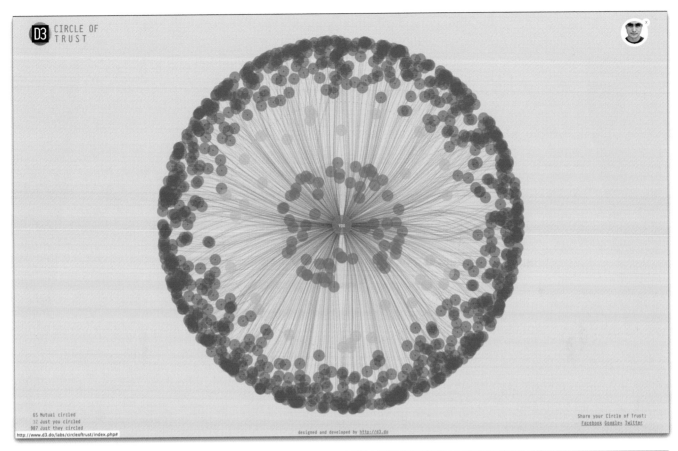

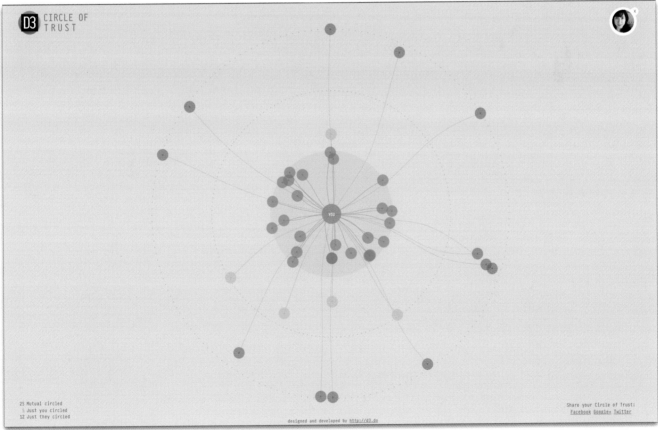

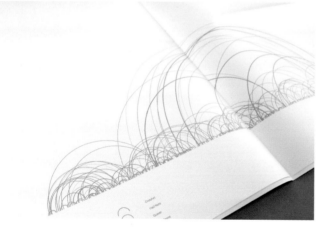

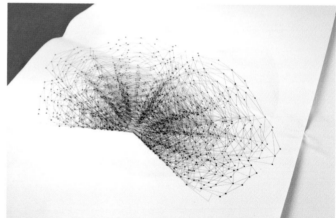

DISPARATE CONNECTIONS

Ⓓ Designer: Brett O'Mahony

Disparate Connections explores the rich avenues of creation, epiphany, insight and imagination that have led to some of the greatest creative masterpieces in history. This exploration aims to unearth and visually represent what these discoveries had in common, what aids epiphany and what guides creation. The compiled studies are illustrated with the use of infographics, in a limited-edition newspaper—comprising posters—called *It Started with the Wheel*, a typographic and data-visualization study that represents every major invention, creation and discovery, from 2340 BC to 2013.

Disparate Connections

Neuroscience,
The Brain &
Creativity

The Creative Myth
Demystifying creativity

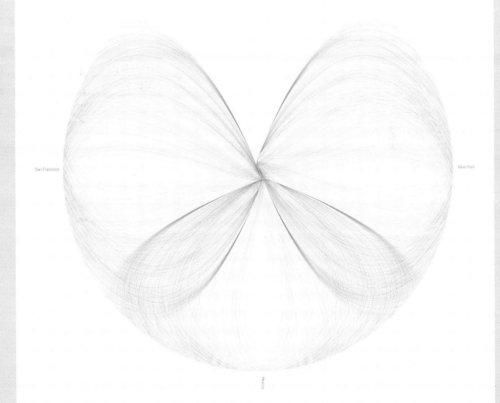

Denver

San Francisco

New York

MEXICO

Insight
Jack Kerouac On The Road
Three Week Burst of Insight

Jack Kerouac's 'On The Road' April 1951

100 Words Per Minute
114000 Words Per Day
798000 Words Per Week
2394000 Words In Total Over Three Weeks

1 Line = 100 Words
1 Section = 1 week
1 Week = 7980 Lines
7980 Lines = 798000 Words

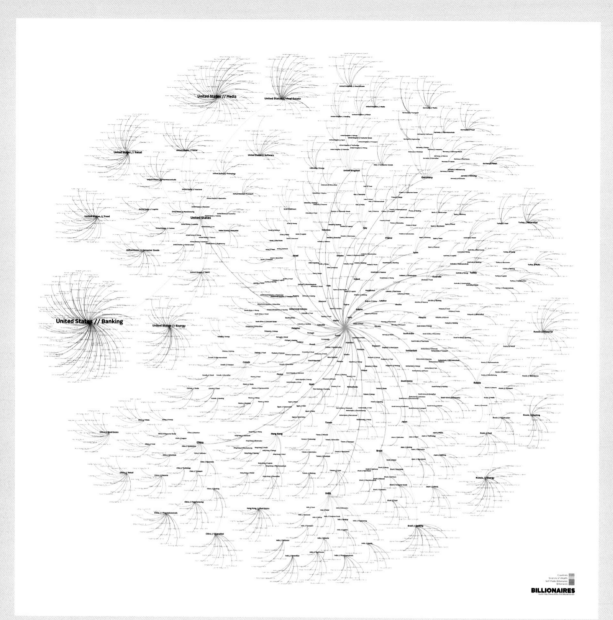

BILLIONAIRES

BILLIONAIRES   ⬍

Ⓓ Designer: Kim Albrecht

Billionaires is a visualization of all humans with a capital of over 1,000,000,000 dollars. The data comes from www.forbes.com/billionaires, but the way the information is visualized provides a very different picture. The 1,600 people are categorized by country and the industry where they made their money, giving an overview of the location and source of wealth. The graphic shows the macro-connections of wealth and their origins.

ANALYSIS OF SPACE   ⬌

Ⓓ Designer: Kim Albrecht

Photographs were uploaded to Amazon's Mechanical Turk, and people from around the world were asked to tag the images. The outcome was a network of words: a tag cloud, which described the content of the images and thus mapped the location. The images were also tagged by the designer. As a result of this process, two overlaying network structures reflected a personal subjective view and the objective view from the cloud. The red labels are personal tags about the area; the black labels are tags from random people from all over the world.

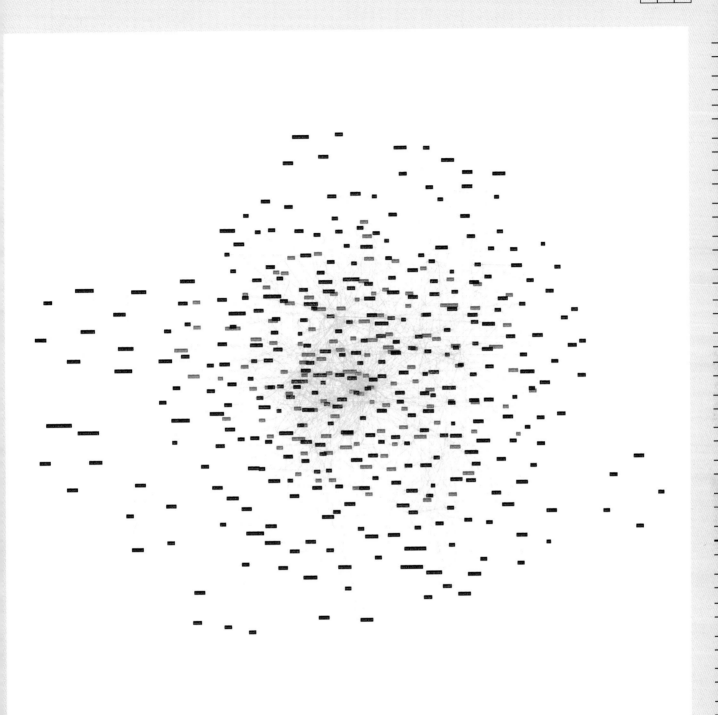

Transports System

Analysing the transport system gives back a wide range in quantity and variety of issues and information available. We focused our work mainly on the infrastructural system nationwide.
Our survey carefully focuses on matters and troubles created at local level by new infrastructures.
It makes a point of laws and rules that regulate the infrastructural net development in European countries.

As far as it is concerned about the analysis of new infrastructures increase, we have pointed out how different roles may interact.
In other words, how citizens can influence the action of the plaintiffs that actually has decisional power in ruling the system.
We have foremost mapped critical areas nationwide. For the BreBeMi highway project we have identified the main plaintiffs and their thinking.

DANIELE BERTOLI
ANDREA DESIATO
PAOLO DUSI
DANIELE FADDA
DANIELE GUIDO
LUCA MASUD
MICHELE MAURI
MAURO NAPOLI

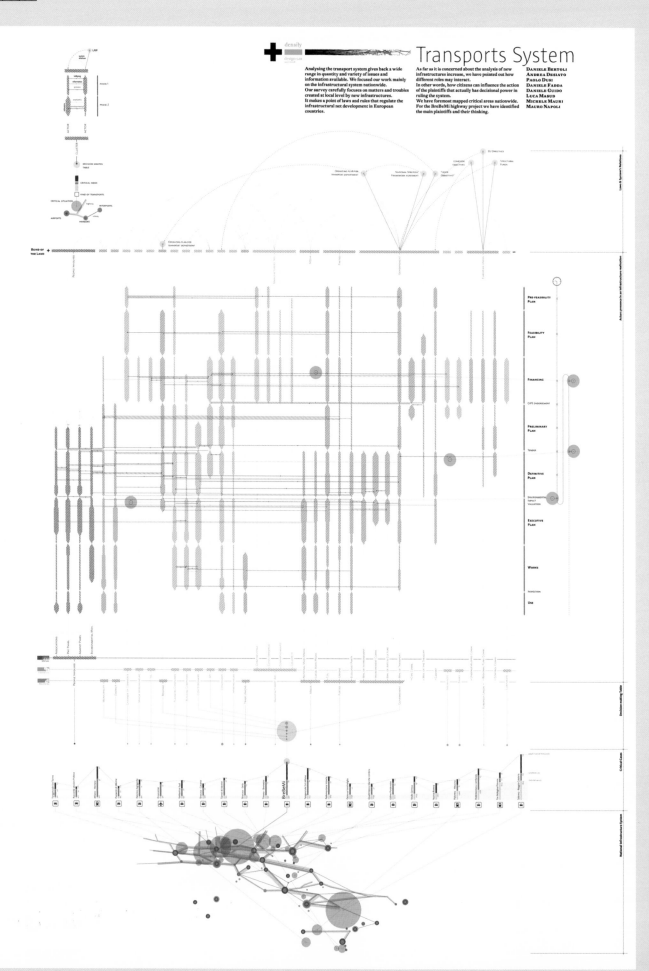

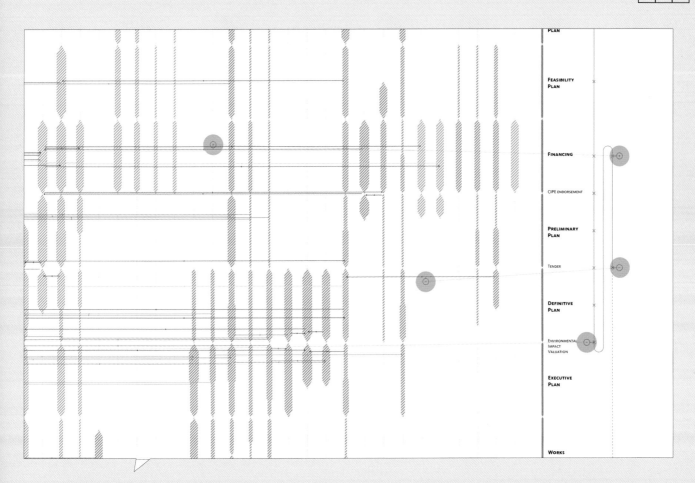

PLAN

FEASIBILITY PLAN

FINANCING

CIPE ENDORSEMENT

PRELIMINARY PLAN

TENDER

DEFINITIVE PLAN

ENVIRONMENTAL IMPACT VALUATION

EXECUTIVE PLAN

WORKS

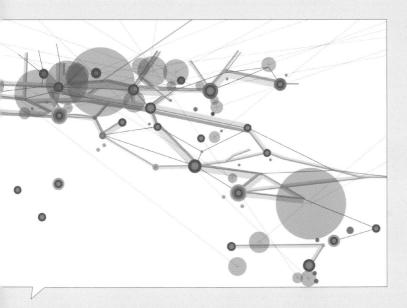

TRANSPORTS SYSTEM

Ⓓ Designer: Daniele Bertoli, Andrea Desiato, Paolo Dusi, Daniele Fadda, Daniele Guido, Luca Masud, Michele Mauri, Mauro Napoli

This infographic deals with a wide range of issues related to the transport system, at an Italian and European level. The survey carefully explores the conflicts created at local level by big infrastructures, such as main roads and high-speed railways.
The map represents each stakeholder's involvement, focusing particularly on citizen groups.

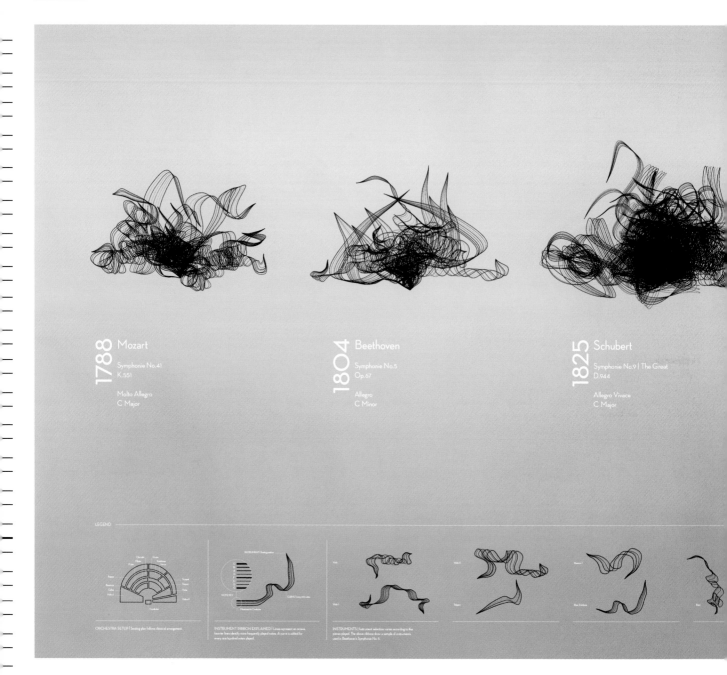

SYMPHONIC COMPLEXITIES

ⓓ Designer: Anna Reinbold

The instrumental contribution to the final movement of six classic symphonies
is visualized in this print. Each visualization is based on the classic seating
arrangement of an orchestra, and considers the number and type of notes
played, showing the complexity involved in playing each of these pieces.

Each instrument is represented by a ribbon comprising eight lines, signifying
the keys of an octave. The weight and curvature of each stroke is determined
by the number of notes played in the final movement.

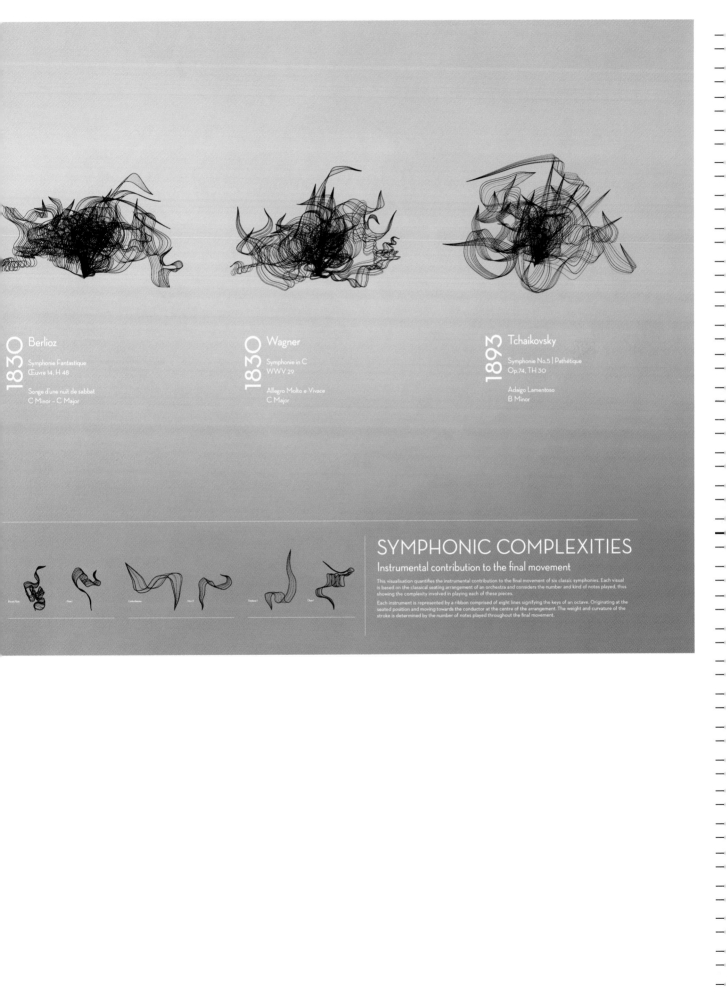

1830 Berlioz

Symphonie Fantastique
Œuvre 14, H 48

Songe d'une nuit de sabbat
C Minor – C Major

1830 Wagner

Symphonie in C
WWV 29

Allegro Molto e Vivace
C Major

1893 Tchaikovsky

Symphonie No.5 | Pathétique
Op.74, TH 30

Adaigo Lamentoso
B Minor

SYMPHONIC COMPLEXITIES
Instrumental contribution to the final movement

This visualisation quantifies the instrumental contribution to the final movement of six classic symphonies. Each visual is based on the classical seating arrangement of an orchestra and considers the number and kind of notes played, thus showing the complexity involved in playing each of these pieces.

Each instrument is represented by a ribbon comprised of eight lines signifying the keys of an octave. Originating at the seated position and moving towards the conductor at the centre of the arrangement. The weight and curvature of the stroke is determined by the number of notes played throughout the final movement.

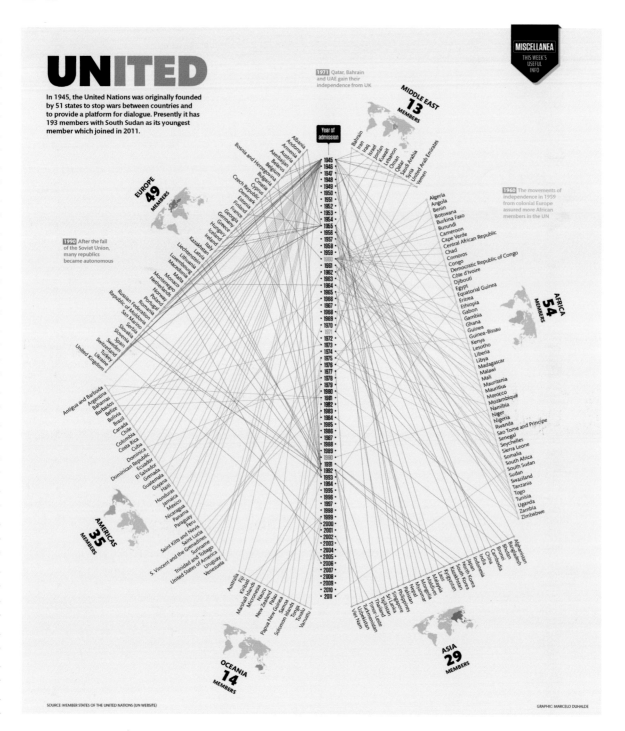

UNITED

In 1945, the United Nations was originally founded by 51 states to stop wars between countries and to provide a platform for dialogue. Presently it has 193 members with South Sudan as its youngest member which joined in 2011.

1971 Qatar, Bahrain and UAE gain their independence from UK

MIDDLE EAST 13 MEMBERS

EUROPE 49 MEMBERS

1960 The movements of independence in 1959 from colonial Europe assured more African members in the UN

1990 After the fall of the Soviet Union, many republics became autonomous

AFRICA 54 MEMBERS

AMERICAS 35 MEMBERS

ASIA 29 MEMBERS

OCEANIA 14 MEMBERS

SOURCE: MEMBER STATES OF THE UNITED NATIONS (UN WEBSITE)

GRAPHIC: MARCELO DUHALDE

UNITED ⇕

Ⓓ Designer: Marcelo Duhalde

With the continents differentiated by colour, this visualization maps out the year when each of the 193 member countries joined the United Nations.

LOSCIL SINE STUDIES ⇄

Ⓓ Designer: Derek Kim
Ⓟ Printer: Seizure Palace

This is a cover and poster for *Sine Studies 1*: a limited edition JAZ Records release by Loscil. The concept behind the art is based on the beauty of sine waves. These waves and their corresponding frequencies were mapped out using an X-Y oscilloscope.

LOSCIL

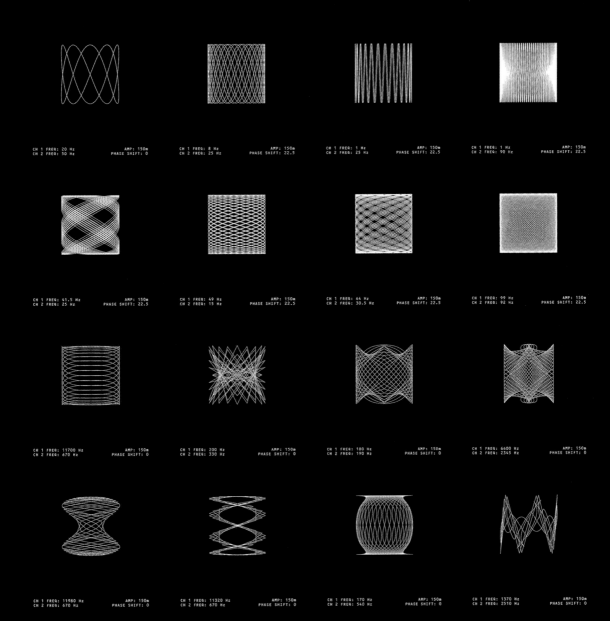

CH 1 FREQ: 20 Hz   AMP: 150m
CH 2 FREQ: 50 Hz   PHASE SHIFT: 0

CH 1 FREQ: 8 Hz   AMP: 150m
CH 2 FREQ: 25 Hz   PHASE SHIFT: 22.5

CH 1 FREQ: 1 Hz   AMP: 150m
CH 2 FREQ: 25 Hz   PHASE SHIFT: 22.5

CH 1 FREQ: 1 Hz   AMP: 150m
CH 2 FREQ: 90 Hz   PHASE SHIFT: 22.5

CH 1 FREQ: 41.5 Hz   AMP: 150m
CH 2 FREQ: 25 Hz   PHASE SHIFT: 22.5

CH 1 FREQ: 49 Hz   AMP: 150m
CH 2 FREQ: 15 Hz   PHASE SHIFT: 22.5

CH 1 FREQ: 64 Hz   AMP: 150m
CH 2 FREQ: 30.5 Hz   PHASE SHIFT: 22.5

CH 1 FREQ: 99 Hz   AMP: 150m
CH 2 FREQ: 92 Hz   PHASE SHIFT: 22.5

CH 1 FREQ: 11700 Hz   AMP: 150m
CH 2 FREQ: 670 Hz   PHASE SHIFT: 0

CH 1 FREQ: 200 Hz   AMP: 150m
CH 2 FREQ: 330 Hz   PHASE SHIFT: 0

CH 1 FREQ: 180 Hz   AMP: 150m
CH 2 FREQ: 190 Hz   PHASE SHIFT: 0

CH 1 FREQ: 6600 Hz   AMP: 150m
CH 2 FREQ: 2345 Hz   PHASE SHIFT: 0

CH 1 FREQ: 11980 Hz   AMP: 150m
CH 2 FREQ: 670 Hz   PHASE SHIFT: 0

CH 1 FREQ: 11320 Hz   AMP: 150m
CH 2 FREQ: 670 Hz   PHASE SHIFT: 0

CH 1 FREQ: 170 Hz   AMP: 150m
CH 2 FREQ: 540 Hz   PHASE SHIFT: 0

CH 1 FREQ: 1370 Hz   AMP: 150m
CH 2 FREQ: 2510 Hz   PHASE SHIFT: 0

SINE STUDIES 1

ALL MUSIC MADE FROM SINE WAVES
©SCOTT MORGAN (SOCAN) 2013
GRAPHIC DESIGN BY NETWORK OSAKA
THANKS TO: JASON ZUMPANO

JAZRECORDS.COM
LOSCIL.CA

SIDE A
—
SS1.1 ELEMENTS

SIDE B
—
SS1.2 UNIT CIRCLE

JAZ
RECORDS

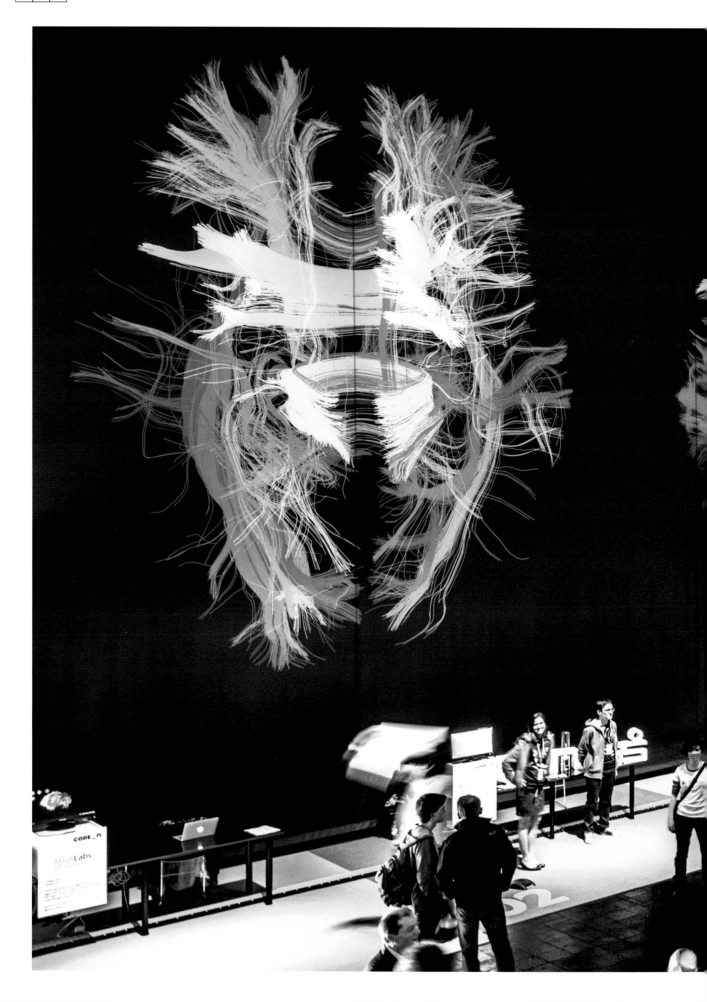

CODE_N

Ⓓ Designer: Kram Weisshaar

A 3,000 m², floor-to-ceiling terapixel graphic manifests the
largesse of big data, the theme of CODE_n 2014. At the
centre of this reimagined forum, an agora-like elevated
platform serves as an ancillary block, with a full range of
culinary programming, an auditorium and a curated public
space. The two raised levels are flanked by wide-set
monumental stairways, one of which is wrapped in a semi-
transparent fabric, which serves as a projection screen.
The result is a semi-public auditorium, which is at once
permeable and specialized.

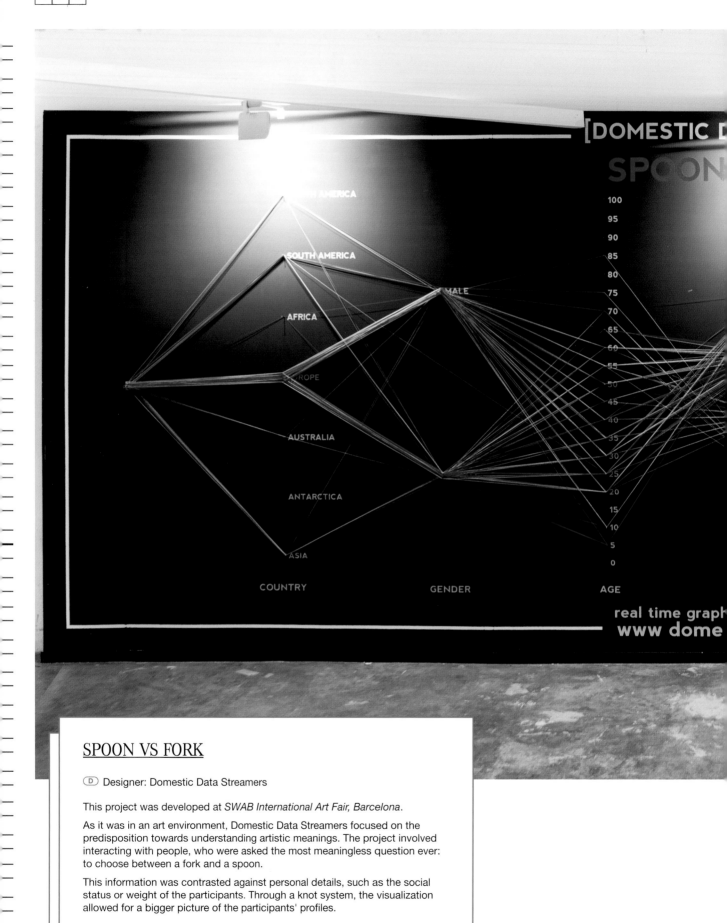

SPOON VS FORK

Ⓓ Designer: Domestic Data Streamers

This project was developed at *SWAB International Art Fair, Barcelona*.

As it was in an art environment, Domestic Data Streamers focused on the predisposition towards understanding artistic meanings. The project involved interacting with people, who were asked the most meaningless question ever: to choose between a fork and a spoon.

This information was contrasted against personal details, such as the social status or weight of the participants. Through a knot system, the visualization allowed for a bigger picture of the participants' profiles.

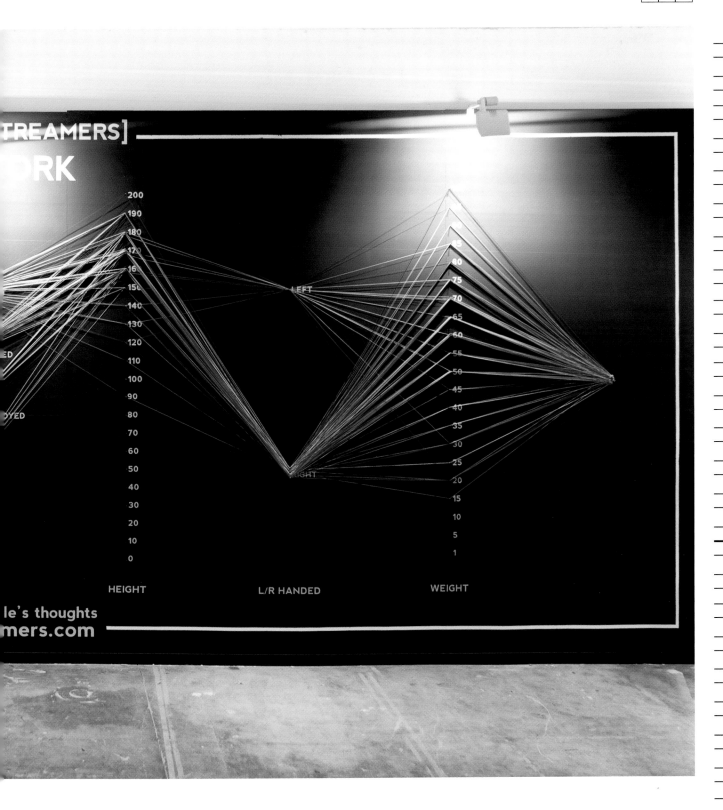

WHAT MADE ME

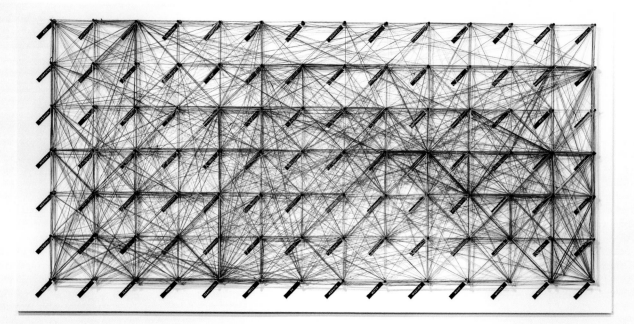

WHAT MADE ME

Ⓓ Designer: Dorota Grabkowska
Ⓟ Photographer: Kuba Kolec

By finding the link between data visualization and spatial design, a three-dimensional and interactive experience was produced, allowing people to become creators of a multi-layered data map. The aim of the project was to explore factors that shape the people of Birmingham, UK, by asking visitors five simple questions, which could be answered by connecting relevant words together with a coloured thread. Through this visual language, participants were able to share the feelings, influences, thoughts and inspirations that make them who they are today.

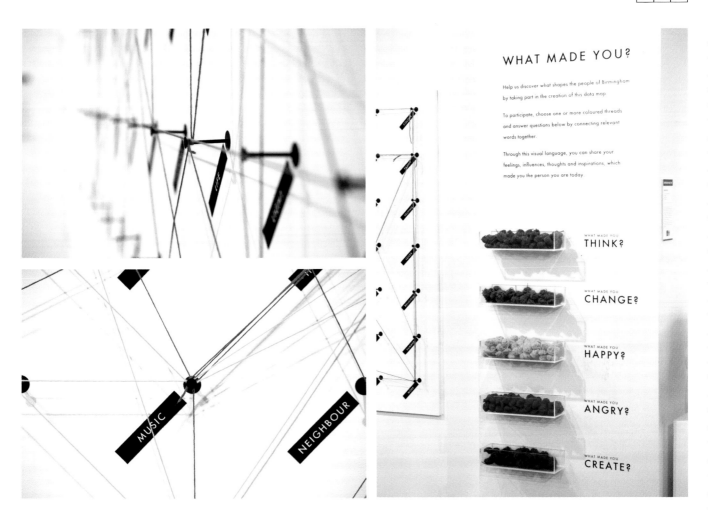

WHAT MADE YOU?

Help us discover what shapes the people of Birmingham by taking part in the creation of this data map

To participate, choose one or more coloured threads and answer questions below by connecting relevant words together.

Through this visual language, you can share your feelings, influences, thoughts and inspirations, which made you the person you are today.

WHAT MADE YOU
THINK?

WHAT MADE YOU
CHANGE?

WHAT MADE YOU
HAPPY?

WHAT MADE YOU
ANGRY?

WHAT MADE YOU
CREATE?

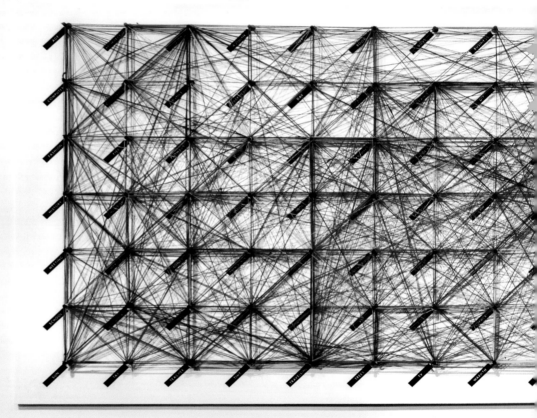

ME

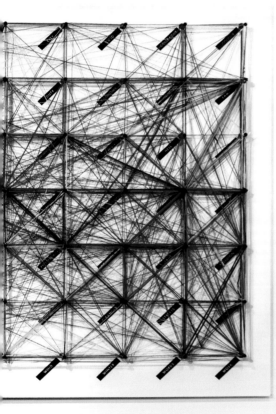

WHAT MADE YOU?

Help us discover what shapes the people of Birmingham
by taking part in the creation of this data map.

To participate, choose one or more coloured threads
and answer questions below by connecting relevant
words together.

Through this visual language, you can share your
feelings, influences, thoughts and inspirations, which
made you the person you are today.

WHAT MADE YOU
THINK?

WHAT MADE YOU
CHANGE?

WHAT MADE YOU
HAPPY?

WHAT MADE YOU
ANGRY?

WHAT MADE YOU
CREATE?

LIGHT STRINGS

Ⓓ Designer: Domestic Data Streamers

Nowadays, we are spending more and more time in front of electronic devices, in activities that have stretched beyond entertainment. In this installation, the designers asked participants how many hours they spend using electronic devices, and how many hours they would like to spend, then contrasted this information against their ages. Each participant was represented by a string of light, which connected all of the answers given by passers-by. It was a statistical experiment, which tried to shed light on the darkest face of technology.

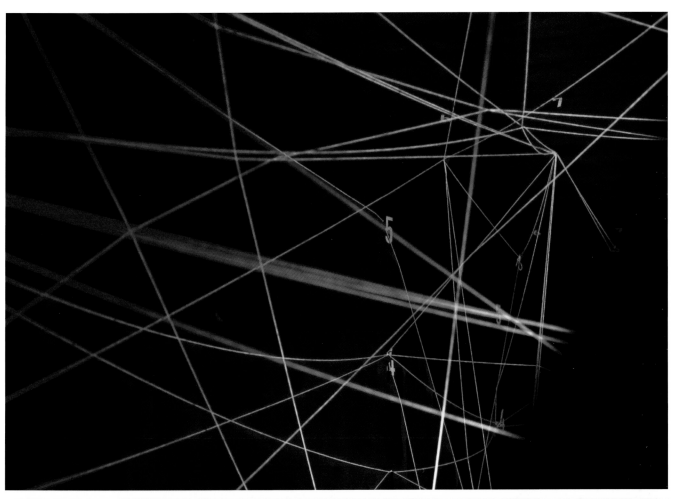

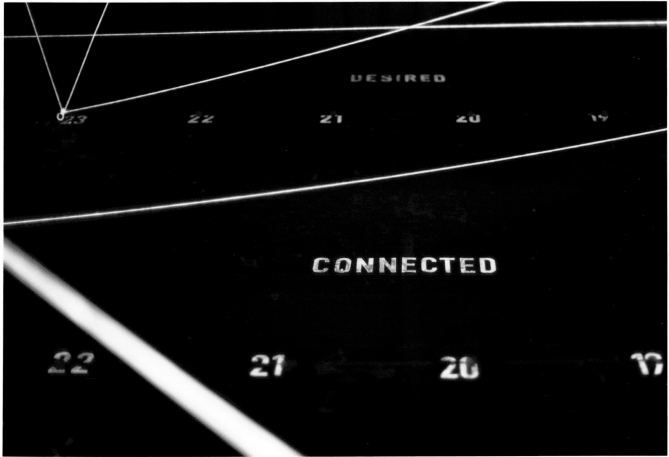

THE SHINING

ⓓ Designer: Valentina D'Efilippo

This project deconstructed the classic film, in order to visualize its internal structure. Far from following the strict rules of written communication, film grammar—which embodies video production knowledge—comprises the body of rules and conventions that are a product of experimentation. It is an accumulation of solutions found through everyday practice of the craft.

The existence of this grammar highlights a fundamental truth: films are crafted, built and shaped, with a purpose in mind. The work aims to exploit the grammar of film, to better understand its semantic features. This exploration could also be used to create a model to compare different films. By applying the same approach to different films, visual comparisons of the cinematographic styles of various directors could be made, and the complexity of the structure of their work could be highlighted.

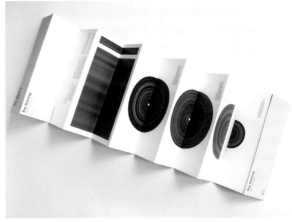

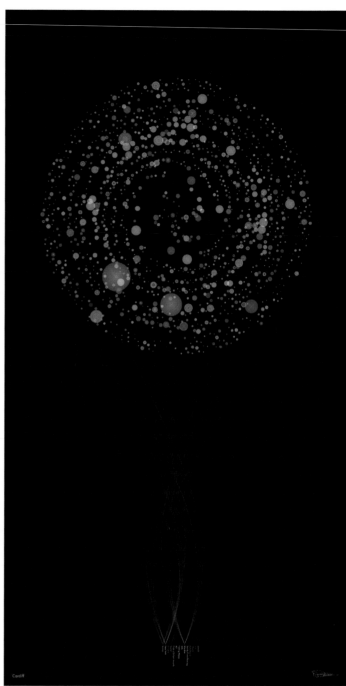

EE DIGITAL CITY PORTRAITS

ⓓ Designer: Brendan Dawes

For the launch of 4G services in eleven UK cities, EE commissioned Brendan Dawes to create a digital portrait for each city, formed from millions of bits of data, as people interacted and talked about the biggest events of the day.

Based on the same mathematics that create the head of a sunflower, time explodes outwards from the centre, with each point representing one minute, allowing a possible 4,320 points—the number of minutes in three days—to cover the day before, during and after the launch of 4G.

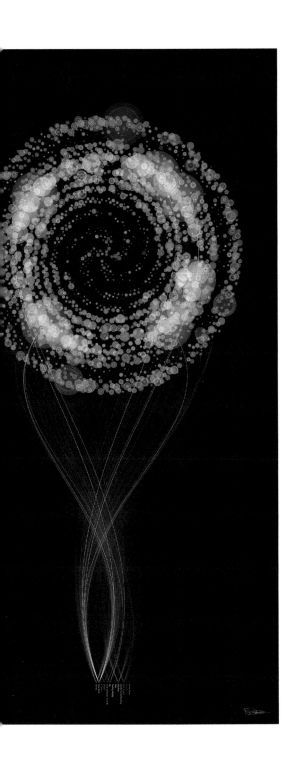

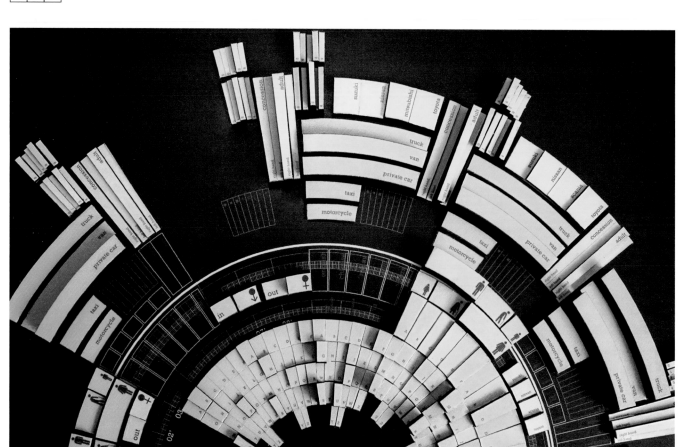

JOURNEY TO THE EAST

Ⓓ Designer: Marselin Acel Widjaja

This project was inspired by data collected during a 37-minute solo journey, in a bus heading towards east Singapore. The aim was to observe as much information as possible in a limited time, including people and surroundings. The data was then presented in a series of infographics, using a handcrafted diagram, to show the quantities of the subjects observed.

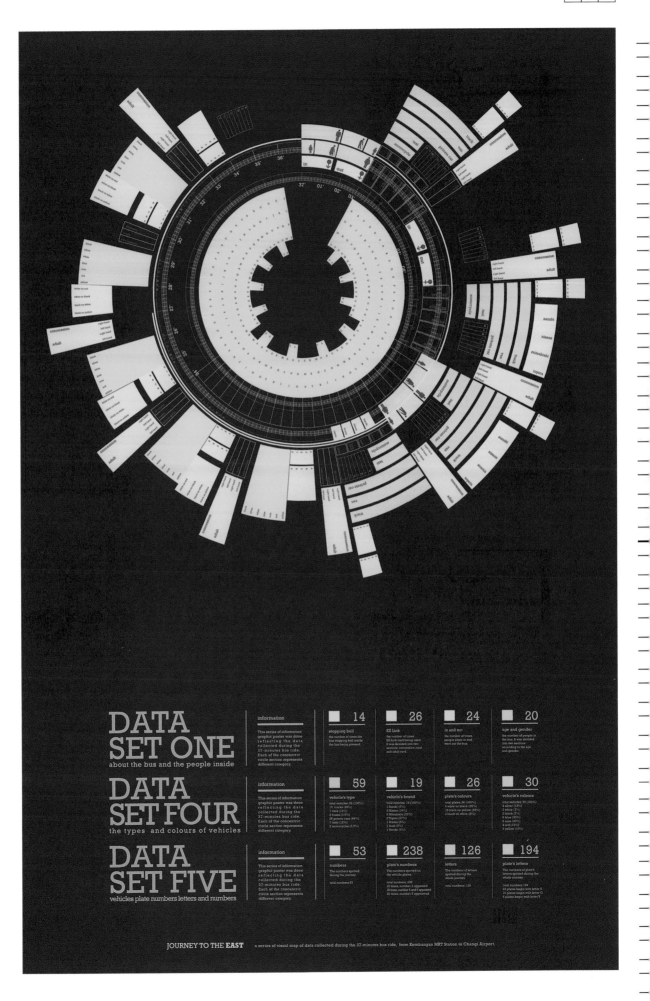

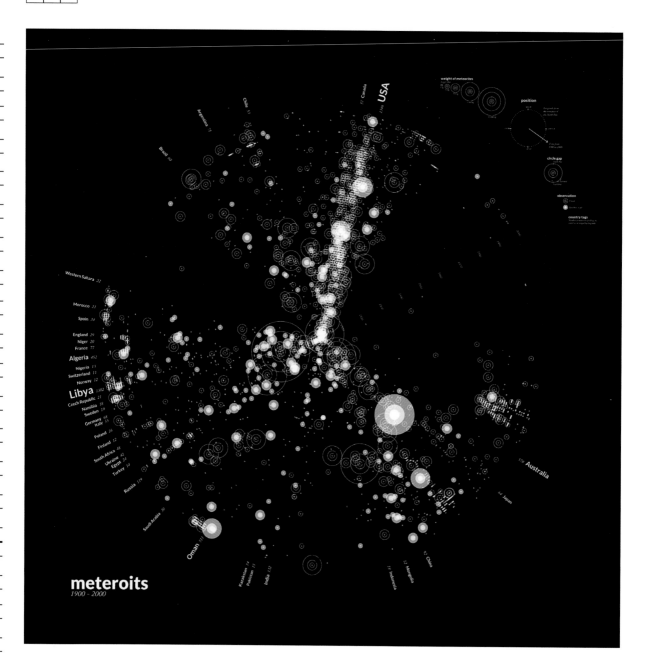

METEORITES ⇕

ⓓ Designer: Kim Albrecht

This is a visualization of all fallen and found meteorites, between 1900 and 2000. The graphic provides a unique perspective on meteorite findings, by comparing time and longitude, on a radial axis. The visualization shows the human bias on the physical locations of found meteorites. For instance, there are two big holes on the longitude of the Atlantic and Pacific Oceans. It shows how the USA has been continuously searching for meteorites over the last 100 years. Strategic searches in Libya and the North and South Poles, over the last 20 years, show up as clusters. There are still more to find.

THE BLACK DATA OF PIEMONTE ⇄

ⓓ Designer: Sara Piccolomini

This visualization shows how many fatal car accidents occur in each province and district of the Piemonte region, Italy. The statistics were highly unexpected: women are better drivers than men, and women are less likely to get into a fatal accident than men. The data also shows an overall decreasing trend in the number of fatal accidents. This is probably due to safer vehicles on the road and increased driver awareness.

THE BLACK DATA OF PIEMONTE

Visualization of the distribution and evolution of fatal car accidents from 1997 to 2011 in Piemonte (Italy)

The visualization shows how many fatal car accidents occur in each province and district of Piemonte region. One of the most unexpected thing is that, statistically speaking, women are better drivers than men: women have much more chances not to have a fatal accident than men. Another thing that can be infer from data is an overall decreasing trend in the number of fatal accidents. It's probably due to safer vehicles on the road and increased awareness of drivers.

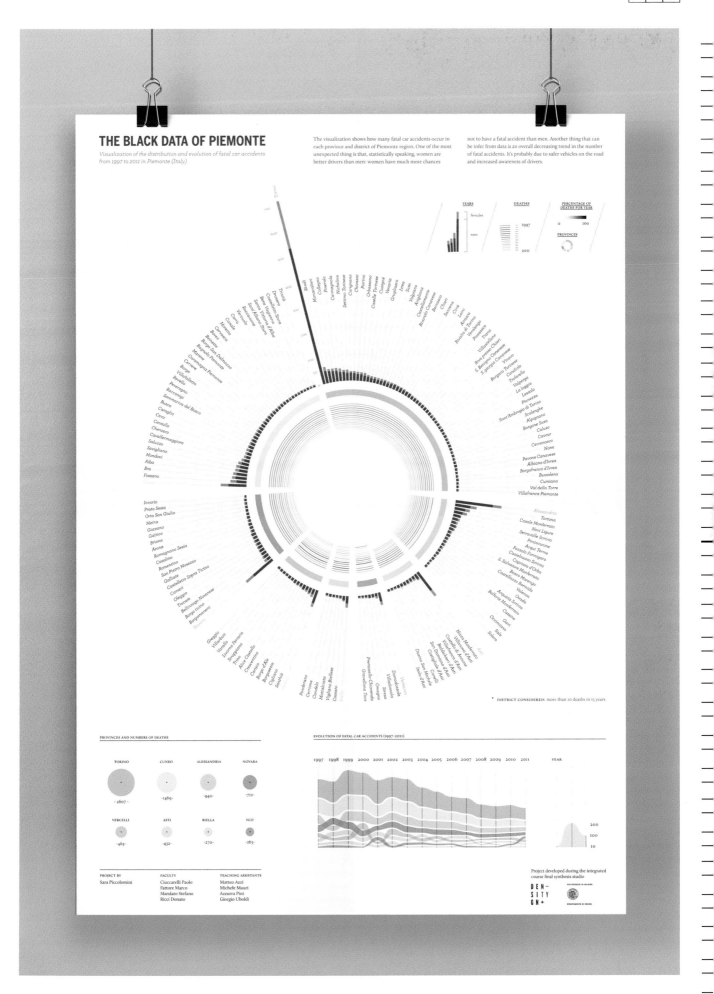

* **DISTRICT CONSIDERED:** more than 10 deaths in 15 years

PROVINCES AND NUMBERS OF DEATHS

TORINO	CUNEO	ALESSANDRIA	NOVARA
- 2607 -	-1469-	-940-	-712-

VERCELLI	ASTI	BIELLA	VCO
-463-	-432-	-270-	-263-

EVOLUTION OF FATAL CAR ACCIDENTS (1997-2011)

1997 1998 1999 2000 2001 2002 2003 2004 2005 2006 2007 2008 2009 2010 2011   YEAR

PROJECT BY
Sara Piccolomini

FACULTY
Ciuccarelli Paolo
Fattore Marco
Mandato Stefano
Ricci Donato

TEACHING ASSISTANTS
Matteo Azzi
Michele Mauri
Azzurra Pini
Giorgio Uboldi

Project developed during the integrated
course final synthesis studio

DEN–
SITY
GN+

POLITECNICO DI MILANO
DIPARTIMENTO DI DESIGN

INFOGRAPHIC - MY TOP 100 FILMS

Ⓓ Designer: Reinhardt Matthysen

This infographic provides an overview of the designer's top one hundred films. The main circle graphic consists of three parts, which show the different trends from his one hundred films. The outer part shows the total worldwide gross revenue of each film, the middle indicates the different genres of each film, and the innermost section of the circle compares his review (dark grey) with IMDB's review (light grey) of each film.

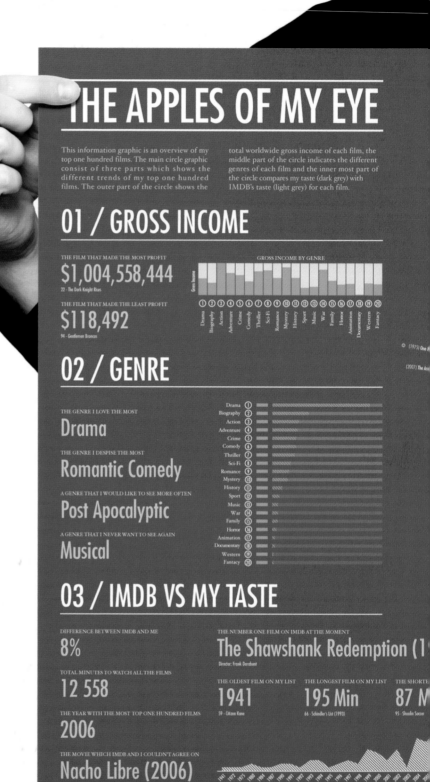

THE APPLES OF MY EYE

This information graphic is an overview of my top one hundred films. The main circle graphic consist of three parts which shows the different trends of my top one hundred films. The outer part of the circle shows the total worldwide gross income of each film, the middle part of the circle indicates the different genres of each film and the inner most part of the circle compares my taste (dark grey) with IMDB's taste (light grey) for each film.

01 / GROSS INCOME

THE FILM THAT MADE THE MOST PROFIT
$1,004,558,444
22 - The Dark Knight Rises

THE FILM THAT MADE THE LEAST PROFIT
$118,492
94 - Gentlemen Broncos

GROSS INCOME BY GENRE

02 / GENRE

THE GENRE I LOVE THE MOST
Drama

THE GENRE I DESPISE THE MOST
Romantic Comedy

A GENRE THAT I WOULD LIKE TO SEE MORE OFTEN
Post Apocalyptic

A GENRE THAT I NEVER WANT TO SEE AGAIN
Musical

Drama ①
Biography ②
Action ③
Adventure ④
Crime ⑤
Comedy ⑥
Thriller ⑦
Sci-Fi ⑧
Romance ⑨
Mystery ⑩
History ⑪
Sport ⑫
Music ⑬
War ⑭
Family ⑮
Horror ⑯
Animation ⑰
Documentary ⑱
Western ⑲
Fantacy ⑳

03 / IMDB VS MY TASTE

DIFFERENCE BETWEEN IMDB AND ME
8%

THE NUMBER ONE FILM ON IMDB AT THE MOMENT
The Shawshank Redemption (1
Director: Frank Darabont

TOTAL MINUTES TO WATCH ALL THE FILMS
12 558

THE OLDEST FILM ON MY LIST
1941
59 - Citizen Kane

THE LONGEST FILM ON MY LIST
195 Min
64 - Schindler's List (1993)

THE SHORTE
87 M
95 - Shaolin Soccer

THE YEAR WITH THE MOST TOP ONE HUNDRED FILMS
2006

THE MOVIE WHICH IMDB AND I COULDN'T AGREE ON
Nacho Libre (2006)

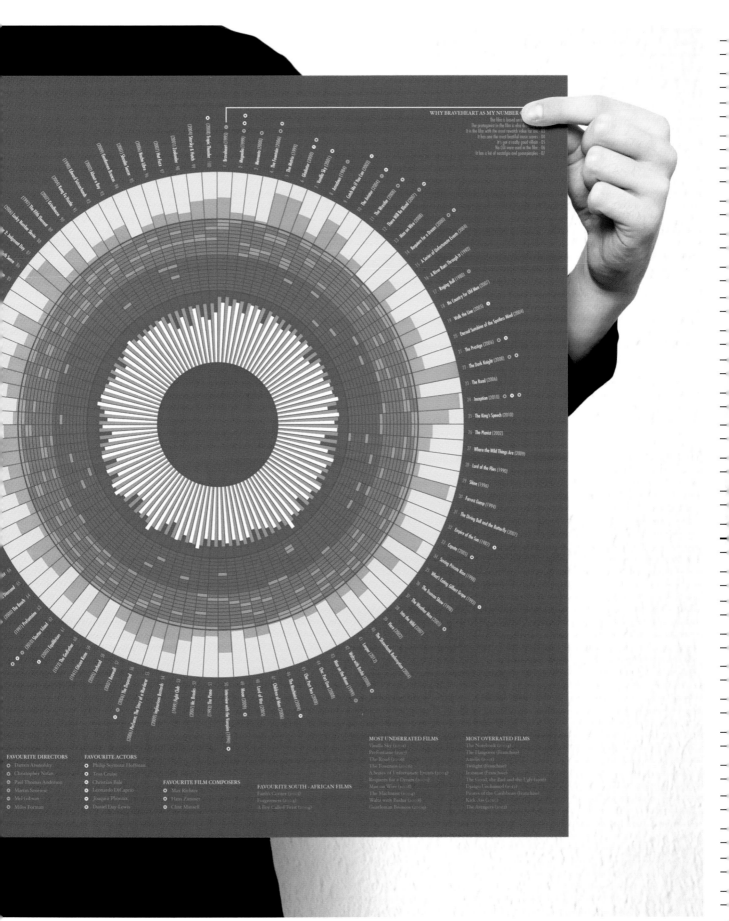

EXISTENTIAL CALCULATOR

Ⓓ Designer: Kelli Anderson

The existential calculator is an interactive
infographic and decision-making tool, which
helps the user decide whether to 'take the job'
or not, using technical means. It organizes the
spectrum of all possible work outcomes—from
pleasurable to spiritually degrading; well-paying
to debt-enhancing; and 'EXCITING' to 'meh…'—
and shows where the reader is likely to land,
based on their input about the potential job.

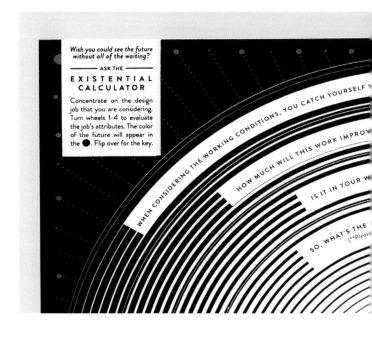

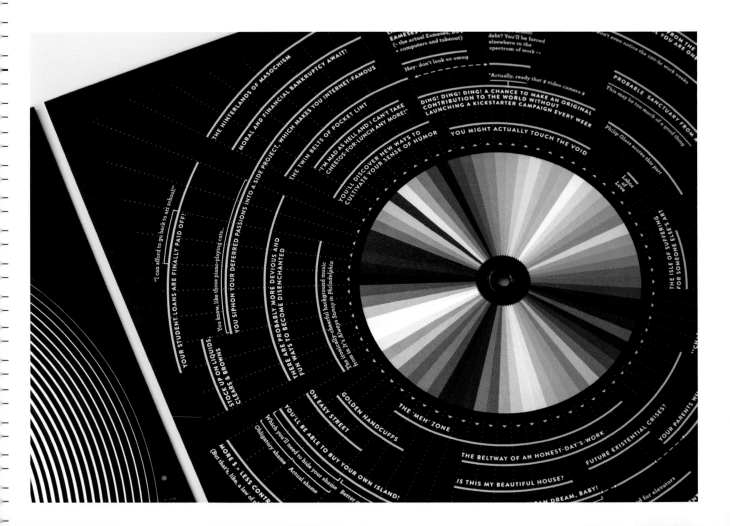

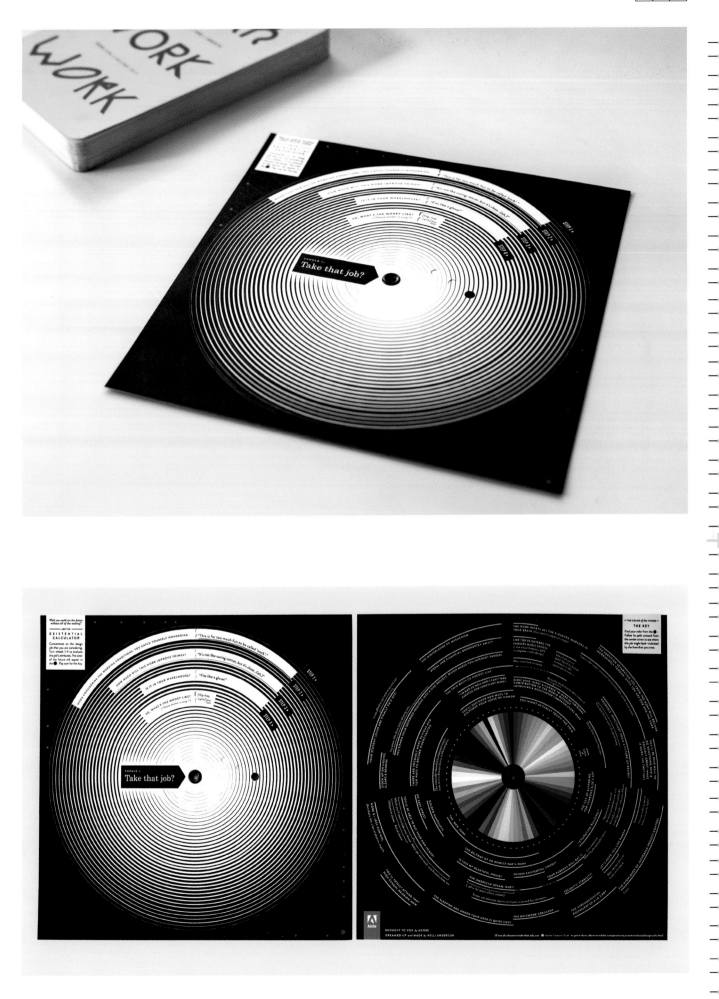

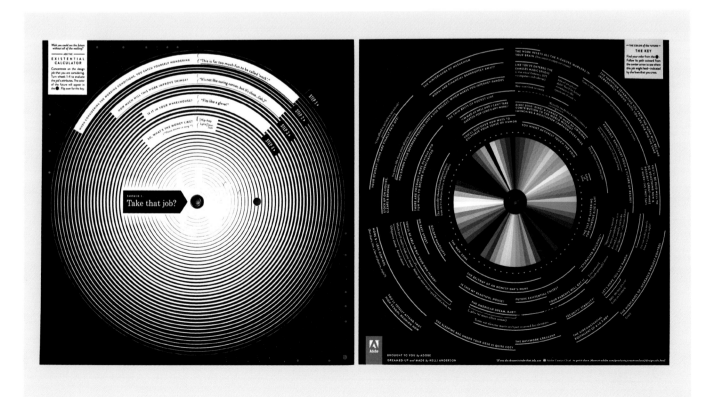

NORSE MYTHOLOGY FAMILY TREE

⇅

Ⓓ Designer: Severino Ribecca

Before the Christianization of Scandinavia and other Germanic nations, stories and myths of great heroes and powerful gods were popular across Nordic-colonized nations. The challenge for this project was to research the numerous popular characters and figures in Norse mythology, and display their relationship to each other through their lineage. This project took place as a sequel to the *Greek Mythology Family Tree Diagram*.

AND THE WINNERS ARE

⇄

Ⓓ Designer: Brett O'Mahony

And The Winners Are is a visual celebration of the medals won during the 2012 Olympic games. The Olympics are a feat of human commitment and achievement, and the medals awarded are a way of commending that dedication. Infographics act as a medium to condense information and communicate written material visually. The five statistics within this project act as a visual link to medals won, through myriad formats. The colour scheme was based on a three-colour format, gold—silver and bronze—to make each aspect of the project consistent with the subject matter.

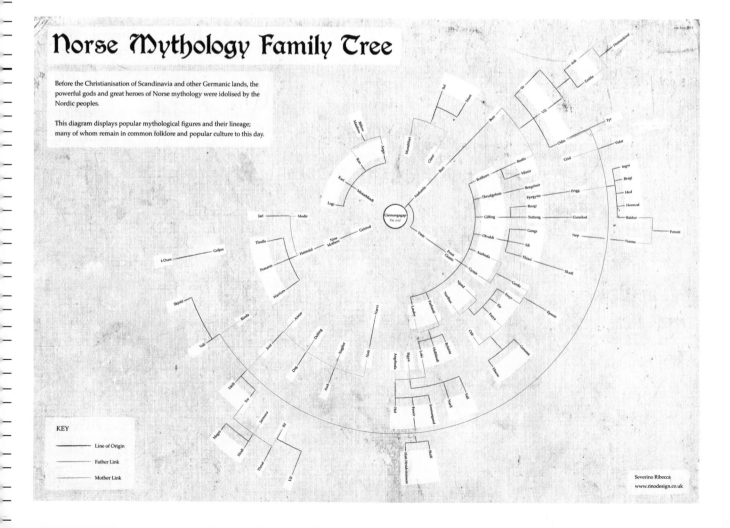

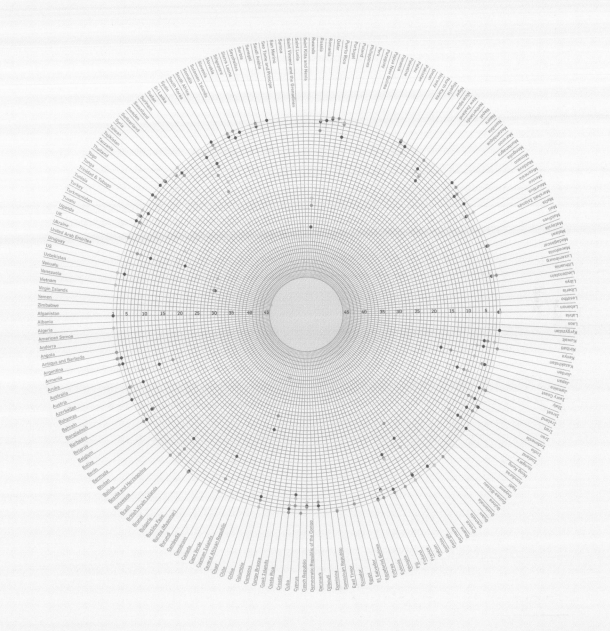

LONDON 2012 OLYMPIC GAMES
MEDAL RANKINGS 2012

A table representing all the participating
countries and the subsequent gold, silver
and bronz medals won during the 2012
Summer Games.

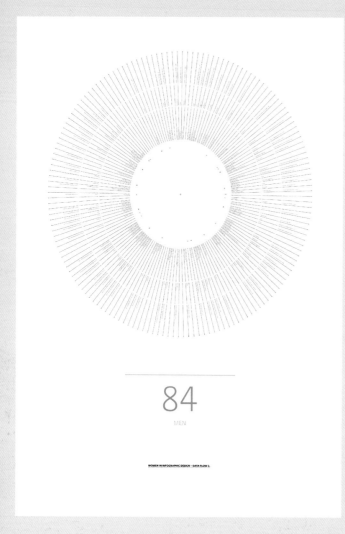

84

MEN

WOMEN IN INFOGRAPHIC DESIGN - DATA FLOW 1.

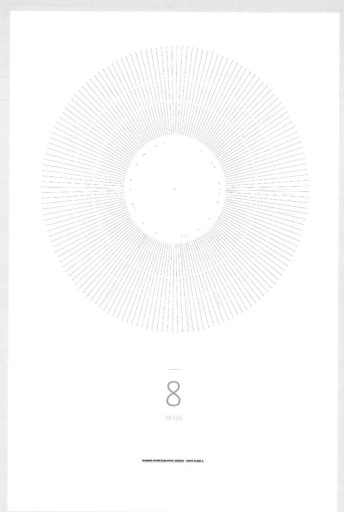

8

MIXED

WOMEN IN INFOGRAPHIC DESIGN - DATA FLOW 2.

WOMEN IN INFOGRAPHIC DESIGN

D Designer: Éva Valicsek

This work uses a *dataflow* to present gender statistics:
84 men, 35 women, 8 mixed studios, and 31 unknown
genders (due to unspecified data), in the infographic
design industry.

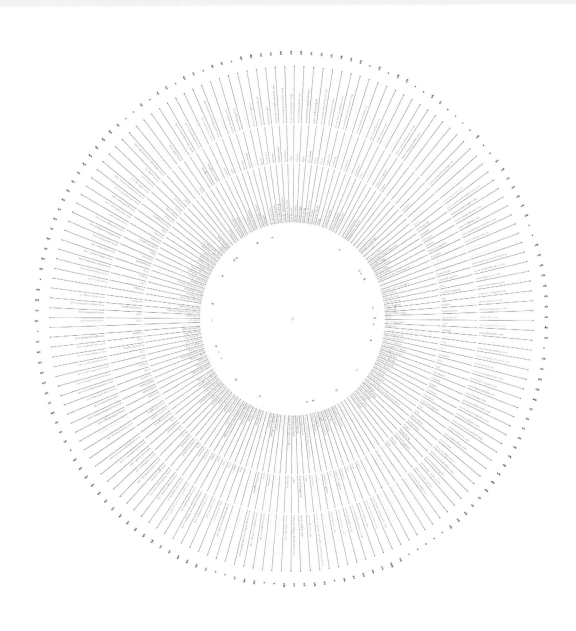

84 · 35 · 8 · 31

MEN   WOMEN   MIXED   UNKNOWN

WOMEN IN INFOGRAPHIC DESIGN – DATA FLOW 2.

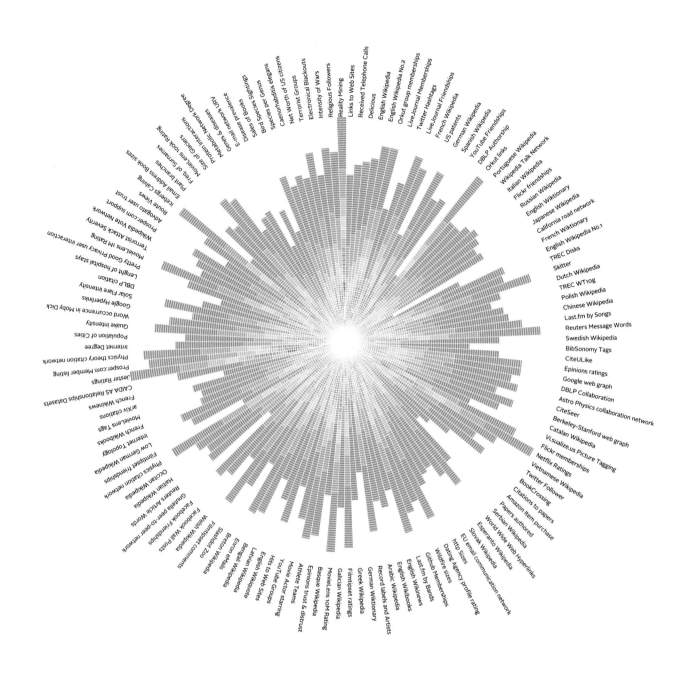

ATLAS OF POWERLAWS

Ⓓ Designer: Kim Albrecht

Kim Albrecht is interested in similarities across social, technological and natural networks. After researching this field, the designer encountered an increasing number of scientific papers and datasets that revealed power laws, mainly in the field of network structures. The idea behind this project was to visualize the diversity of these power laws, but also to look at differences in his findings.

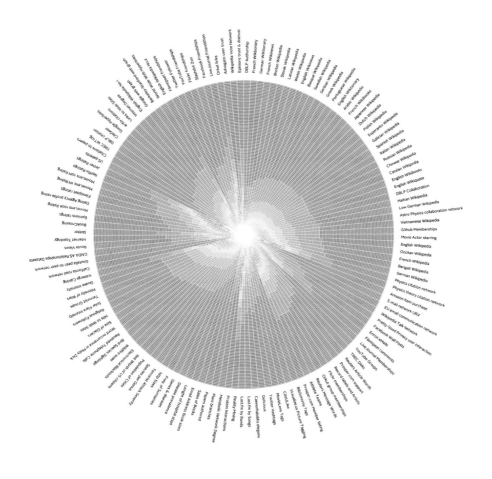

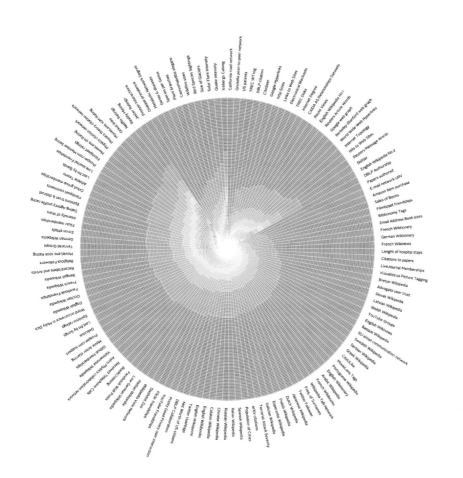

A YEAR IN STEPS

Ⓓ Designer: Carey Spies
Ⓓ Data: Moves by ProtoGeo

A Year in Steps catalogues an entire year's worth of pedometer data. Information was recorded using several iOS tracking applications, such as *Moves* and *Argus*. The visualization shows three different cities and walking trends in each of them. Dips in April and May indicate increased driving in Los Angeles, a city notorious for residents being unable to walk from place to place. In contrast to that is the spike in September, in Seattle, a much smaller and mobile city.

A YEAR IN STEPS

300+ DAYS OF MOVES AND ARGUS STEP TRACKING

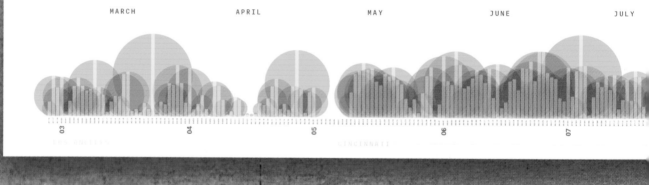

MARCH   APRIL   MAY   JUNE   JULY

03   04   05   06   07

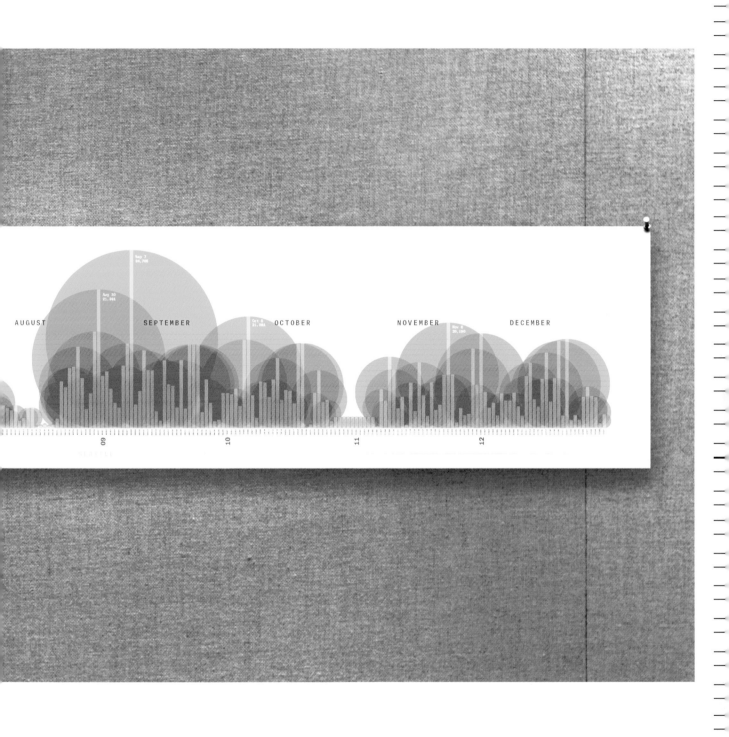

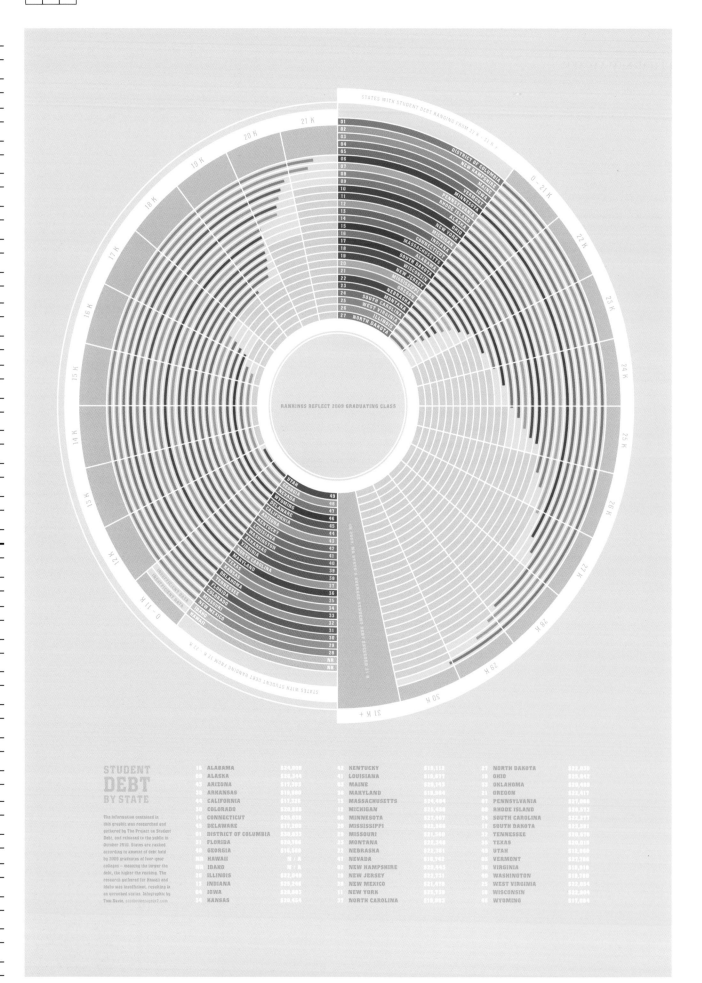

STUDENT
DEBT
BY STATE

STUDENT DEBT

 Designer: Tom Davie

Student Debt compared the average student debt held by students graduating from American universities and colleges. Available information for all fifty US states was used, in order to show which states provided the best financial outcomes for their recent graduates.

←

ON THE MOVE

→

Ⓓ Designer: Carey Spies
Ⓓ Data: Moves by ProtoGeo

On the Move is a representation of the designer's total steps taken each week. *Moves* (a mobile application) recommends 10,000 steps a day for a healthy lifestyle, which adds up to over 50,000 steps per week (shown in pink). By stacking them, you can see the clear size differences between each week, and how the overall step count changes between working in Los Angeles, and living and studying at university, in Cincinnati.

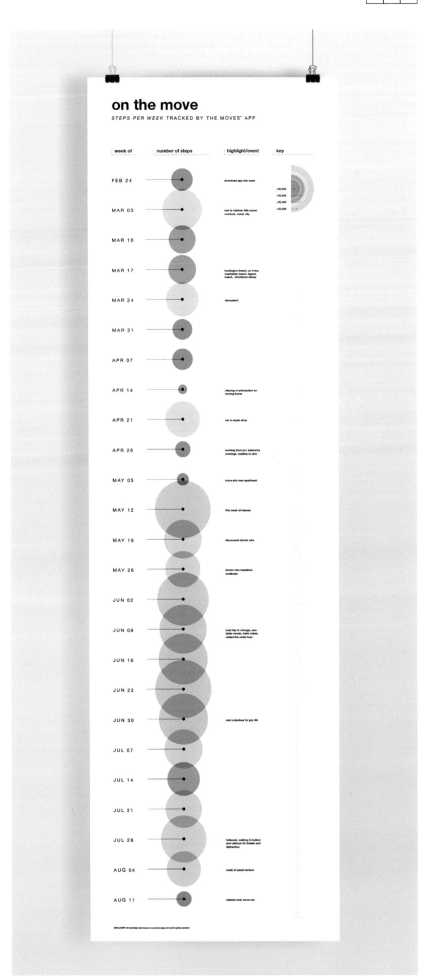

Radial Bar Chart

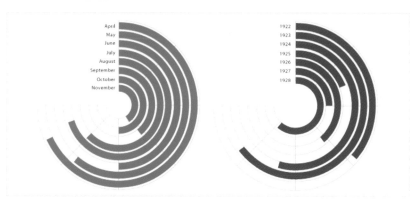

Description

A Radial/Circular Bar Chart is simply a Bar Chart plotted on a polar coordinate system, rather than on a cartesian one.

The problem with Radial Bar Charts is that lengths can be misinterpreted. Each bar on the outside gets relatively longer to the last, even if they represent the same value. This is because each bar has to be at a different radii, so each bar is judged by its angle. Our visual systems are better at interpreting straight lines, so the cartesian bar chart is better for comparing values. Therefore, Radial Bar Charts are used primarily for aesthetic reasons.

Functions

(Comparisons)   (Relationships)

Anatomy

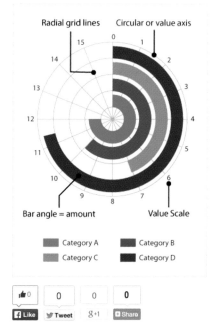

👍 0   0   0   0

f Like   🐦 Tweet   g+1   ➕ Share

THE DATA VISUALIZATION CATALOGUE   ⇅

Ⓓ Designer: Severino Ribecca

The Data Visualization Catalogue is an online reference tool for different data visualization methods, and a way to help viewers find the right method for their data. This is an on-going project, where the designer makes frequent updates with new reference methods.

TOMA - TIMELINE OF MODERN ART   ⇆

Ⓓ Designer: Miguel Coelho

This infographic poster aims to create a visual representation of the most prominent artistic movements, from 1867 to 1976. It illustrates their distribution over time, the beginning and end of each movement, and the main artists that gave expression to each one. World Wars I and II are also marked, to show the movements that intersected these two important historical periods.

ToMA - Timeline of Modern Art

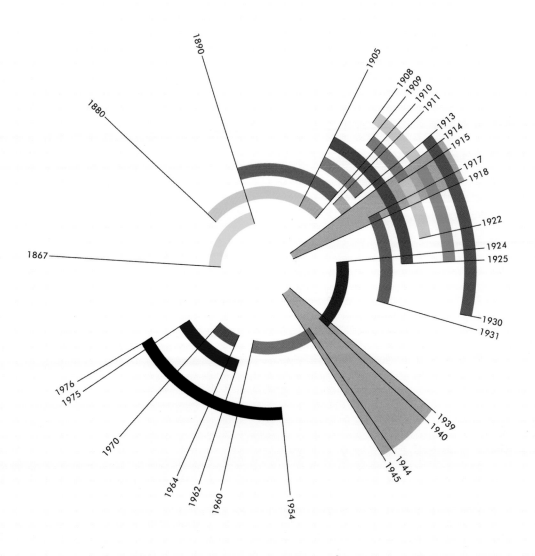

1867
1880
1890
1905
1908
1909
1910
1911
1913
1914
1915
1917
1918
1922
1924
1925
1930
1931
1939
1940
1944
1945
1954
1960
1962
1964
1970
1975
1976

IMPRESSIONISM

Alfred Sisley
Edgar Degas
Édouard Manet
Camille Pissarro
Claude Monet
Pierre-Auguste Renoir

POST-IMPRESSIONISM

Amedeo Modigliani
Auguste Renoir
Georges Seurat
Henri de Toulouse-Lautrec
Paul Cézanne
Paul Gauguin
Paul Signac
Vincent Van Gogh

FAUVISM

André Derain
Henri Matisse
Maurice de Vlaminck

**ART NOVEAU
VIENNA SECESSION
JUGENDSTIL**

Antoni Gaudi
Aubrey Beardsley
Gustav Klimt
Henri de Toulouse-Lautrec

EXPRESSIONISM

Edvard Munch
Egon Schiele
Marc Chagall
Oskar Kokoschka

**DIE BRÜCKE
(THE BRIDGE)**

Ernst Ludwig Kirchner
Karl Schmidt-Rottluff

**DER BLAUE REITER
(THE BLUE RIDER)**

Alexej von Jawlensky
August Macke
Franz Marc
Wassily Kandinsky

CUBISM

Fernand Léger
Francis Picabia
Georges Braque
Juan Gris
Pablo Picasso

FUTURISM

Carlo Carrà
Filippo T. Marinetti
Giacomo Balla
Gino Severini
Umberto Boccioni

DADA

André Breton
Francis Picabia
Hans Arp
Hugo Pall
Kurt Schwitters
Marcel Duchamp
Max Ernst
Raoul Hausmann
Tristan Tzara

CONSTRUCTIVISM

Alexander Rodchenko
El Lissitzky
Kasimir Malevich
László Moholy-Nagy
Naum Gabo
Vladimir Tatlin

SUPREMATISM

Aleksandra Ekster
Ivan Klinn
Kazimir Malevich
Lyubov Popova
Olga Rozanova

**DE STIJL
(NEOPLASTICISM)**

Bart van der Leck
Piet Mondrian
Theo van Doesburg
Vilmos Huszár

SURREALISM

André Breton
Francis Picabia
Giorgio de Chirico
Juan Miró
M. C. Escher
Man Ray
René Magritte
Salvador Dali

**ABSTRACT
EXPRESSIONISM**

Adolph Gottlieb
Arshile Gorky
Franz Kline
Hans Hofmann
Jackson Pollock
Mark Rothko
Robert Motherwell
Willem de Kooning

POP ART

Andy Warhol
David Hockney
Jasper Johns
Robert Indiana
Robert Rauschenberg
Roy Lichtenstein
Yves Klein

OP ART

Bridget Riley
Richard Amuszkiewicz
Victor Vasarely

MINIMALISM

Frank Stella
John McCracken
John McLaughlin
Robert Morris
Sol LeWitt
Yves Klein

WORLD WAR I & II

METRO AREA ↕

Ⓓ Designer: Hey

Poster featuring the New York Metro area, produced for the *Lapsus Graphic Showcase*.

VISUAL TEST ⇆

Ⓓ Designer: NICEWORK

Test visualization of the St. Bride Library collection.

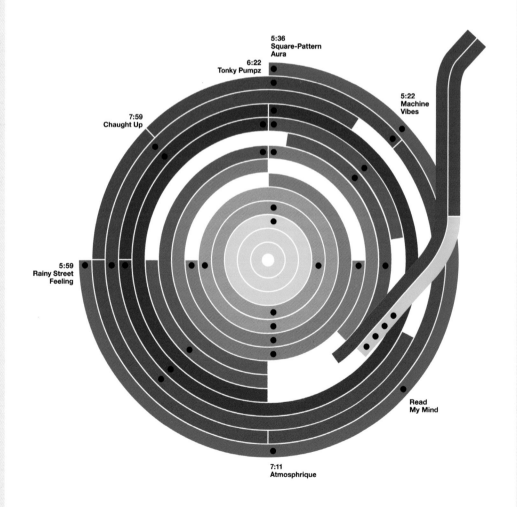

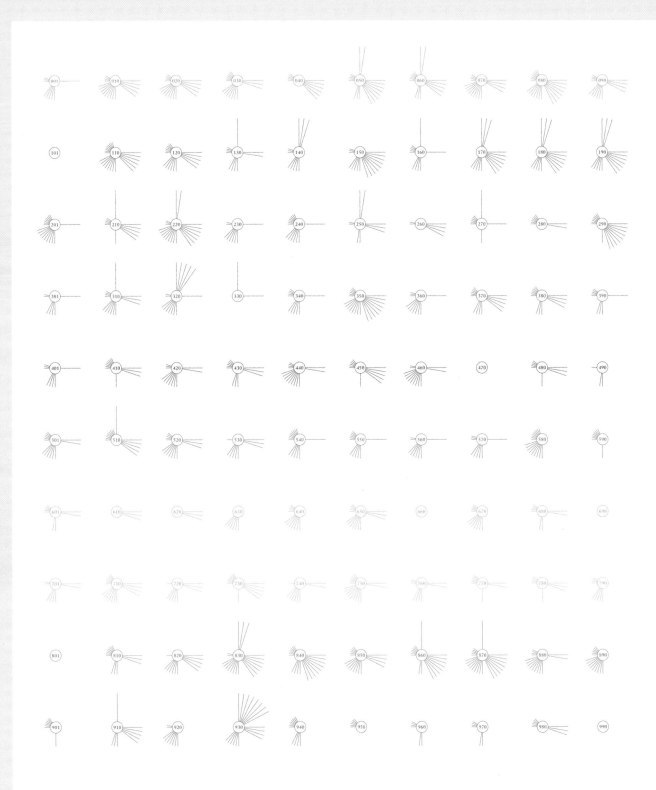

000 thought / intellectual activity / channels of communication
001 generalities
010 language(s)
020 press law / freedom of press / regulation of printing
030 intellectual property / copyright / piracy
040 literary history / popular literature / reading / authorship
050 library science
060 newspaper and magazine industry / the press
070 book trade / publishing / bookselling
080 advertising and publicity
090 book collecting

100 writing systems
110 semiotics / notations / history of the alphabet
120 non-latin scripts and letterforms
130 latin scripts and letterforms
140 shorthand / stenography
150 lettering / writing in general
160 typefounding and related trades
170 type specimens
180 type specimens
190 type specimens

200 art and design / illustration / colour / ink
201 generalities
210 general history of art and design
220 local history of art and design
230 theory of art and design
240 general design
250 graphic design
260 ornament and pattern
270 illustration
280 colour
290 ink and associated materials

300 printing
301 generalities
310 general history of printing
320 local history of printing
330 special classes of printing
340 study of printing history / historiography of printing
350 structure of the printing industries
360 economics of printing
370 management
380 education / training
390 printing science

400 preparatory printing processes / pre-press
401 generalities
410 copy and images for reproduction
420 composing generally / hand composition
430 typewriters / keyboards and similar devices
440 mechanical composition
450 electronic composition and imaging systems
460 photography
470 vacant
480 relief platemaking / photoengraving
490 storage and materials handling

500 printing processes / letterpress
501 generalities
510 printers' manuals
520 short text on printing
530 printing presses / machines and equipment
540 handpresses (letterpress) / printing at the hand press
550 jobbing platen / platen press operation
560 cylinder letterpress machines and presswork
570 rotary letterpress machines and presswork
580 flexography / aniline printing
590 minor relief-printing methods

600 lithography
601 generalities
610 general history of lithography
620 local history of lithography
630 special classes of lithographic establishment
640 industrial lithography
650 lithographic techniques
660 vacant
670 artists' lithographic printing
680 lithographic surfaces, machinery and presswork
690 vacant

700 printmaking / other industrial printing processes
701 generalities
710 printmaking and picture printing processes
720 intaglio printmaking processes
730 relief printmaking processes
740 photo-mechanical printing or printmaking processes
750 screen printing processes
760 photogravure printing / rotogravure
770 electronic printing processes / non-impact printing
780 other industrial printing processes / duplicating
790 combination industrial printing methods

800 written and printed matter / paper / bookbinding
801 generalities
810 bibliographical technique
820 enumerative bibliographies
830 paper and associated materials
840 bookbinding / print finishing and conservation
850 manuscripts
860 printed books
870 non-book printed matter
880 packaging industry / converting
890 format substitution / typography

900 noteworthy examples of...
901 publishers' work / newspapers / chained books
910 music / non-latin printing / works in shorthand
920 artists' and designers' work
930 printers' work
940 products of prepress systems
950 letterpress printing
960 lithographic printing
970 printmaking and other industrial printing processes
980 bindings / chapbooks / broadsides

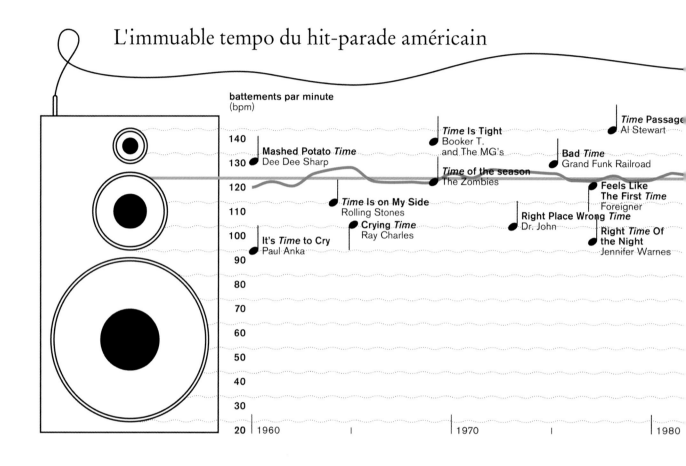

L'immuable tempo du hit-parade américain

battements par minute
(bpm)

140 — **Mashed Potato** *Time*
130 — Dee Dee Sharp

Time Is Tight
Booker T.
and The MG's

Time Passage
Al Stewart

Bad *Time*
Grand Funk Railroad

Time of the season
The Zombies

120

Time Is on My Side
Rolling Stones

110

Crying *Time*
Ray Charles

Right Place Wrong *Time*
Dr. John

Feels Like
The First *Time*
Foreigner

100 — It's *Time* to Cry
Paul Anka

90

Right *Time* **Of
the Night**
Jennifer Warnes

80

70

60

50

40

30

20 | 1960 | | 1970 | | 1980

BEATS PER MINUTE

Ⓓ Designer: Benjamin Schulte
Ⓐ Agency: Largenetwork
Ⓔ Editor: Benjamin Bollmann
Ⓒ Client: Hémisphères

This infographic visualizes the average tempo of
popular songs from the US charts, between 1960 and
2010. The sound waves floating out of the speaker
show the scale of the chart. It is noteworthy that the
average bmp of the songs is 119.8.

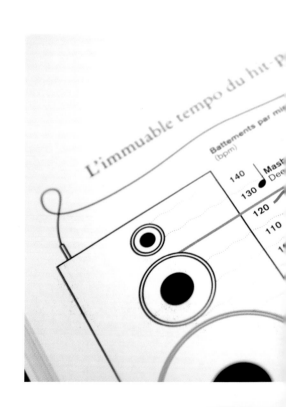

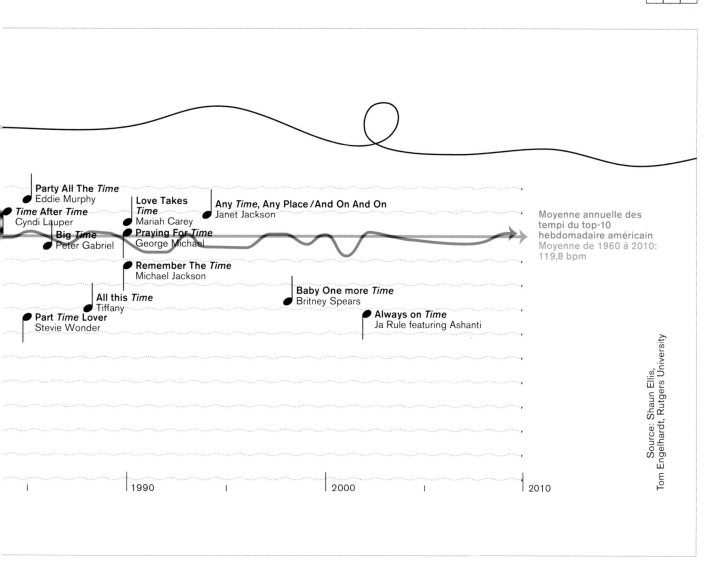

Party All The *Time*
Eddie Murphy

Time* After *Time
Cyndi Lauper

Big *Time*
Peter Gabriel

Love Takes *Time*
Mariah Carey

Praying For *Time*
George Michael

Any *Time*, Any Place / And On And On
Janet Jackson

Remember The *Time*
Michael Jackson

All this *Time*
Tiffany

Baby One more *Time*
Britney Spears

Part *Time* Lover
Stevie Wonder

Always on *Time*
Ja Rule featuring Ashanti

Moyenne annuelle des
tempi du top-10
hebdomadaire américain
Moyenne de 1960 à 2010:
119,8 bpm

1990   2000   2010

Source: Shaun Ellis,
Tom Engelhardt, Rutgers University

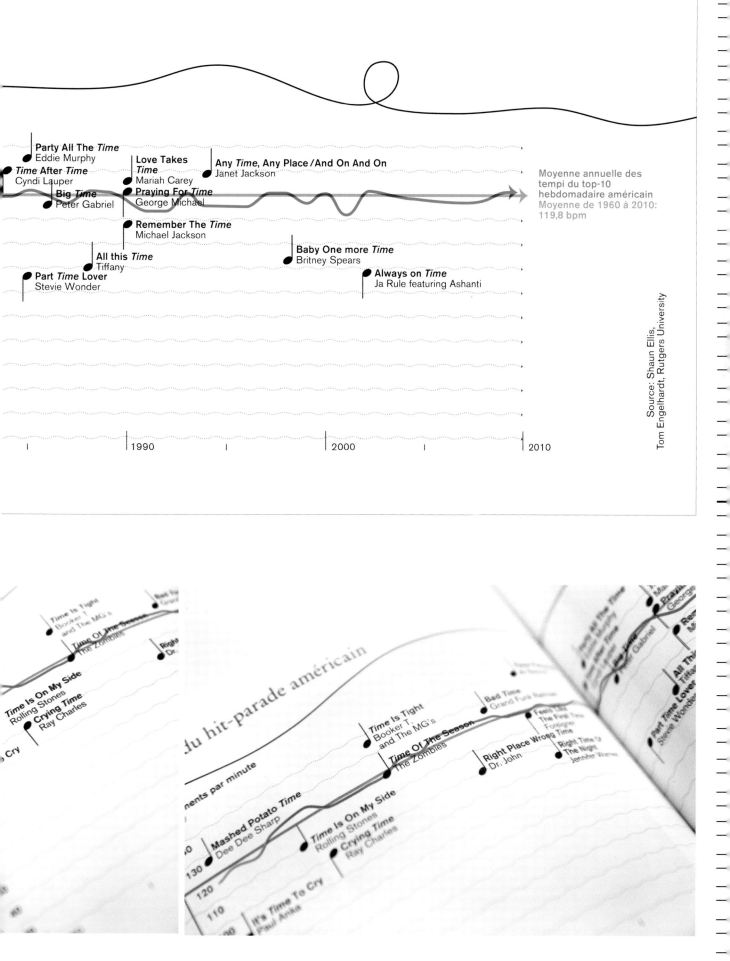

du hit-parade américain

***Time* Is Tight**
Booker T.
and The MG's

***Time* Of The Season**
The Zombies

Right Place Wrong *Time*
Dr. John

Bad *Time*
Grand Funk Railroad

**Right *Time* to
The Night**
Jennifer Warnes

Mashed Potato *Time*
Dee Dee Sharp

***Time* Is On My Side**
Rolling Stones

Crying *Time*
Ray Charles

It's *Time* To Cry
Paul Anka

130

120

110

...ments par minute

THE LIFE OF A WOODEN PENCIL

Ⓓ Designer: Marcelo Duhalde

This is a visualization of a simple experiment to see how long a drawing pencil lasts. In the process, the designer used the same pencil to complete six large (A3-size) drawings. Every turn in the sharpener was also counted.

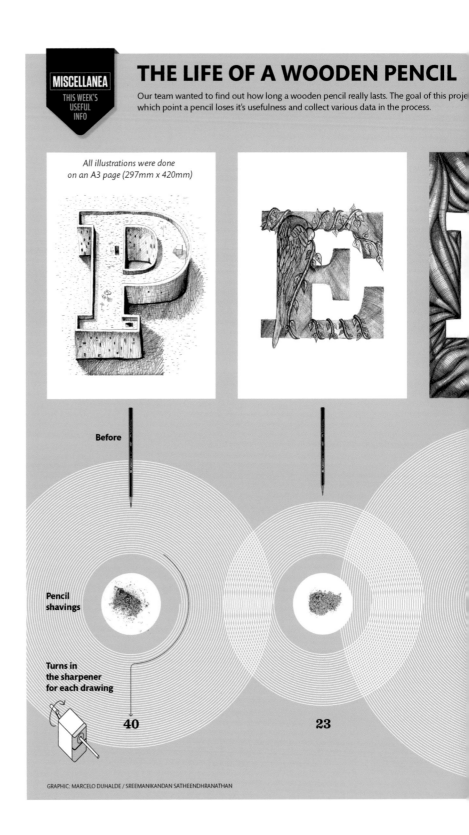

MISCELLANEA THIS WEEK'S USEFUL INFO

THE LIFE OF A WOODEN PENCIL

Our team wanted to find out how long a wooden pencil really lasts. The goal of this proje which point a pencil loses it's usefulness and collect various data in the process.

All illustrations were done on an A3 page (297mm x 420mm)

Before

Pencil shavings

Turns in the sharpener for each drawing

40

23

GRAPHIC: MARCELO DUHALDE / SREEMANIKANDAN SATHEENDHRANATHAN

Before and after
Actual pencil

e up to

(17.5 cm)

(2.7 cm)

All elements are
scaled at 18%

After

It took a total of 236 turns
in the sharpener to make 6
drawings and reduce the
pencil into this pile of
shavings

18

42

57

Bien gérer la critique sur internet

Comment le fabricant de yahourts Paul doit-il répondre à un avis négatif sur sa page Facebook pour éviter de ruiner sa réputation en ligne?

Un internaute publie un avis négatif sur Facebook.

Vos yahourts sentent mauvais

Paul

Internautes

Paul utilise un système automatique de veille comme par exemple Social Mention.

Paul n'utilise pas de système automatique de veille.

...

Aussitôt alerté, Paul s'excuse.

Nous allons vous envoyer gratuitement de nouveaux paquets de yahourts

Aussitôt alerté, Paul réfute la critique.

Vous avez laissé trop longtemps vos yahourts hors du frigo!

Quelques jours passent. De nombreux autres commentaires corroborent la plainte initiale.

Les miens aussi sentent mauvais

Les miens aussi sentent mauvais

Paul achète des mots clés Google liés au produit incriminé pour le référencer sous son meilleur jour.

Très rapidement, les internautes s'enflamment car eux aussi constatent l'odeur.

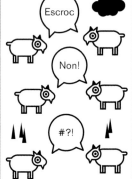

Escroc

Non!

#?!

Paul s'excuse.

Nous allons vous envoyer gratuitement de nouveaux paquets de yahourts

Paul réfute la critique.

Vous avez laissé trop longtemps vos yahourts hors du frigo!

Paul publie sur son blog une vidéo qui présente ses méthodes de fabrication artisanales.

Risques élevés de dommages durables.

Ouh, la vache!

Dommage sur une longue période mais revalorisation de la marque possible.

Pas sérieux, cette marque

TM

Moi, je la trouve pas mal

La nouvelle de l'incident se répand partout sur internet et la presse traditionnelle s'empare du dossier.

#?!

#?!   Presse locale

Dommages très importants et durables sur la réputation.

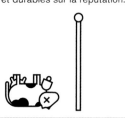

Dommages faibles sur la réputation. Revalorisation de la marque aux yeux des utilisateurs.

TM

E-REPUTATION   ←

D Designer: Benjamin Schulte
A Agency: Largenetwork
E Editor: Benjamin Bollmann
C Client: Hémisphères

The infographic *E-Reputation* shows the different ways a company can respond to negative criticism on social networks, and their consequences.

Paul the Cow is a producer of yoghurt. He receives criticism about the quality of his products. He has four different ways of reacting, resulting in four different consequences, some of which can be fatal.

ENCRYPTION   →

D Designer: Benjamin Schulte
A Agency: Largenetwork
E Editor: Benjamin Bollmann
C Client: Reflex

Encryption deals with different options for encrypting our digital communications on the Internet. It explains how to encrypt your emails with PGP, and how the TOR network is helping users surf the Internet anonymously, preventing web servers from recognizing their IP addresses. You can even encrypt your emails using quantum cryptography, which is quite complicated, but extremely safe.

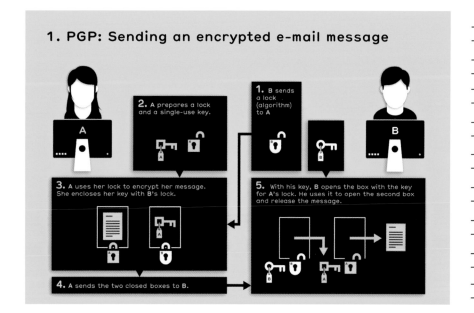

1. PGP: Sending an encrypted e-mail message

1. B sends a lock (algorithm) to A
2. A prepares a lock and a single-use key.
3. A uses her lock to encrypt her message. She encloses her key with B's lock.
4. A sends the two closed boxes to B.
5. With his key, B opens the box with the key for A's lock. He uses it to open the second box and release the message.

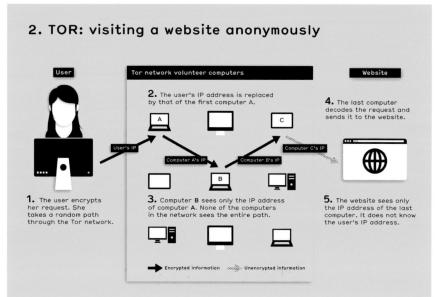

2. TOR: visiting a website anonymously

User | Tor network volunteer computers | Website

1. The user encrypts her request. She takes a random path through the Tor network.
2. The user's IP address is replaced by that of the first computer A.
3. Computer B sees only the IP address of computer A. None of the computers in the network sees the entire path.
4. The last computer decodes the request and sends it to the website.
5. The website sees only the IP address of the last computer. It does not know the user's IP address.

User's IP — Computer A's IP — Computer B's IP — Computer C's IP

→ Encrypted information   //// Unencrypted information

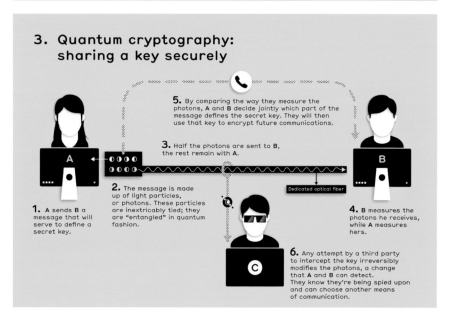

3. Quantum cryptography: sharing a key securely

1. A sends B a message that will serve to define a secret key.
2. The message is made up of light particles, or photons. These particles are inextricably tied; they are "entangled" in quantum fashion.
3. Half the photons are sent to B, the rest remain with A.
4. B measures the photons he receives, while A measures hers.
5. By comparing the way they measure the photons, A and B decide jointly which part of the message defines the secret key. They will then use that key to encrypt future communications.
6. Any attempt by a third party to intercept the key irreversibly modifies the photons, a change that A and B can detect. They know they're being spied upon and can choose another means of communication.

Dedicated optical fiber

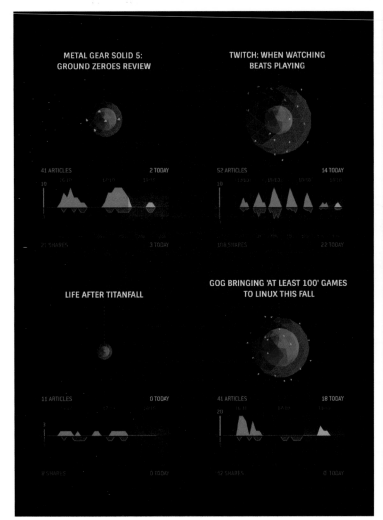

ACTUALITÉS

Ⓓ Designer: Dataveyes, Antidot
Ⓒ Client: Paris Science Museum
(La Cité des Sciences)

⇅

This is a real-time ambient environment created for a video game exhibition at *La Cité des Sciences*. This visualization aimed to make users aware of the most prevalent topics in video games, but also of differences in coverage between general, new and specialist sources, blogs, and social networks. The data describing current news is translated into an artistic landscape, where current news topics are represented by planets, their echo on social networks by a surrounding halo, and recent articles, by orbiting satellites. These elements come to life and feed off the fluctuation of current news, which acts as a data-fuelled energy source.

BODY PARTS

Ⓓ Designer: Grundini

⇄

How much are you worth?

Bodyparts is an infographic produced for Esquire Magazine. It details how a person's specific body parts add up to the approximate value of a car.

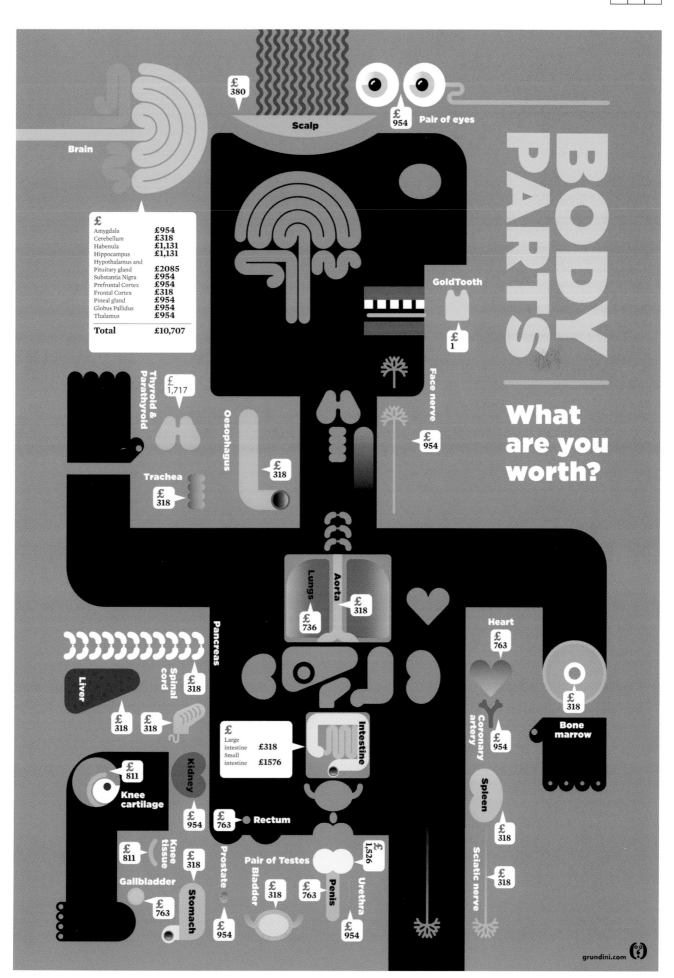

BODY PARTS

What are you worth?

Brain

£	
Amygdala	£954
Cerebellum	£318
Habenula	£1,131
Hippocampus	£1,131
Hypothalamus and Pituitary gland	£2085
Substantia Nigra	£954
Prefrontal Cortex	£954
Frontal Cortex	£318
Pineal gland	£954
Globus Pallidus	£954
Thalamus	£954
Total	**£10,707**

Scalp — £380

Pair of eyes — £954

Gold Tooth — £1

Face nerve — £954

Thyroid & Parathyroid — £1,717

Oesophagus

Trachea — £318

Oesophagus — £318

Lungs — £736

Aorta — £318

Heart — £763

£318

Pancreas — £318

Spinal cord — £318

Liver

£318 £318

Coronary artery — £954

Spleen — £318

Bone marrow

Sciatic nerve — £318

£	
Large intestine	£318
Small intestine	£1576

Intestine

Knee cartilage — £811

Kidney — £954

Rectum — £763

£1,526

Knee tissue — £811

£318

Gallbladder

Stomach — £763

Prostate

Bladder

Pair of Testes

Penis — £763

Urethra — £954

£318

£954

grundini.com

STREET DOMESTIC

Ⓓ Designer: Domestic Data Streamers

Street Domestic is a real-time infographic about people's moods over 24 hours, on a specific square in Barcelona. The research involves a flux of data, and compares the ages and feelings of the people involved.

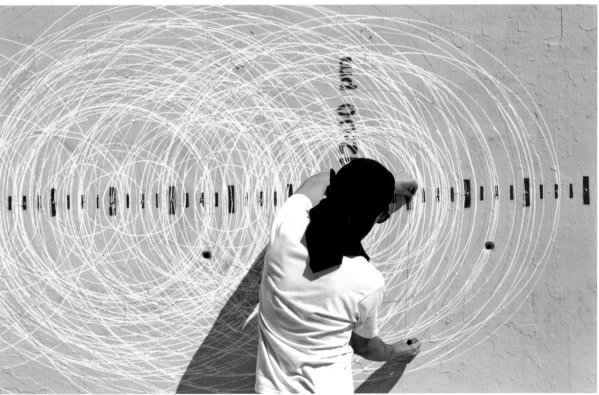

BEHANCE PORTFOLIO REVIEW

(AD) Art Director: Domestic Data Streamers

Behance is one of the biggest creative communities in the world, a platform to showcase and discover new work from any creative field. Domestic Data Streamers was invited to participate in the Barcelona Portfolio Reviews, to create a voting system for candidates for the closing talk at the event.

Seven panels were displayed with the work of each designer available to do the talk. By generating an ephemeral laboratory, where data is literally turned into liquid, votes cast by attendees could be measured and visually perceived.

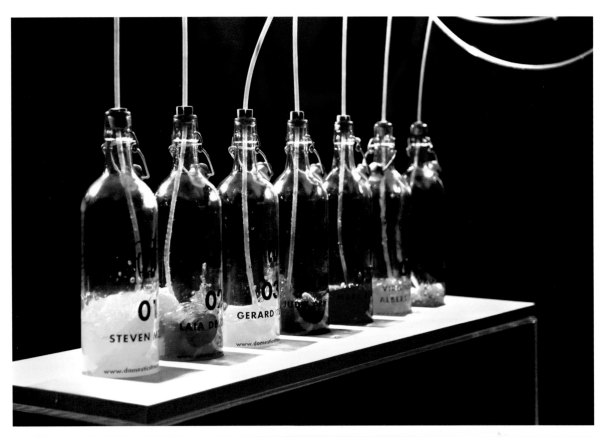

THE INTERNET MAP

Ⓓ Designer: Ruslan Enikeev

The Internet Map is a bi-dimensional presentation of links between websites on the Internet. Every site is a circle on the map, and its size is determined by website traffic: the larger the quantity of traffic, the bigger the circle. Users switching between websites form links. The stronger the link, the closer the websites tend to arrange themselves with respect to each other. It encompasses over 350,000 websites, from 196 countries, and all domain zones. Information about more than two million links between the websites has joined some of them together, into topical clusters.

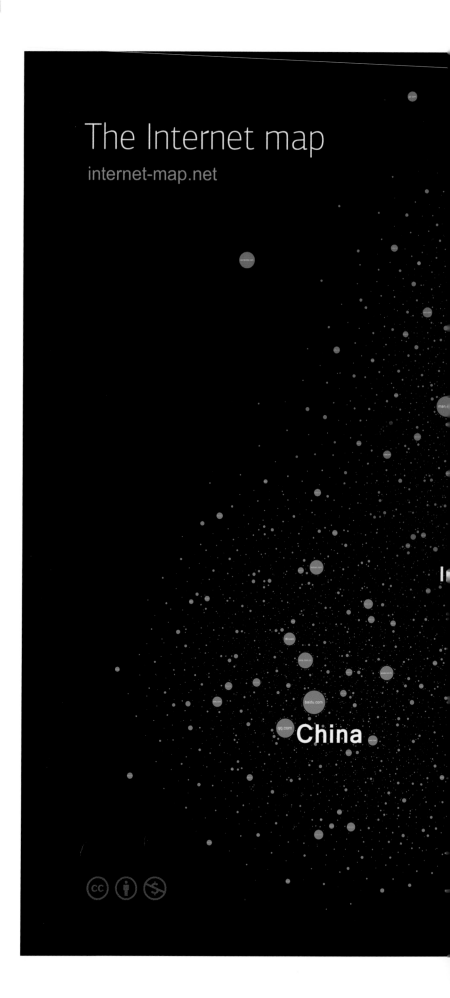

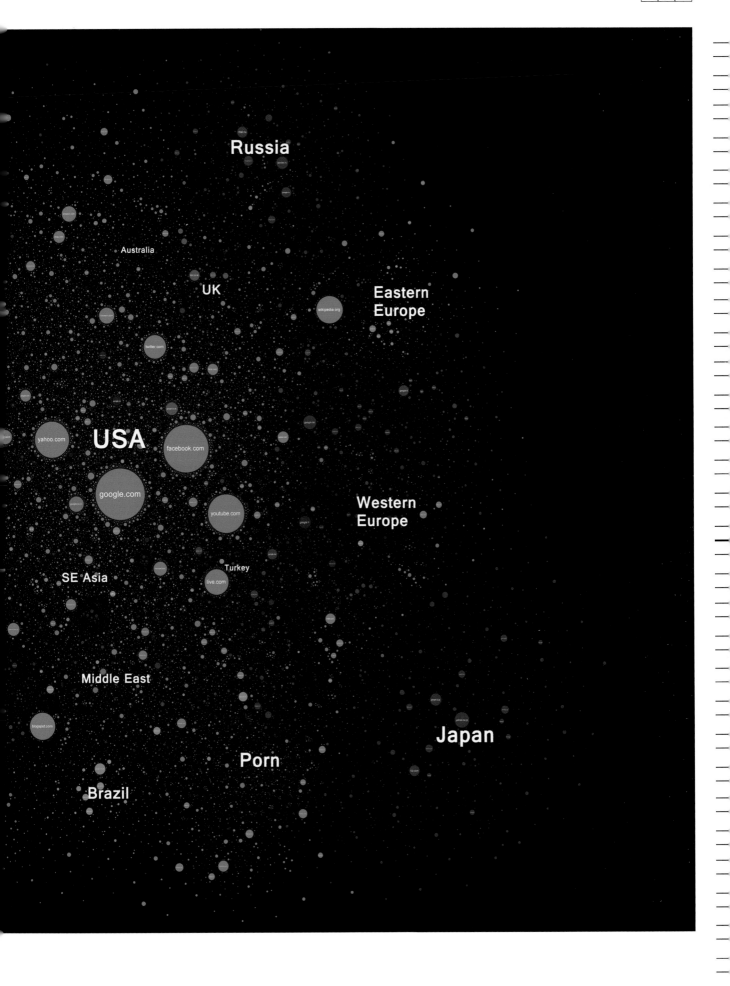

MAP OF AMSTERDAM

Ⓓ Designer: Archie's Press   ↓↑

A letterpress-printed map of Amsterdam, designed to orient the user, with strategically included landmarks and essentials about the region.

MAP OF NEW ORLEANS

Ⓓ Designer: Archie's Press   ⇆

Best explored by bike, the eccentricities of New Orleans are simplified into its key elements, culminating in a letterpress-printed map for the curious explorer.

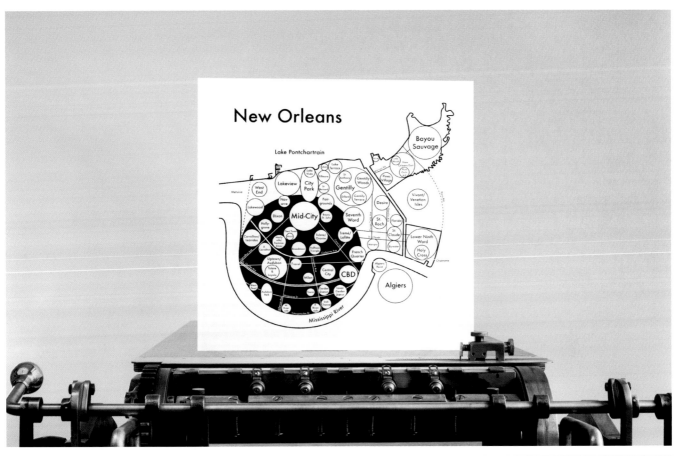

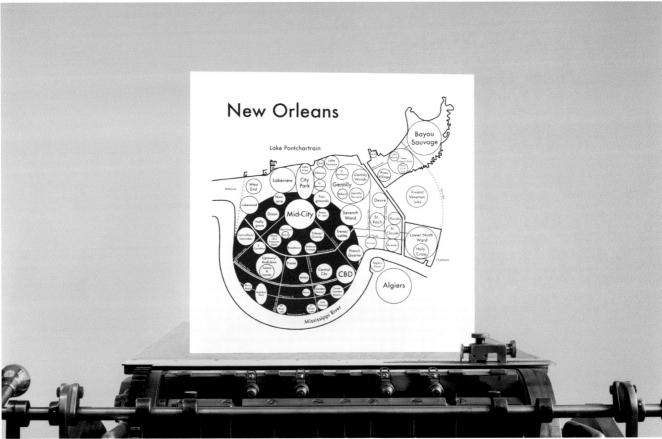

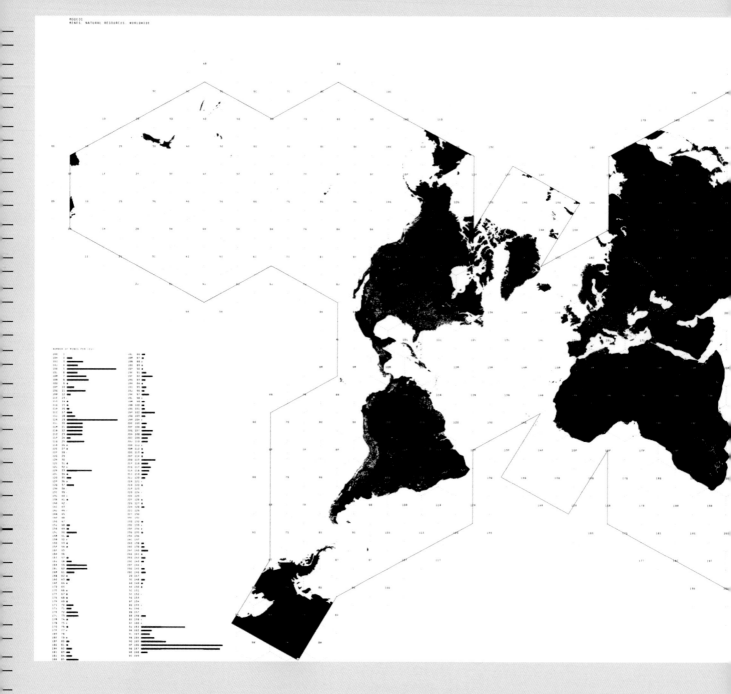

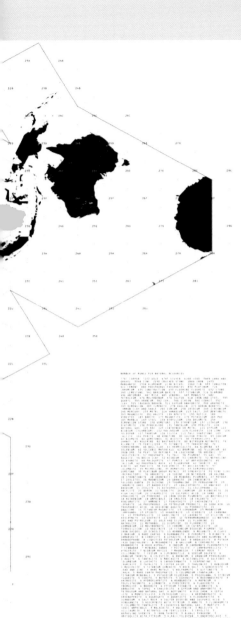

WORLD DOCS

Ⓓ Designer: Andreas Schlegel
and Patrick Kochlik

Natural resources form the tangible basis of the global
capitalist economy. Their occurrence, mining, trade and
depletion have massive environmental and geopolitical
implications. *World Docs* collects publicly available data
about these implications from various online data resources,
including the CIA factbook, USGS, Wikipedia, and
nationmaster.com, and transforms them into a data narrative.
The result is a board-game-inspired collection of tangible
assets: maps, diagrams and information cards, which foster
an informed, associative and open-ended discourse.

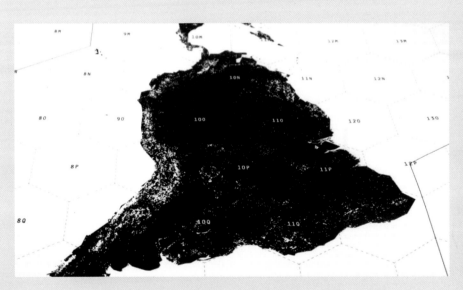

ZEOLITES, 26 MAGNESIUM, 26 GRANITE,
LLERS EARTH, 25 OLIVINE, 25 TOURMALI
ROMITE ORES, 23 BADDELEYITE, 23 CHAL
DIUM, 21 ZEOLITE, 21 ASTROPHYLLITE,
YLITE, 21 BORON, 21 SODALITE, 20 CA
H CALCIUM, 20 STAUROLITE, 19 SULFUR
LERITE, 19 PYROXENE, 19 IRON OXIDE
UTHENIUM, 18 AMPHIBOLE, 18 SMELTER
GMATITE, 17 AMMONIA, 17 PEROVSKITE
RITE, 16 PHOSPHORUS, 16 PETROLEUM
HORIC ACID, 16 AEGIRINE-AUGITE, 1
IME, 14 TITANIUM MAGNETITE, 13 CO
NDS, 13 EPIDOTE, 13 VANADINITE,
PYROPHYLLITE, 12 GADOLINITE, 12
NITE, 12 GOETHITE, 12 COKE, 11 F
PETROLEUM, 11 GOLD AND SILVER,
TE, 11 METHANOL, 11 DIOPSIDE, 1
UM, 10 MOLYBDENITE, 10 CHROME,
ICON, 10 KAOLINITE, 10 TITANIU

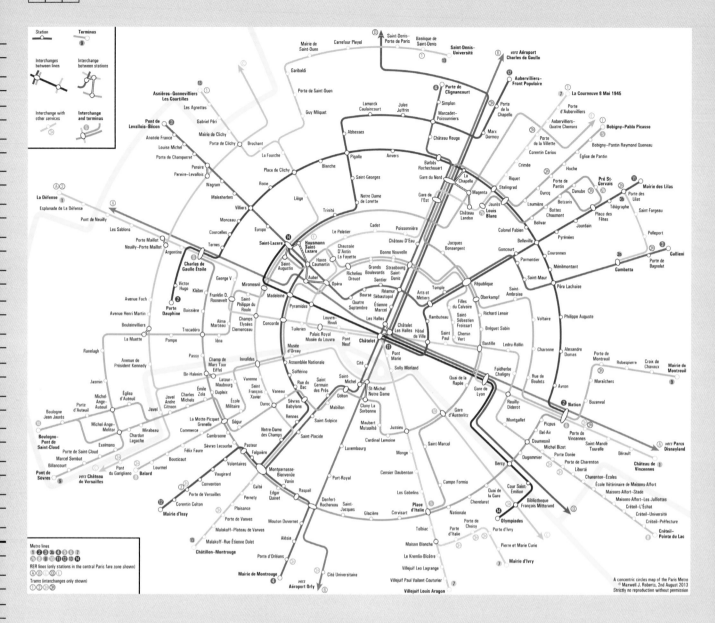

A concentric circles map of the Paris Metro
© Maxwell J. Roberts, 2nd August 2013
Strictly no reproduction without permission

MAPS IN CIRCLES

Ⓓ Designer: Maxwell Roberts

Originally inspired by the London "Overground" orbital railway, *Maps in Circles* is an exploration of global subway networks. It uses a novel technique involving concentric circles and spikes, which results in visual maps with breathtaking levels of coherence, which force cities into unprecedented levels of organization.

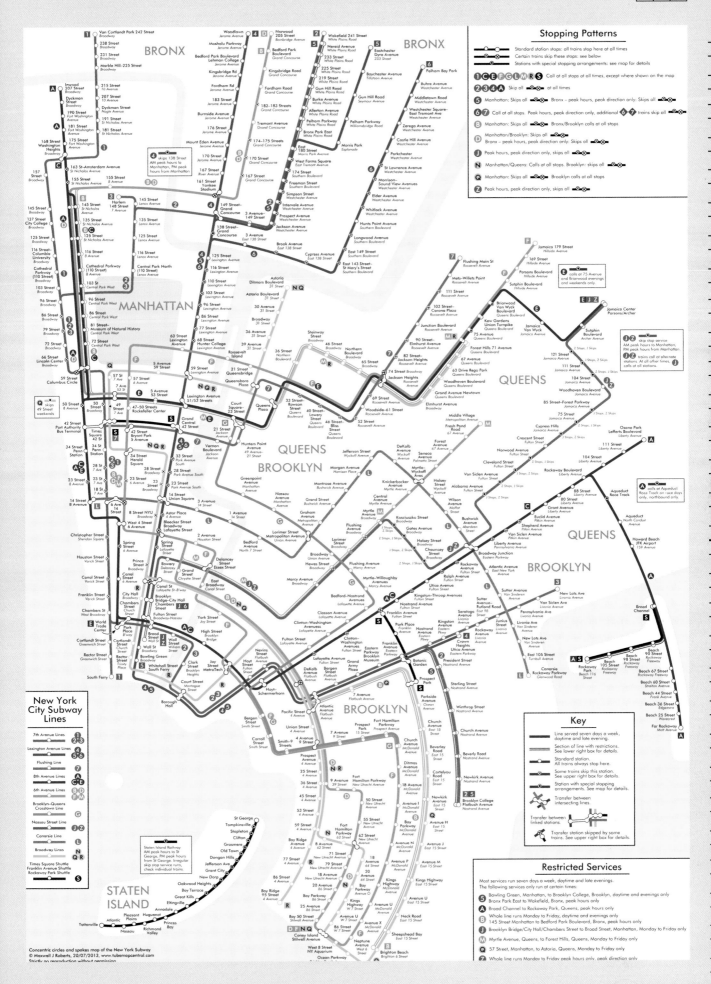

Concentric circles and spokes map of the New York Subway
© Maxwell J Roberts, 20/07/2013. www.tubemapcentral.com
Strictly no reproduction without permission

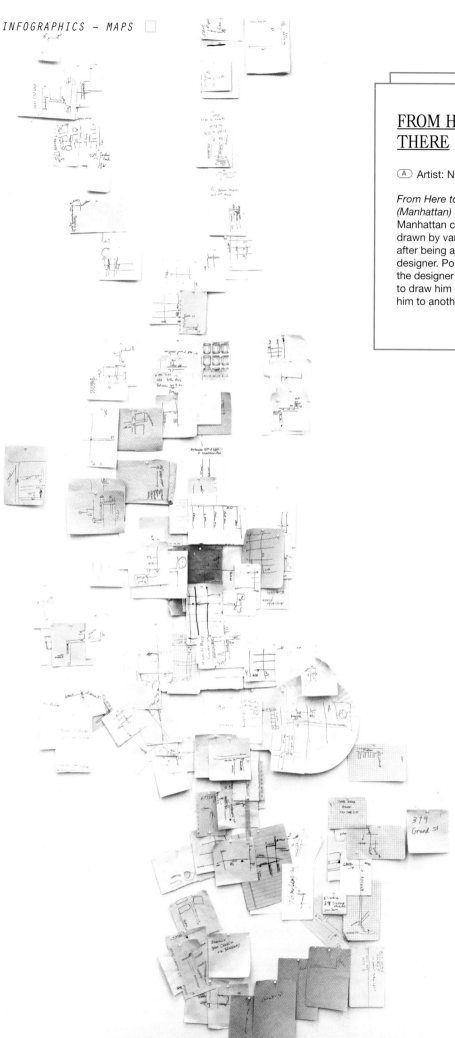

FROM HERE TO THERE

Ⓐ Artist: Nobutaka Aozaki

From Here to There (Manhattan) is a map of Manhattan composed of maps drawn by various pedestrians, after being approached by the designer. Posing as a tourist, the designer asked pedestrians to draw him a map, to direct him to another location.

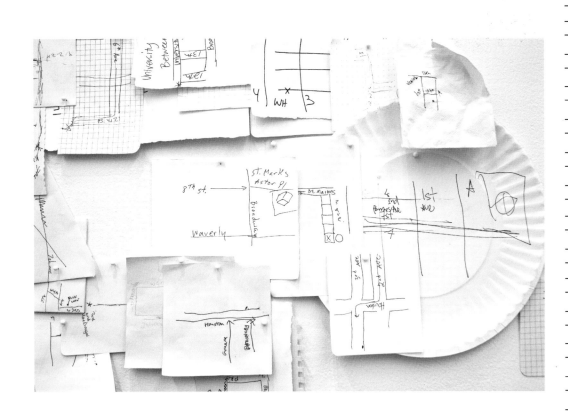

If the world were a village of 100 people

SKIN COLOUR

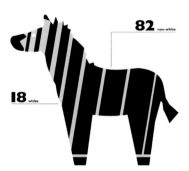

82 non-white

18 white

If the world were a village of 100 people

FREEDOM

48 can't speak, act according to their faith and conscience due to harassment, imprisonment, torture or death

52 can

If the world were a village of 100 people

AGE

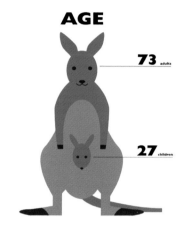

73 adults

27 children

If the world were a village of 100 people

RELIGION

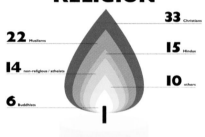

33 Christians

22 Muslims

15 Hindus

14 non-religious / atheists

10 others

6 Buddhists

If the world were a village of 100 people

COMPUTERS

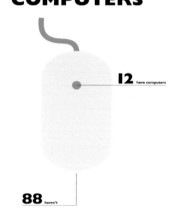

12 have computers

88 haven't

If the world were a village of 100 people

FOOD

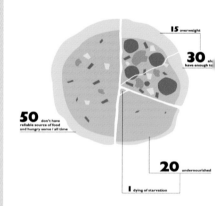

15 overweight

30 al... have enough to...

50 don't have reliable source of food and hungry some / all time

20 undernourished

I dying of starvation

THE WORLD OF 100

Ⓓ Designer: Toby Ng

If the world were a village of 100 people, what would its composition be? This set of 20 posters is built on statistics about population spread around the world, based on various classifications. The numbers are turned into infographics, as a way to help the viewer interpret them.

If the world were a village of 100 people

NATIONALITY

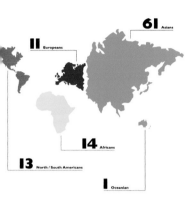

61 Asians

11 Europeans

14 Africans

13 North / South Americans

1 Oceanian

If the world were a village of 100 people

LANGUAGE

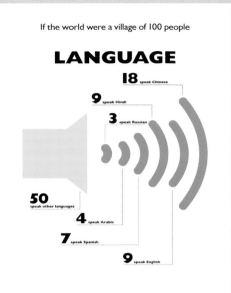

18 speak Chinese

9 speak Hindi

3 speak Russian

50 speak other languages

4 speak Arabic

7 speak Spanish

9 speak English

If the world were a village of 100 people

MONEY

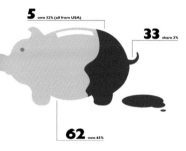

5 own 32% (all from USA)

33 share 3%

62 own 65%

If the world were a village of 100 people

FEAR

20 live in fear of death by bombardment armed attack, landmines, or of rape or kidnapping by armed groups

80 don't

THE WORLD OF 100 POSTCARDS

If the world were a village of 100 people, how would the composition be? In 20 classifications, each illustrated by vibrant, distinctive graphics, the spread of population is more than dull numbers on paper. Let this series of postcards tour you around — Look, this is the world we are living in.

Toby Ng

SKIN COLOUR

82

18

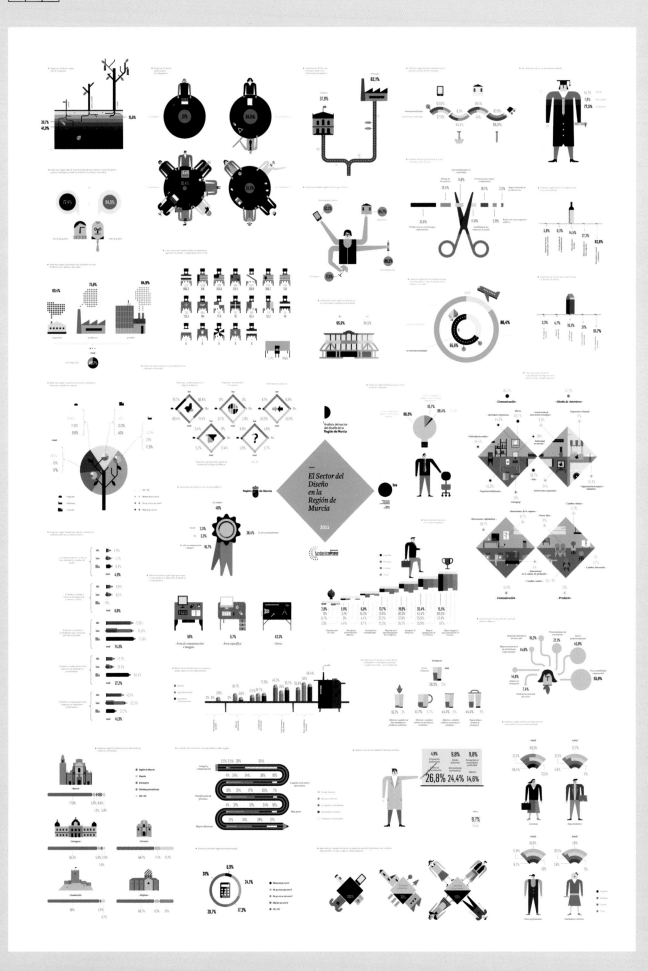

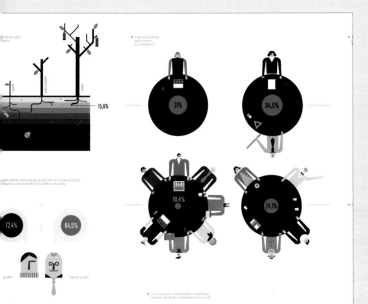

DESIGN IN MURCIA

Ⓓ Designer: Romualdo Faura
Ⓒ Client: Obs Murcia (Consejería de Cultura de la Región de Murcia)

This is a series of infographics for the first Murcia Design report, commissioned by the Murcia Design Centre (Spain). The idea was to brighten up the statistics in the report, using pictures. Two colours were used, to give a touch of seriousness to the pictures.

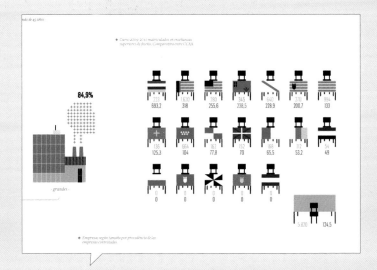

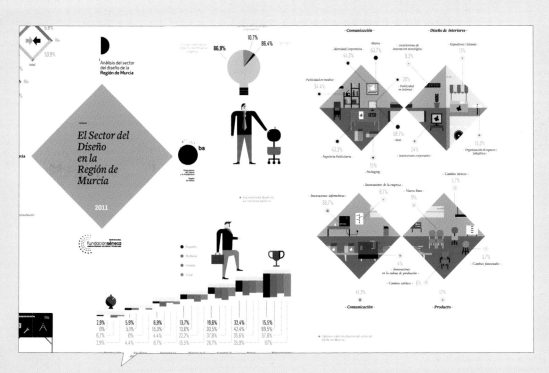

CULTURA

ROPA

CURIOSIDADES

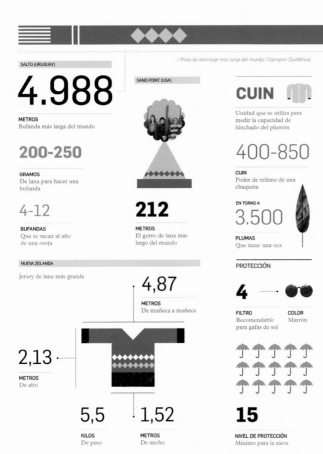

SALTO (URUGUAY)

4.988

METROS
Bufanda más larga del mundo

200-250

GRAMOS
De lana para hacer una bufanda

4-12

BUFANDAS
Que se sacan al año de una oveja

NUEVA ZELANDA
Jersey de lana más grande

2,13

METROS
De alto

SAND POINT (USA)

212

METROS
El gorro de lana más largo del mundo

4,87

METROS
De muñeca a muñeca

5,5

KILOS
De peso

1,52

METROS
De ancho

= Pista de aterrizaje más larga del mundo / Upington (Sudáfrica)

CUIN

Unidad que se utiliza para medir la capacidad de hinchado del plumón

400-850

CUIN
Poder de relleno de una chaqueta

EN TORNO A

3.500

PLUMAS
Que tiene una oca

PROTECCIÓN

4

FILTRO
Recomendable para gafas de sol

COLOR
Marrón

15

NIVEL DE PROTECCIÓN
Mínimo para la nieve

HARBIN (CHINA)
La escultura de nieve más grande del mundo

200

METROS
Largo

35

METROS
Alto

TAEBAEK CITY (COREA DEL SUR)

5.387

PARTICIPANTES
En la mayor guerra de bolas de nieve

57.200.000

RESULTADOS
De la palabra Nieve en Google

MAINE

37,21

METROS
Altura del mayor muñeco de nieve

BISMARCK (USA)

8.962

PERSONAS
Haciendo ángeles de nieve simultáneamente

22
ENERO

Día Mundial de la Nieve

GRAN BRETAÑA

0,01

MILÍMETROS
Altura del muñeco de nieve más pequeño

0,001

MILÍMETROS
Tamaño de la nariz

ESQUIMALES

30

TONALIDADES
De blanco que reconocen los esquimales

70.000

ESQUIMALES
Que se estiman en el mundo

▲ CANADÁ
▲ GROENLANDIA
▲ ALASKA
▲ SIBERIA

KUHTAI (AUSTRIA)

12,1

METROS
Diámetro del iglú más grande

8,1

METROS
Altura del interior

14   15

INFOGRAPHICS OF SNOW

Ⓓ Designer: Romualdo Faura
Ⓒ Client: Pelonio/Mercedes Benz

This series of infographics is created for *ALUD*, a magazine published by Mercedes Benz. They are all related to snow: ski resorts, snow sports, weather, glaciers and more.

ESQUÍ

ESTACIONES

3.600

Estaciones de esquí en el mundo

4.000

KM²
El ámbito de esquí
mundial

22.300

REMONTES
en el parque mundial

FRANCIA

Dominio de esquí
más grande del mundo

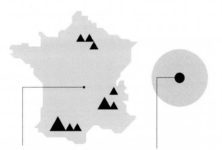

357

ESTACIONES
De esquí en Francia

18

%
De los remontes
del mundo

DOLOMITI SUPERSKI

Estación de esquí más grande

1.200

KILÓMETROS
de pistas

12

ÁREAS

CHACALTAYA (BOL)

5.300

METROS
A mayor altura

CERRO CASTOR

195

METROS
A menor altura

CERVINIA (ITA)

25

KILÓMETROS
Longitud de uno de los
descenso más largos

ESPAÑA

36

ESTACIONES
En España

700

KILÓMETROS
Superficie
esquiable

TELESILLA

BRECKENRIDGE

3.963

METROS
Telesilla más alto
del mundo

15

KM/H
La velocidad media
de un telesilla

LA NUBE NO ES INVISIBLE

Ⓓ Designer: Relajaelcoco
Ⓒ Client: Yorokobu Magazine

The Cloud is not Invisible is a monthly double-page infographic produced for *Yorokobu* Magazine, a Spanish publication about creativity, trends, design and communication. The mission was to create a sparkling and amazing composition, using a black and white outline illustration style, tempered with a soft colour palette. The final result is a huge infographic structure, with several levels of information, focusing mainly on content hierarchy.

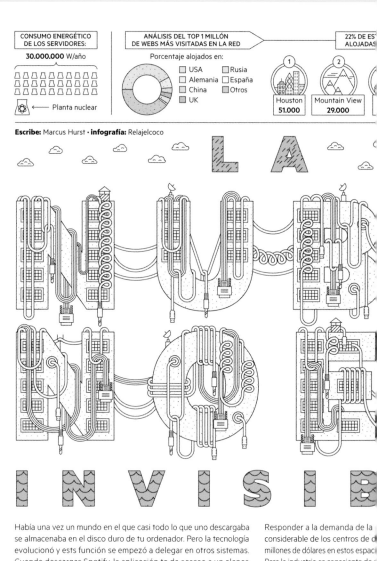

CONSUMO ENERGÉTICO DE LOS SERVIDORES:
30.000.000 W/año
← Planta nuclear

ANÁLISIS DEL TOP 1 MILLÓN DE WEBS MÁS VISITADAS EN LA RED
Porcentaje alojados en:
☐ USA ☐ Rusia
☐ Alemania ☐ España
☐ China ☐ Otros
☐ UK

22% DE ES... ALOJADAS...

1 Houston **51.000**
2 Mountain View **29.000**

Escribe: Marcus Hurst · **infografía:** Relajelcoco

Había una vez un mundo en el que casi todo lo que uno descargaba se almacenaba en el disco duro de tu ordenador. Pero la tecnología evolucionó y ests función se empezó a delegar en otros sistemas. Cuando descargas Spotify, la aplicación te da acceso a un elenco enorme de canciones pero ninguna se queda grabada en tu ordenador. Aquella canción está guardada en los bajos de un centro de datos lleno de servidores que almacenan esa información sustituyendo a tu disco duro. Las páginas web que hoy visitas se alojan aquí también.

Responder a la demanda de la ... considerable de los centros de d... millones de dólares en estos espac... Pero la industria es consciente de ... La energía que gastan sigue sie... fuentes fósiles. Los niveles de efic... y los recursos necesarios para mar... son enormes. La nube está aquí p...

EDIFICIOS CURIOSOS UTILIZADOS PARA ALMACENAR SERVIDORES

PIONEN DATA CENTER (SUECIA)
(un búnker de la guerra fría a 30 m bajo tierra)

CLUMEQ, UNIVERSITÉ LAVAL (CANADÁ)
(interior de un acelerador de partículas remodelado)

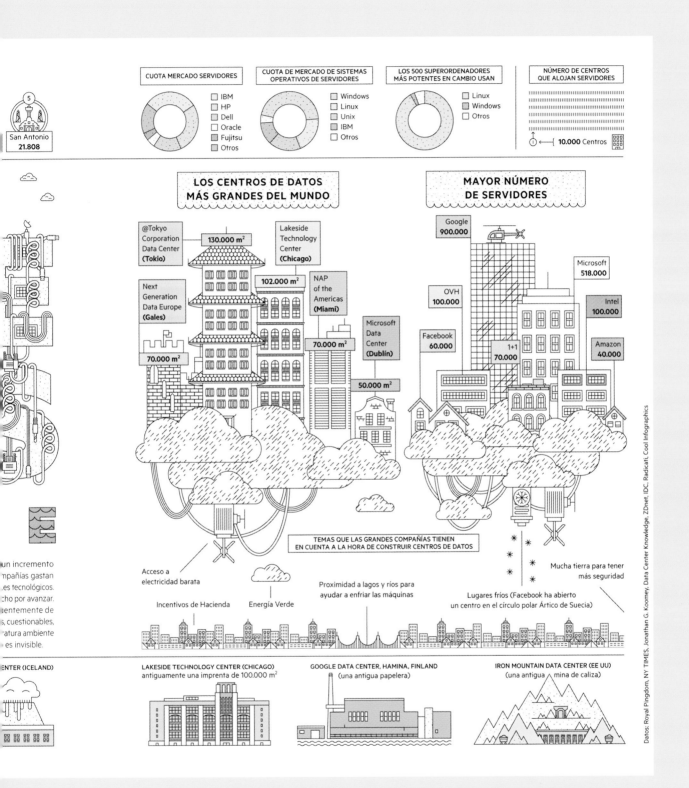

- ☐ IBM
- ☐ HP
- ☐ Dell
- ☐ Oracle
- ☐ Fujitsu
- ☐ Otros

CUOTA DE MERCADO DE SISTEMAS OPERATIVOS DE SERVIDORES

- ☐ Windows
- ☐ Linux
- ☐ Unix
- ☐ IBM
- ☐ Otros

LOS 500 SUPERORDENADORES MÁS POTENTES EN CAMBIO USAN

- ☐ Linux
- ☐ Windows
- ☐ Otros

NÚMERO DE CENTROS QUE ALOJAN SERVIDORES

⊕ ⟵⟶ 10.000 Centros

(5)
San Antonio
21.808

LOS CENTROS DE DATOS MÁS GRANDES DEL MUNDO

MAYOR NÚMERO DE SERVIDORES

@Tokyo Corporation Data Center **(Tokio)** — 130.000 m²

Lakeside Technology Center **(Chicago)** — 102.000 m²

Next Generation Data Europe **(Gales)**

NAP of the Americas **(Miami)** — 70.000 m²

Microsoft Data Center **(Dublín)** — 50.000 m²

70.000 m²

Google 900.000

Microsoft 518.000

OVH 100.000

Intel 100.000

Facebook 60.000

1+1 70.000

Amazon 40.000

TEMAS QUE LAS GRANDES COMPAÑÍAS TIENEN EN CUENTA A LA HORA DE CONSTRUIR CENTROS DE DATOS

Acceso a electricidad barata

Incentivos de Hacienda

Energía Verde

Proximidad a lagos y ríos para ayudar a enfriar las máquinas

Lugares fríos (Facebook ha abierto un centro en el círculo polar Ártico de Suecia)

Mucha tierra para tener más seguridad

un incremento
mpañías gastan
les tecnológicos.
cho por avanzar.
entemente de
s, cuestionables,
ratura ambiente
es invisible.

ENTER (ICELAND)

LAKESIDE TECHNOLOGY CENTER (CHICAGO)
antiguamente una imprenta de 100.000 m²

GOOGLE DATA CENTER, HAMINA, FINLAND
(una antigua papelera)

IRON MOUNTAIN DATA CENTER (EE UU)
(una antigua mina de caliza)

Datos: Royal Pingdom, NY TIMES, Jonathan G. Koomey, Data Center Knowledge, ZDnet, IDC, Radicati, Cool Infographics

VEWLIX L

ビュウリックス

TAITO VEWLIX-L

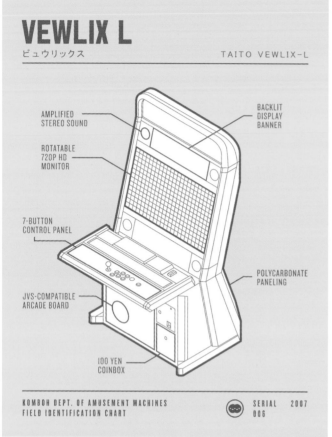

AMPLIFIED
STEREO SOUND

ROTATABLE
720P HD
MONITOR

7-BUTTON
CONTROL PANEL

JVS-COMPATIBLE
ARCADE BOARD

100 YEN
COINBOX

BACKLIT
DISPLAY
BANNER

POLYCARBONATE
PANELING

KOMBOH DEPT. OF AMUSEMENT MACHINES
FIELD IDENTIFICATION CHART

SERIAL   2007
006

DONKEY KONG

ドンキーコング

TKG4-UP

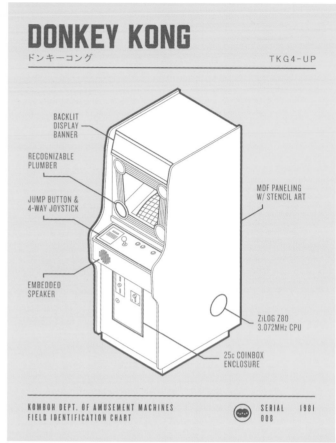

BACKLIT
DISPLAY
BANNER

RECOGNIZABLE
PLUMBER

JUMP BUTTON &
4-WAY JOYSTICK

EMBEDDED
SPEAKER

MDF PANELING
W/ STENCIL ART

ZiLOG Z80
3.072MHz CPU

25c COINBOX
ENCLOSURE

KOMBOH DEPT. OF AMUSEMENT MACHINES
FIELD IDENTIFICATION CHART

SERIAL   1981
008

VS.SYSTEM

任天堂VS.システム

MDS-TBL

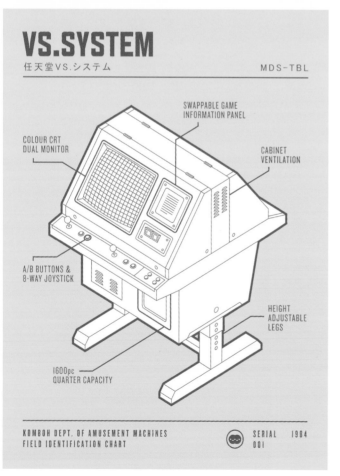

SWAPPABLE GAME
INFORMATION PANEL

COLOUR CRT
DUAL MONITOR

CABINET
VENTILATION

A/B BUTTONS &
8-WAY JOYSTICK

HEIGHT
ADJUSTABLE
LEGS

1600pc
QUARTER CAPACITY

KOMBOH DEPT. OF AMUSEMENT MACHINES
FIELD IDENTIFICATION CHART

SERIAL   1984
001

AMUSEMENT MACHINE
FIELD IDENTIFICATION KIT

Ⓓ Designer: KOMBOH

Arcades are all but dead in most places in the
world. This kit is intended to help millennials
identify these forgotten relics of a past age.

MULTI VIDEO SYS.

ネオジオMVS   MVS-1-25

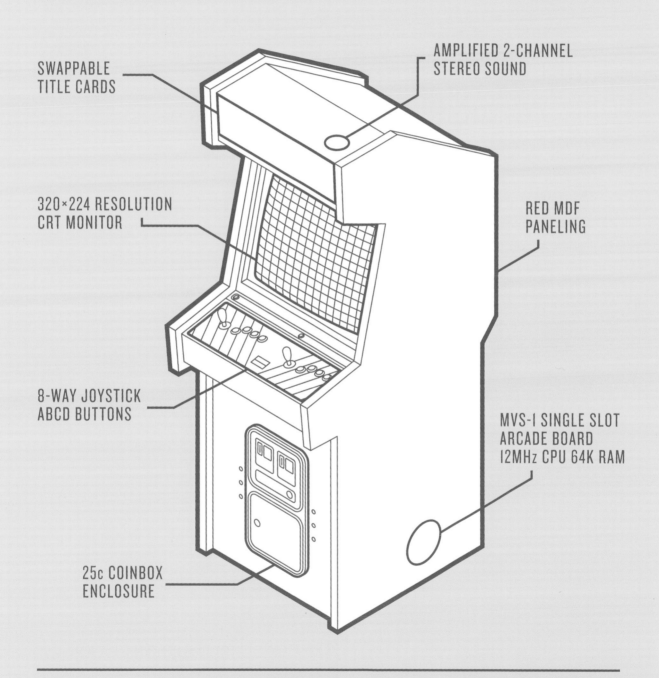

SWAPPABLE
TITLE CARDS

AMPLIFIED 2-CHANNEL
STEREO SOUND

320×224 RESOLUTION
CRT MONITOR

RED MDF
PANELING

8-WAY JOYSTICK
ABCD BUTTONS

MVS-1 SINGLE SLOT
ARCADE BOARD
12MHz CPU 64K RAM

25c COINBOX
ENCLOSURE

ICE CREAM

Ⓓ Designer: MGMT. design

Ice cream was originally invented by the Chinese in 200 BC. Legend has it that the Emperor kept it a secret, until Marco Polo visited and allegedly took the production technique back to Italy. Created during a heatwave in the summer of 2013, Ice Cream showcases different ways to enjoy a scoop (or two) of ice cream.

STOCKS

 →

Ⓓ Designer: Hey

Illustrations for *Fortune* magazine, on the 15 best stocks for 2013.

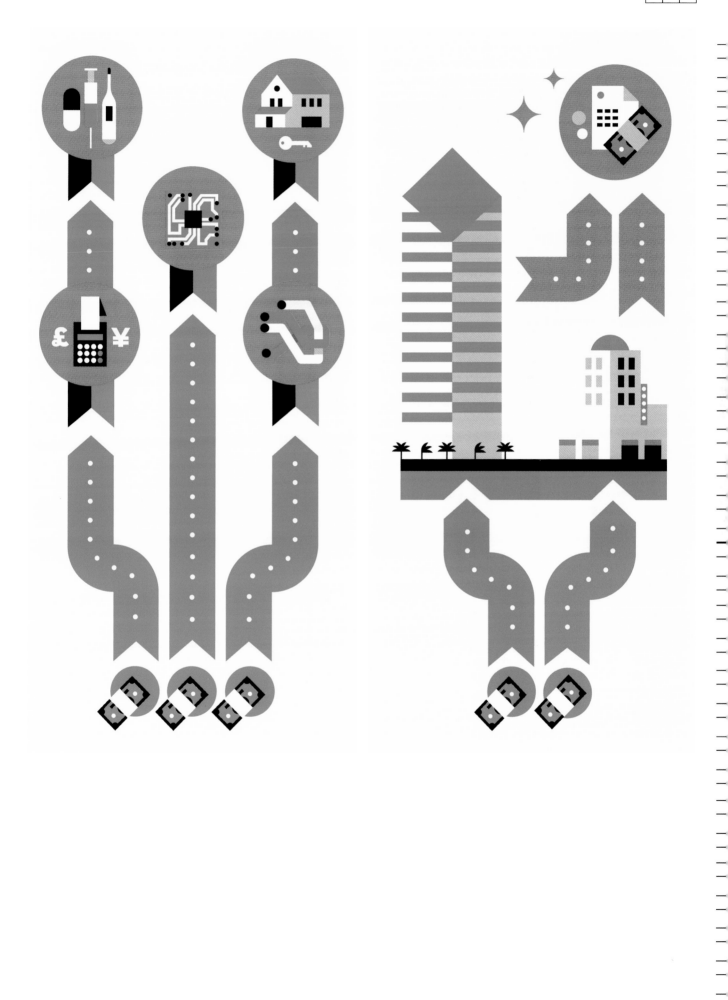

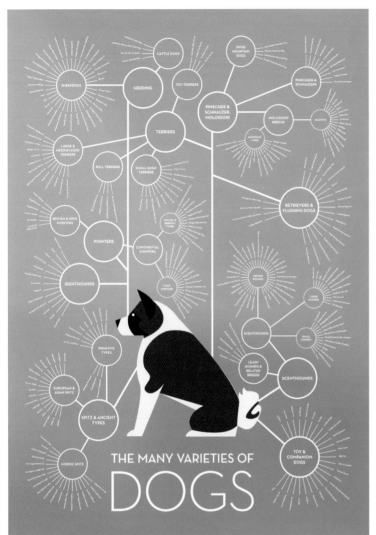

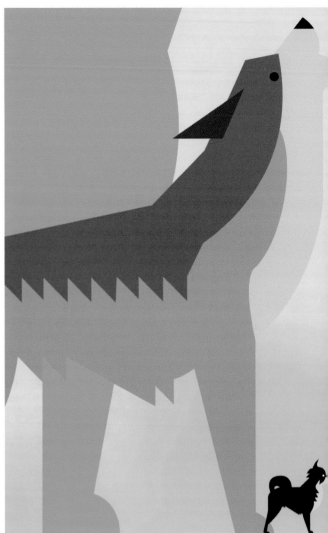

HISTORY OF DOGS

ⒹDesigner: Anna Reinbold

The wolf in our living rooms. How much 'wolfness' is left in man's best friend?

Dogs display the greatest variation in size of any known species. Despite the wide diversity in their appearance, numerous domestic dogs can be traced back to domestication of the grey wolf, 15,000 years ago. Genetic diversity has declined in favour of selective breeding, and features such as short legs can be linked to a single gene mutation.

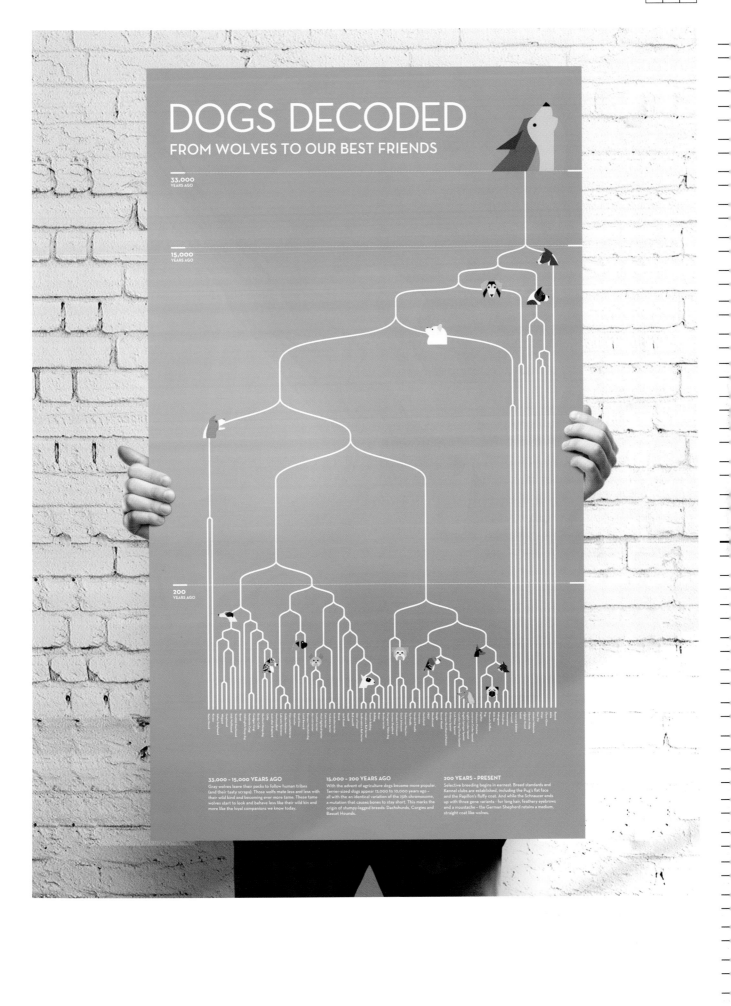

DOGS DECODED
FROM WOLVES TO OUR BEST FRIENDS

33,000 YEARS AGO

15,000 YEARS AGO

200 YEARS AGO

33,000 – 15,000 YEARS AGO
Gray wolves leave their packs to follow human tribes (and their tasty scraps). Those wolfs mate less and less with their wild kind and becoming ever more tame. These tame wolves start to look and behave less like their wild kin and more like the loyal companions we know today.

15,000 – 200 YEARS AGO
With the advent of agriculture dogs become more popular. Terrier-sized dogs appear 12,000 to 10,000 years ago – all with the an identical variation of the 15th chromosome, a mutation that causes bones to stay short. This marks the origin of stumpy-legged breeds: Dachshunds, Corgies and Basset Hounds.

200 YEARS – PRESENT
Selective breeding begins in earnest. Breed standards and Kennel clubs are established, including the Pug's flat face and the Papillon's fluffy coat. And while the Schnauzer ends up with three gene variants – for long hair, feathery eyebrows and a moustache – the German Shepherd retains a medium, straight coat like wolves.

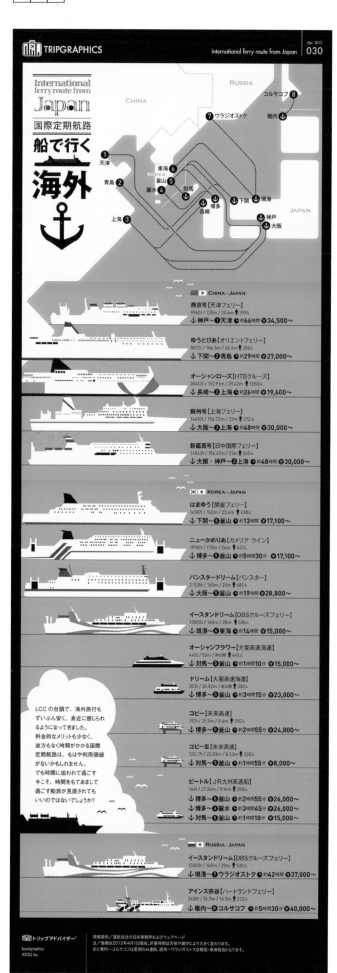

TRIPGRAPHICS#30 ←

Ⓓ Designer: bowlgraphics
Ⓡ Researcher: ATOLL Inc.
Ⓒ Client: TripAdvisor Japan

A route map of international
ferries from Japan. All the
illustrations of vessels are drawn
on a comparative scale.

METROMIN →

Ⓘ Illustrator: bowlgraphics
Ⓓ Designer: groovision
Ⓒ Client: Starts Publishing
Corporation
A distribution map of beers,
showing production regions, and
brands guests can drink during
the Tokyo Midtown World Beer
Festival.

Tokyo Midtown　東京ミッドタウン

WORLD BEER FESTIVAL

ワールド ビア フェスティバル、実施中！

ビールとは、世界中どこを旅しても出会えるもの。
その数の分だけ、「我がビールが一番！」をうたう国や地域があるわけで、飲み比べてみるとスゴく楽しい。
というわけで、各地のビールを様々、味わってみませんか？
ただ今、東京ミッドタウンでは、「ワールド ビア フェスティバル」を実施中です（6月30日まで）!!

世界のビールを楽しもう！！

ワールド ビア フェスティバル「世界のビールを楽しもう!!」では、まずどの国や地域にどんなビールがあるのかをチェックすることが大切です。そこで、ここでは16の参加店が提供している各地のビールをご紹介！ 飲みたいビールを見つけたら、いざ、お店へ足を運んでみましょう。

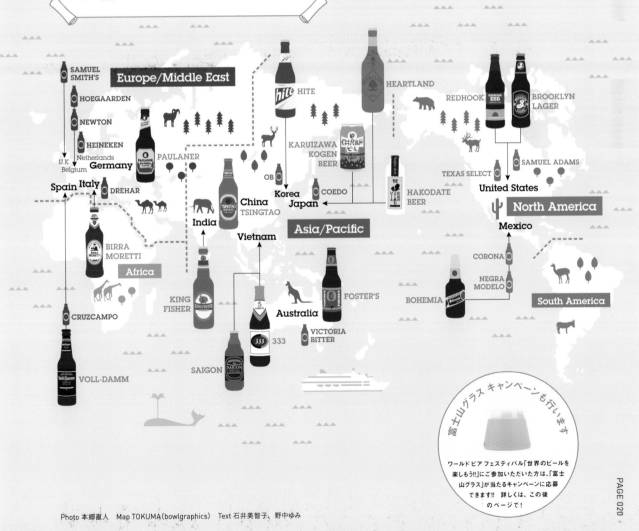

富士山グラス キャンペーンも行います

ワールド ビア フェスティバル「世界のビールを楽しもう!!」にご参加いただいた方は、「富士山グラス」が当たるキャンペーンに応募できます!! 詳しくは、この後のページで！

Photo 本郷直人　Map TOKUMA（bowlgraphics）　Text 石井美智子、野中ゆみ

TOP GROSSING
FOREING FILMS
OF ALL TIME

MISCELLANEA
THIS WEEK'S
USEFUL
INFO

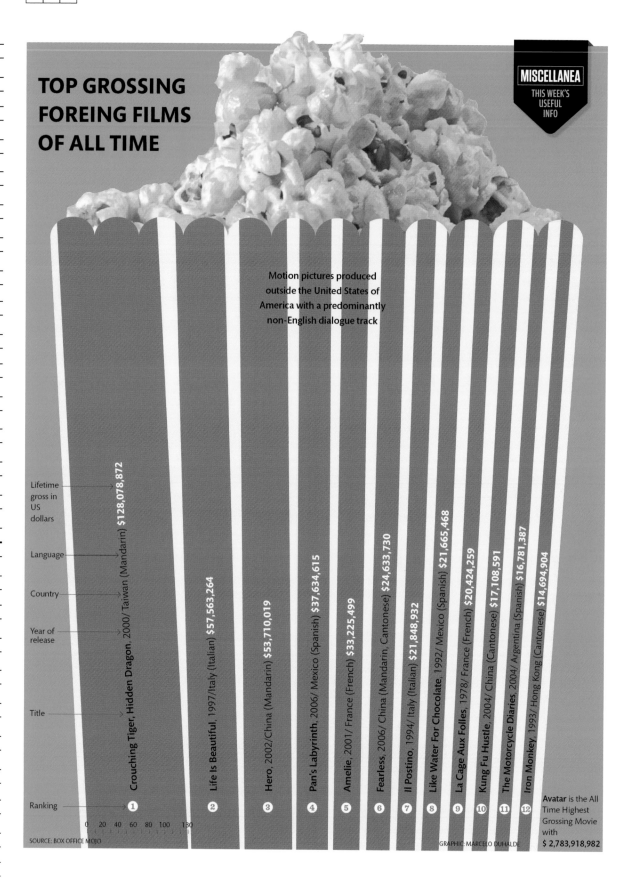

Motion pictures produced
outside the United States of
America with a predominantly
non-English dialogue track

Lifetime
gross in
US
dollars

Language

Country

Year of
release

Title

Ranking

1. Crouching Tiger, Hidden Dragon, 2000/ Taiwan (Mandarin) **$128,078,872**
2. Life Is Beautiful, 1997/Italy (Italian) **$57,563,264**
3. Hero, 2002/China (Mandarin) **$53,710,019**
4. Pan's Labyrinth, 2006/ Mexico (Spanish) **$37,634,615**
5. Amelie, 2001/ France (French) **$33,225,499**
6. Fearless, 2006/ China (Mandarin, Cantonese) **$24,633,730**
7. Il Postino, 1994/ Italy (Italian) **$21,848,932**
8. Like Water For Chocolate, 1992/ Mexico (Spanish) **$21,665,468**
9. La Cage Aux Folles, 1978/ France (French) **$20,424,259**
10. Kung Fu Hustle, 2004/ China (Cantonese) **$17,108,591**
11. The Motorcycle Diaries, 2004/ Argentina (Spanish) **$16,781,387**
12. Iron Monkey, 1993/ Hong Kong (Cantonese) **$14,694,904**

0 20 40 60 80 100 130

Avatar is the All
Time Highest
Grossing Movie
with
$ 2,783,918,982

SOURCE: BOX OFFICE MOJO

GRAPHIC: MARCELO DUHALDE

GROSSING FILMS

Ⓓ Designer: Marcelo Duhalde

A comparison of the top grossing foreign films of all time.

←

A BEGINNER'S GUIDE TO WINE

Ⓓ Designer: Anna Reinbold

Wine can be complicated. This guide provides an overview of the correct terminology used by wine lovers, without forgetting the little details to look out for when choosing a nice bottle.

→

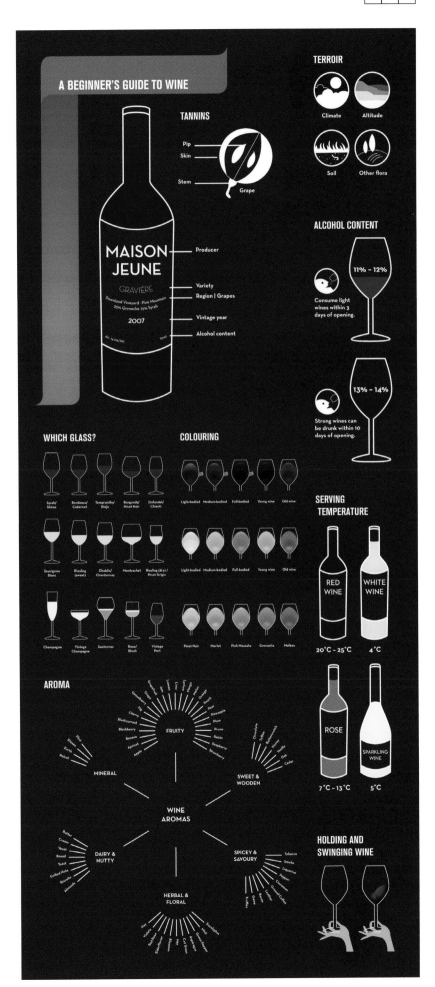

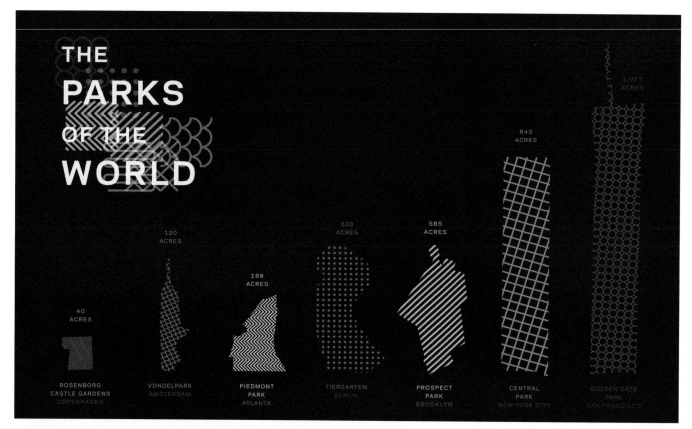

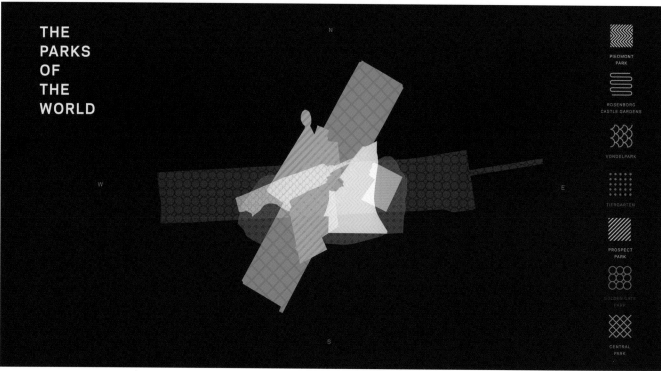

THE PARKS OF THE WORLD

Ⓓ Designer: Mikell Fine Iles

A series of infographics created to comparatively visualize the characteristics of the large urban parks visited by the designer, in 2011. The variables investigated include: size, shape, position on map, annual visitors, and date of inception.

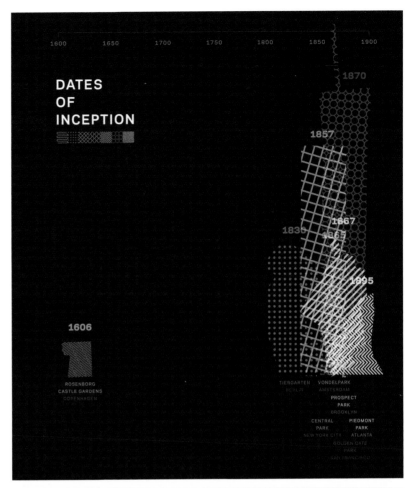

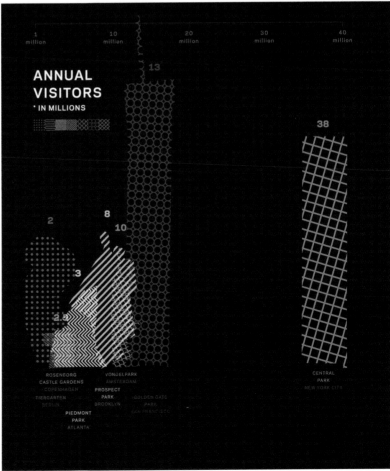

COMPLEMENTI OGGETTI 2011

Ⓓ Designer: Davide Mottes
ⒶⒹ Art Director: Francesco Franchi
Ⓔ Editor: Elisa Furlan
Ⓟ Photographer: F38F

Complementi Oggetti is a fashion infographic section developed for *IL (Intelligence in Lifestyle)*, the monthly magazine issued by *Il Sole 24 Ore*.

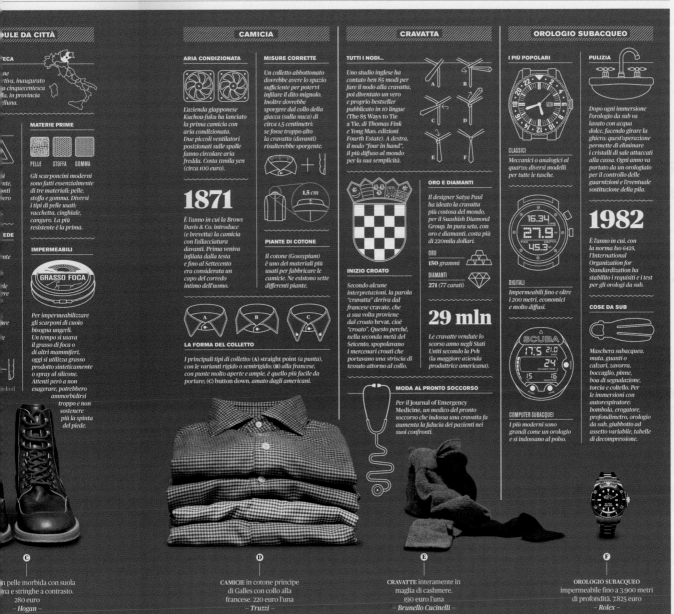

...ULE DA CITTÀ

...ECA

...ne
...tiva, inaugurato
...a cinquecentesca
...la, in provincia
...lluna.

MATERIE PRIME

PELLE   STOFFA   GOMMA

Gli scarponcini moderni sono fatti essenzialmente di tre materiali: pelle, stoffa e gomma. Diversi i tipi di pelle usati: vacchetta, cinghiale, canguro. La più resistente è la prima.

...EDE

IMPERMEABILI

GRASSO FOCA

Per impermeabilizzare gli scarponi di cuoio bisogna ungerli. Un tempo si usava il grasso di foca o di altri mammiferi, oggi si utilizza grasso prodotto sinteticamente o spray al silicone. Attenti però a non esagerare, potrebbero ammorbidirsi troppo e non sostenere più la spinta del piede.

Ⓒ

...n pelle morbida con suola
...na e stringhe a contrasto.
280 euro
– Hogan –

CAMICIA

ARIA CONDIZIONATA

L'azienda giapponese Kuchou-fuku ha lanciato la prima camicia con aria condizionata. Due piccoli ventilatori posizionati sulle spalle fanno circolare aria fredda. Costa 11mila yen (circa 100 euro).

1871

È l'anno in cui la Brows Davis & Co. introduce (e brevetta) la camicia con l'allacciatura davanti. Prima veniva infilata dalla testa e fino al Settecento era considerata un capo del corredo intimo dell'uomo.

MISURE CORRETTE

Un colletto abbottonato dovrebbe avere lo spazio sufficiente per potervi infilare il dito mignolo. Inoltre dovrebbe sporgere dal collo della giacca (sulla nuca) di circa 1,5 centimetri: se fosse troppo alto la cravatta (davanti) risulterebbe sporgente.

1,5 cm

PIANTE DI COTONE

Il cotone (Gossypium) è uno dei materiali più usati per fabbricare le camicie. Ne esistono sette differenti piante.

LA FORMA DEL COLLETTO

Ⓐ   **Ⓑ**   **Ⓒ**

I principali tipi di colletto: (A) straight point (a punta), con le varianti rigido o semirigido; (B) alla francese, con punte molto aperte e ampie, è quello più facile da portare; (C) button down, amato dagli americani.

Ⓓ

CAMICIE in cotone principe
di Galles con collo alla
francese. 220 euro l'una
– Truzzi –

CRAVATTA

TUTTI I NODI...

Uno studio inglese ha contato ben 85 modi per fare il nodo alla cravatta, poi diventato un vero e proprio bestseller pubblicato in 10 lingue (The 85 Ways to Tie a Tie, di Thomas Fink e Yong Mao, edizioni Fourth Estate). A destra, il nodo "four in hand", il più diffuso al mondo per la sua semplicità.

A   B   C   D   E   F

INIZIO CROATO

Secondo alcune interpretazioni, la parola "cravatta" deriva dal francese cravate, che a sua volta proviene dal croato hrvat, cioè "croato". Questo perché, nella seconda metà del Seicento, spopolavano i mercenari croati che portavano una striscia di tessuto attorno al collo.

ORO E DIAMANTI

Il designer Satya Paul ha ideato la cravatta più costosa del mondo, per il Suashish Diamond Group. In pura seta, con oro e diamanti, costa più di 220mila dollari.

ORO
150 grammi

DIAMANTI
271 (77 carati)

29 mln

Le cravatte vendute lo scorso anno negli Stati Uniti secondo la Pvh (la maggiore azienda produttrice americana).

MODA AL PRONTO SOCCORSO

Per il Journal of Emergency Medicine, un medico del pronto soccorso che indossa una cravatta fa aumenta la fiducia dei pazienti nei suoi confronti.

Ⓔ

CRAVATTE interamente in
maglia di cashmere.
190 euro l'una
– Brunello Cucinelli –

OROLOGIO SUBACQUEO

I PIÙ POPOLARI

CLASSICI

Meccanici o analogici al quarzo; diversi modelli per tutte le tasche.

DIGITALI

Impermeabili fino e oltre i 200 metri, economici e molto diffusi.

16.34 TIME
27.9
45.3

SCUBA
17.5 21.0
24
15 16

COMPUTER SUBACQUEI

I più moderni sono grandi come un orologio e si indossano al polso.

PULIZIA

Dopo ogni immersione l'orologio da sub va lavato con acqua dolce, facendo girare la ghiera: quest'operazione permette di eliminare i cristalli di sale attaccati alla cassa. Ogni anno va portato da un orologiaio per il controllo delle guarnizioni e l'eventuale sostituzione della pila.

1982

È l'anno in cui, con la norma Iso 6425, l'International Organization for Standardization ha stabilito i requisiti e i test per gli orologi da sub.

COSE DA SUB

Maschera subacquea, muta, guanti o calzari, zavorra, boccaglio, pinne, boa di segnalazione, torcia e coltello. Per le immersioni con autorespiratore: bombola, erogatore, profondimetro, orologio da sub, giubbotto ad assetto variabile, tabelle di decompressione.

Ⓕ

OROLOGIO SUBACQUEO
impermeabile fino a 3.900 metri
di profondità. 7.825 euro
– Rolex –

DONOSTI

Infografía Alimentaria Básica: Pintxo

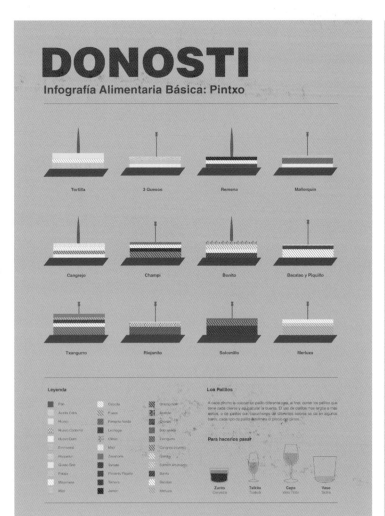

NÁPOLES

Infografía Alimentaria Básica: Pizza

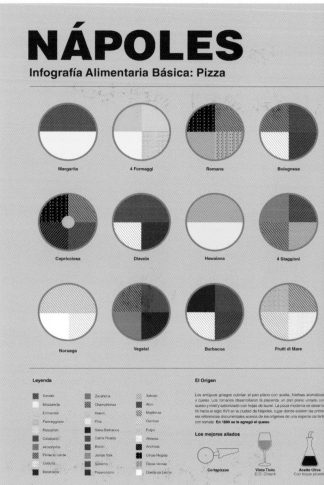

INFO FOOD

Ⓓ Designer: David Padrosa (L'esstudi)

Born out of a love for design and food,
colloquial food items from five different cities
are systematically reimagined.

TOKYO

Infografía Alimentaria Básica: Sushi

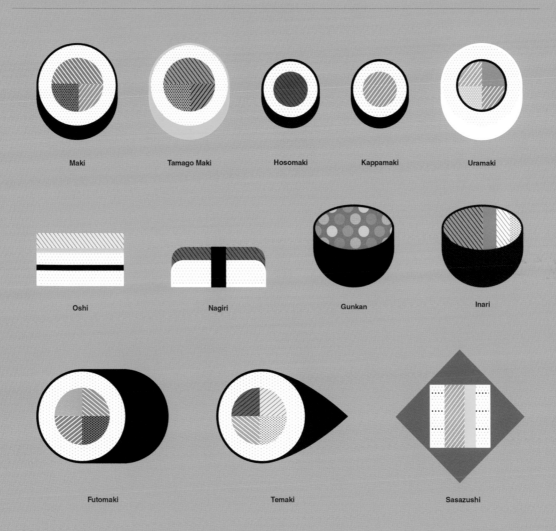

Maki — Tamago Maki — Hosomaki — Kappamaki — Uramaki

Oshi — Nagiri — Gunkan — Inari

Futomaki — Temaki — Sasazushi

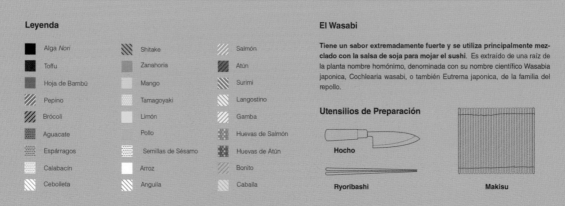

Leyenda

Alga *Nori*	Shitake	Salmón
Toffu	Zanahoria	Atún
Hoja de Bambú	Mango	Surimi
Pepino	Tamagoyaki	Langostino
Brócoli	Limón	Gamba
Aguacate	Pollo	Huevas de Salmón
Espárragos	Semillas de Sésamo	Huevas de Atún
Calabacín	Arroz	Bonito
Cebolleta	Anguila	Caballa

El Wasabi

Tiene un sabor extremadamente fuerte y se utiliza principalmente mezclado con la salsa de soja para mojar el sushi. Es extraído de una raíz de la planta nombre homónimo, denominada con su nombre científico Wasabia japonica, Cochlearia wasabi, o también Eutrema japonica, de la familia del repollo.

Utensilios de Preparación

Hocho

Ryoribashi

Makisu

DESIGN X FOOD

Ⓓ Designer: Ryan MacEachern

Ryan MacEachern's daily food consumption
is translated into pie charts, using food
photography as a medium.

61%
protein
61%/15%
937kcal

4%
carbs
4%/55%
62kcal

35%
fat
35%/30%
537kcal

calories
1536/ 2500kcal

78%
fat
78%/30%
2860kcal

1%
carbs
1%/55%
27kcal

23%
protein
23%/15%
638kcal

calories
2778/ 2500kcal

4%
carbs
4%/55%
25kcal

14%
fat
14%/30%
78kcal

82%
protein
82%/15%
459kcal

calories
559/ 2500kcal

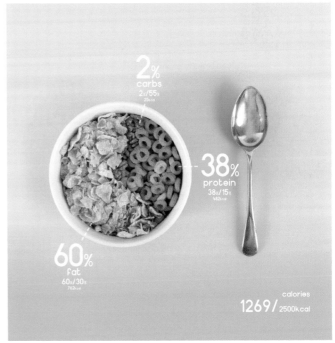

2%
carbs
2%/55%
25kcal

38%
protein
38%/15%
482kcal

60%
fat
60%/30%
762kcal

calories
1269/ 2500kcal

LURIE'S NETWORK

Ⓓ Designer: Kelli Anderson

Illustrated using paper, *Lurie's Network* is an infographic webpage, showing the world and connections of Daniel Lurie, founder of the *Tipping Point* community.

DANIEL LURIE

by Lorainne Ipwich

Raised in a long tradition of San Francisco philanthropy, Lurie is the son of Rabbi Brian Lurie and Mimi Haas.

At 34, he is emerging as a leader for a new generation that is tackling poverty.

CAROLINE FROMM LURIE
Stepmother

BECCA PROWDA
Wife · Barnard college grad

TAYA LURIE
Daughter · 2 years old

BENEFICIARIES

3,236,500 — KIPP BAY AREA SCHOOLS

702K — SF CHILD ABUSE PREVENTION CENTER

1,302,000 — CANAL ALLIANCE

100K — UJIMA FAMILY RECOVERY SERVICES

1,490,000 — FRESH LIFELINES FOR YOUTH

125K — COMMUNITY HOUSING PARTNERSHIP

402K — GATEWAY TO COLLEGE NATIONAL NETWORK

155K — NURSE-FAMILY PARTNERSHIP

1,788,775 — FIRST PLACE FOR YOUTH

1,360,000 — NEW DOOR VENTURES

789.3K — RAVENSWOOD FAMILY HEALTH CENTER

481K — EASTSIDE COLLEGE PREP SCHOOL

2,700,000 — SINGLE STOP BAY AREA

331K — CENTER FOR EMPLOYMENT OPPORTUNITIES

1,786,000 — INNVISION SHELTER NETWORK

2,404,475 — READING PARTNERS

100K — GENESYS WORKS

1,826,860 — HOMELESS PRENATAL PROGRAM

710K — WAGES

1,655,000 — YEAR UP

270K — MISSION ASSET FUND

890K

SF STATE GUARDIAN SCHOLARS PROGRAM

LARKIN STREET YOUTH SERVICES

540K

481K — NEXT STEP LEARNING CENTER

4,073,000 — ASPIRE PUBLIC SCHOOLS

510K — BELL

1,330,000 — ROCKETSHIP EDUCATION

THE STRIDE CENTER

698K

1,956,000 — BUILD

246K — THE BREAD PROJECT

225K — JOBTRAIN

335K — SWORDS TO PLOWSHARES

2,129,000 — CENTER FOR YOUTH WELLNESS

2,110,000 — COMPASS FAMILY SERVICES

225K — SUNNY HILLS SERVICES

691K

BAYVIEW CHILD HEALTH CENTER

150K — COLLEGE TRACK

645K — UPWARDLY GLOBAL

125K — CITIZEN SCHOOLS

504K — SHELTER

1,845,000 — RUBICON PROGRAMS INC.

340K — OPPORTUNITY JUNCTION

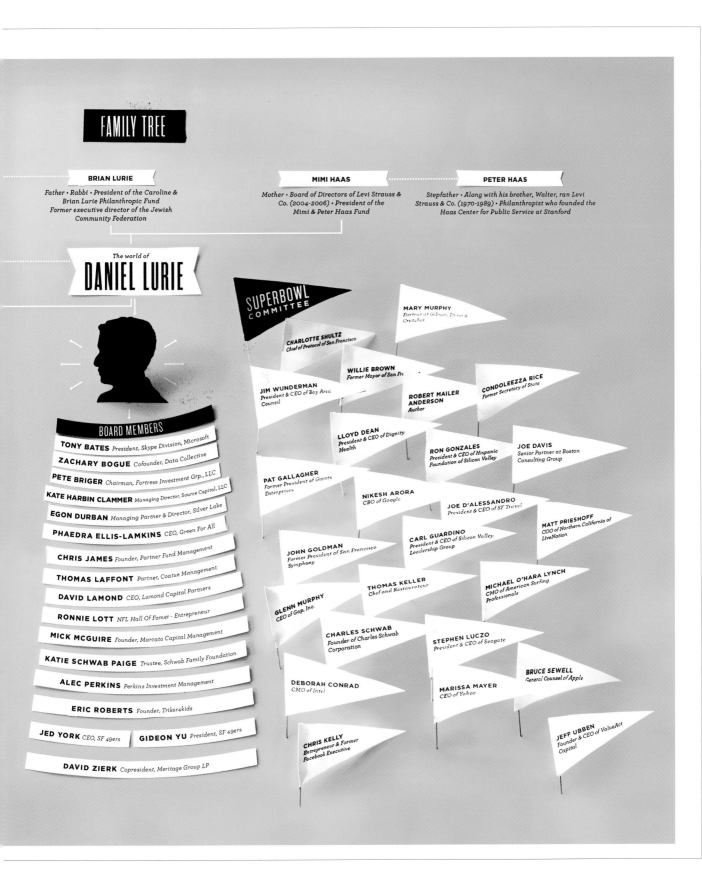

FAMILY TREE

BRIAN LURIE
Father • Rabbi • President of the Caroline & Brian Lurie Philanthropic Fund Former executive director of the Jewish Community Federation

MIMI HAAS
Mother • Board of Directors of Levi Strauss & Co. (2004-2006) • President of the Mimi & Peter Haas Fund

PETER HAAS
Stepfather • Along with his brother, Walter, ran Levi Strauss & Co. (1970-1989) • Philanthropist who founded the Haas Center for Public Service at Stanford

The world of
DANIEL LURIE

BOARD MEMBERS

TONY BATES *President, Skype Division, Microsoft*

ZACHARY BOGUE *Cofounder, Data Collective*

PETE BRIGER *Chairman, Fortress Investment Grp., LLC*

KATE HARBIN CLAMMER *Managing Director, Source Capital, LLC*

EGON DURBAN *Managing Partner & Director, Silver Lake*

PHAEDRA ELLIS-LAMKINS *CEO, Green For All*

CHRIS JAMES *Founder, Partner Fund Management*

THOMAS LAFFONT *Partner, Coatue Management*

DAVID LAMOND *CEO, Lamond Capital Partners*

RONNIE LOTT *NFL Hall Of Famer - Entrepreneur*

MICK MCGUIRE *Founder, Marcato Capital Management*

KATIE SCHWAB PAIGE *Trustee, Schwab Family Foundation*

ALEC PERKINS *Perkins Investment Management*

ERIC ROBERTS *Founder, Triksr4kids*

JED YORK *CEO, SF 49ers*   **GIDEON YU** *President, SF 49ers*

DAVID ZIERK *Copresident, Meritage Group LP*

SUPERBOWL COMMITTEE

MARY MURPHY *Partner at Gibson, Dunn & Crutcher*

CHARLOTTE SHULTZ *Chief of Protocol of San Francisco*

WILLIE BROWN *Former Mayor of San Fra*

JIM WUNDERMAN *President & CEO of Bay Area Council*

ROBERT MAILER ANDERSON *Author*

CONDOLEEZZA RICE *Former Secretary of State*

LLOYD DEAN *President & CEO of Dignity Health*

RON GONZALES *President & CEO of Hispanic Foundation of Silicon Valley*

JOE DAVIS *Senior Partner at Boston Consulting Group*

PAT GALLAGHER *Former President of Giants Enterprises*

NIKESH ARORA *CBO of Google*

JOE D'ALESSANDRO *President & CEO of SF Travel*

MATT PRIESHOFF *COO of Northern California of LiveNation*

JOHN GOLDMAN *Former President of San Francisco Symphony*

CARL GUARDINO *President & CEO of Silicon Valley Leadership Group*

THOMAS KELLER *Chef and Restaurateur*

MICHAEL O'HARA LYNCH *CMO of American Surfing Professionals*

GLENN MURPHY *CEO of Gap, Inc.*

CHARLES SCHWAB *Founder of Charles Schwab Corporation*

STEPHEN LUCZO *President & CEO of Seagate*

BRUCE SEWELL *General Counsel of Apple*

DEBORAH CONRAD *CMO of Intel*

MARISSA MAYER *CEO of Yahoo*

CHRIS KELLY *Entrepreneur & Former Facebook Executive*

JEFF UBBEN *Founder & CEO of ValueAct Capital*

Onion / *Lök* / 玉葱

Sweet potato
Sötpotatis / さつまいも

Green onion
Purjolök / 長葱

Chinese cabbage
Salladskål / 白菜

Cucumber
Gurka / きゅうり

White radish
Rättika / 大根

Mushroom / *Svamp*
マッシュルーム

Carrot
Morot / 人参

Parsnip / *Palsternacka*
パースニップ

Pea / *Ärt* / 絹さや

Aubergine
Aubergine / 茄子

Spinach
Spenat / ほうれん草

Allium
Gräslök / あさつき

MAIN VEGETABLES
HUVUDGRÖNSAKER / 主な野菜

They are the accessible vegetables in Sweden that can be used for Japanese cooking. Two of them are used as substitutes for other vegetables.

Detta är de tillgängliga grönsakerna i Sverige som kan användas för japansk matlagning. Två av dem används som ersättningar för andra grönsaker.

これらが、スウェーデンでも手に入りやすい、日本食に使える野菜の数々です。このうち2つは、別の野菜の代用品として使われています。

WHITE RADISH / *RÄTTIKA* / 大根

This is used a lot both raw and cooked. It is common to have meat/fish with grated white radish, too. It removes the fishy smell and supports digestion at the same time.

Den används mycket både rå och tillagad. Det är också vanligt att servera kött/fisk med riven rättika. Den tar bort fisklukt och hjälper samtidigt matsmältningen.

そのままでも調理してもよく使われます。大根おろしを肉や魚に添えるのも一般的です。魚の生臭さを消すと同時に、消化の助けとなります。

MUSHROOM / *SVAMP* / マッシュルーム

Shitake mushroom is one of the essential ingredients, especially for getting bouillon. However, they are difficult to find in Sweden and therefore are substituted with usual mushrooms in this book.

Shitake svamp är en av de grundläggande ingredienserna, särskilt för att göra buljong. Den är dock svårt att hitta i Sverige och därför ersättas den med vanlig svamp i boken.

しいたけは日本食には欠かせない旨味のある食材ですが、スウェーデンでは手に入りにくいため、この本ではマッシュルームで代用されています。

PARSNIP / *PALSTERNACKA* / パースニップ

This is used as a substitute for burdock in this book. It is a little sweeter than burdock, but have a similar flavor, and is more accessible in Sweden.

Den används som ersättning för svartrot i boken. Det är lite sötare än svartrot men luktar likadant, och mer lätttillgänglig i Sverige.

この本で、ごぼうの代用として使われています。ごぼうより少し甘みがありますが、風味が似ていて、スウェーデンで手に入りやすい食材です。

12

13

GUITE TO THE FOREIGN JAPANESE KITCHEN

Ⓓ Designer: Moé Takemura

Today, we look for pleasure and excitement in food, in addition to safety and reliability, in a struggle between our interests in multicultural food and awareness of environmental and health issues. This infographic reflects this dilemma, and introduces traditional Japanese home cooking in a way that is appropriate to the modern Swedish lifestyle.

GUIDE TO THE FOREIGN JAPANESE KITCHEN
GUIDE TILL DET UTLÄNDSKA JAPANSKA KÖKET
海外で作る日本食案内

MOÉ TAKEMURA

DEEP FRIED VEGETABLES (TEMPURA)
FRITERADE GRÖNSAKER (TEMPURA)
天ぷら

1 sweet potato	*1 sötpotatis*	さつまいも　1個
8-12 asparaguses	*8-12 sparrisar*	アスパラガス 8-12本
8 mushrooms	*8 svampar*	きのこ 8-12個
1 onion	*1 lök*	玉葱　1玉
2 dl flour	*2 dl mjöl*	小麦粉　2 dl
1.5 ts. baking powder	*1.5 tsk bakpulver*	ベーキングパウダー
1 ts. salt	*1 tsk salt*	小さじ 1.5
2 dl cold water	*2 dl kallt vatten*	塩　小さじ1
1 Tb. white wine	*1 msk vitt vin*	冷水　2 dl
Cooking oil	*Matolja*	酒　大さじ1
		油

Slice sweet potato and onion. Cut asparaguses into 4-5 cm pieces and mushrooms into half.

Skiva sötpotatisen och löken. Skär sparrisarna i ca 4-5 cm långa bitar och dela svampen i halvor.

さつまいもと玉葱は薄くスライスする。アスパラガス
は4-5cmの長さに、きのこは半分に切る。

Mix flour, baking powder, salt, water and white wine.

Rör ihop mjöl, bakpulver, salt, vatten och vitt vin till en smet.

小麦粉、ベーキングパウダー、塩、水、酒を
軽く混ぜ合わせる。

Dip the vegetables in the batter.
(Take the onion slices in the end.)

*Doppa grönsakerna i smeten.
(Ta den skivade löken i slutet.)*

野菜に衣をつける。（玉葱は最後に。）

Deep fry them in high heated cooking oil.
Tempura tastes the best when it's newly fried.

*Fritera grönsakerna i oljan på hög värme.
Tempura är godast nyfriterad.*

野菜を高温の油で揚げる。
揚げたてをお召し上がりください。

76　　　　　　　　　　　　　　　　　　　　　　　77

RICE WITH GREEN SOYA BEANS
RIS MED GRÖNA SOJABÖNOR
豆ごはん

250 g green soya beans (defrosted)	*250 g gröna sojabönor (tinade)*	枝豆 250g
2.5 dl rice	*2.5 dl ris*	米 2.5dl
0.5 ts. salt	*0.5 tsk salt*	塩 小さじ0.5
5 dl water	*5 dl vatten*	水 5dl

Cook rice and green soya beans together in a pot
as you normally cook rice.

*Koka ris och gröna sojabönor tillsammans
i en kastrull som du vanligtvis kokar ris.*

材料を鍋に入れ、白ごはんを炊くのと同じ要領で炊く。

82　　　　　　　　　　　　　　　　　　　　　　　83

thunderstorm

typhoon

meiyu   the east asian rainy season

may   jun   jul   aug   sep

ILHA FORMOSA

Ⓓ Designer: Tien-Min Liao

These infographics are part of a promotional set designed to introduce Taiwan. Typical, everyday facts about the country are translated into usable data, and paper illustration is used to create the graphics.

is 2,150 mm, about
an rainfall. However,
concentrated from

season
the result of annual
Asia. Each year, the
es from northeast
which comes from
nsistent precipitation
the late spring and
non is called Meiyu.

oct

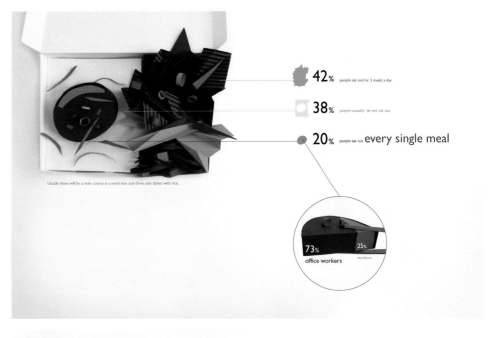

42% people eat out I or 2 meals a day

38% people usually do not eat out

20% people eat out **every single meal**

Usually there will be a main course in a lunch box and three side dishes with rice.

73%
office workers

25%
students

900   800   700   1,000   1,100   **1,200** km

cycling around the entire island

Cycling around the entire island has become more and more popular in recent years.
Some students do it as a celebration for their graduation, while more people view it as
a challenge and adventure. The ages of the participants are from nine to eighty years old.
It usually takes 6~12 days to finish. The total lenghth is about 1,200km.

2200 years ago
traditional chinese
characters appeard
The modern shapes of traditional Chinese
characters first appeared in Han Dynasty.

1950s
simplified chinese
characters appeared
The government of the People's
Republic of China simplified the
Chinese characters.

taiwan
hong kong
macau

mainland china

fish
ancient chinese characters

fish with tail
traditional chinese characters

fish witout tail
simplified chinese characters

traditional chinese characters

Traditional Chinese characters have been used for 2200 years. The modern shapes of traditional Chinese characters
first appeared with the emergence of clerical script during the Han Dynasty (206 BCE – 220 CE), and have been more
or less stable since the 5th century (during the Southern and Northern Dynasties).

The government of the People's Republic of China simplified and standardized the Chinese characters in the 1950s.
Many characters lost their own meanings after they are simplified. They were used in Mainland China starting in the
1950s. Unlike Simplified Chinese characters, Traditional Chinese characters show the original hieroglyphic meaning
and the beauty of the structure. They are still used in Taiwan, Hong Kong and Macau.

MONDAY   Vegetables

THURSDAY   Condiments

TUESDAY   Meats

WEDNESDAY   Whole Wheat & Grains

SATURDAY   Vegetables

SUNDAY   Rest Day

A BALANCED BLOG

Ⓓ Designer: Column Five
Ⓒ Client: LinkedIn Marketing Solutions

Using food groups as a metaphor for various types of blog content, the infographic is intended to help content marketers plan their blog budgets, so as to achieve their desired success.

A Well-Balanced Blog

It's no secret that blogging is a foundational element of successful content marketing. In fact, **67%** of marketers created blogs last year. While blogging can deliver solid results, it does require significant time, commitment, and strategy. Here, we break down the types of content that your readers prefer to consume, to help you plan and execute efficient and impactful blog entries throughout the week.

Breaking Down Your Meal

This is how much time and energy you should be spending
on each type of content.

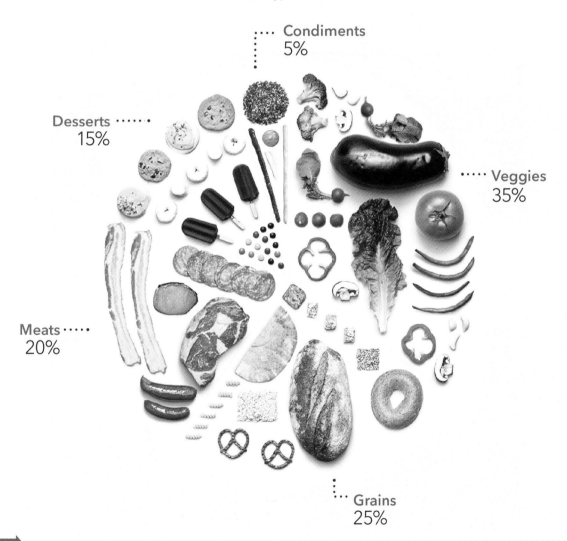

Condiments
5%

Desserts
15%

Veggies
35%

Meats
20%

Grains
25%

Follow this recommended diet, and learn more about how to boost
your impact and reach online by visiting **marketing.linkedin.com.**

Inspired by HubSpot's blog post, "5 Types of Posts to Feed Your Business Blog."

Linked in. Marketing Solutions

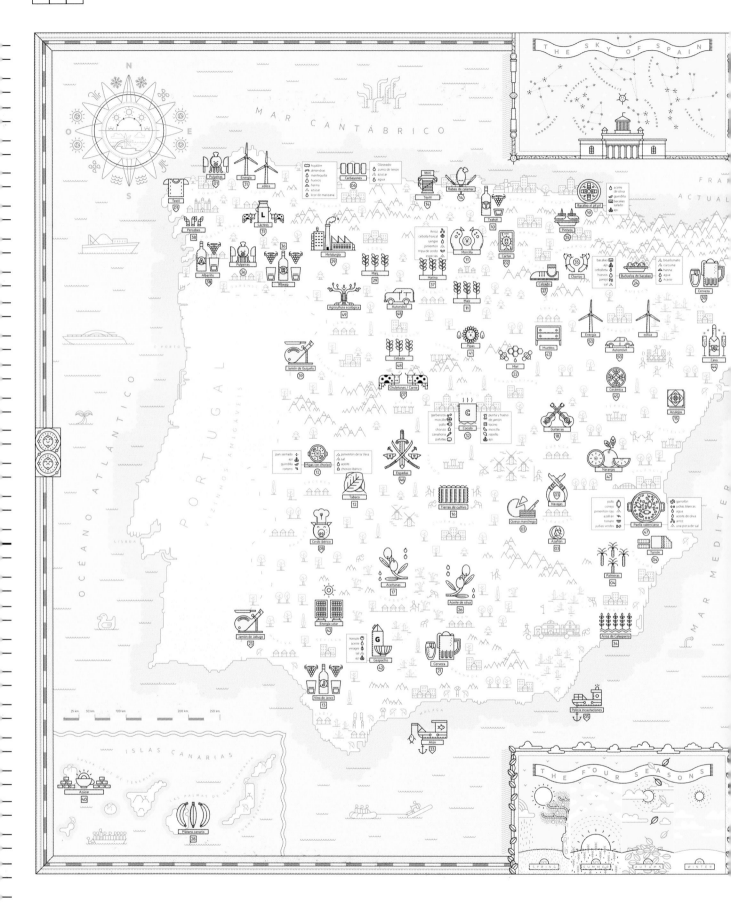

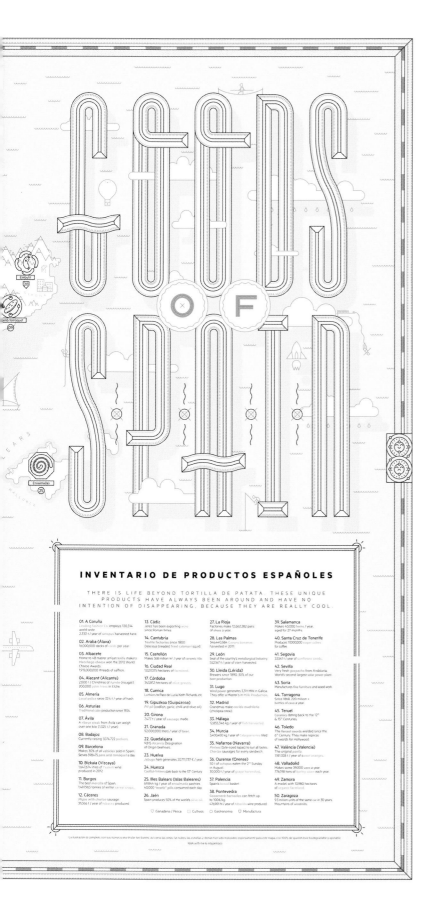

GOODS OF SPAIN

Ⓓ Designer: Relajaelcoco

A full-colour, illustrated poster produced in collaboration with *Replace with Me*, intended to represent the most important Spanish exports, from regions such as Palencia and Valencia.

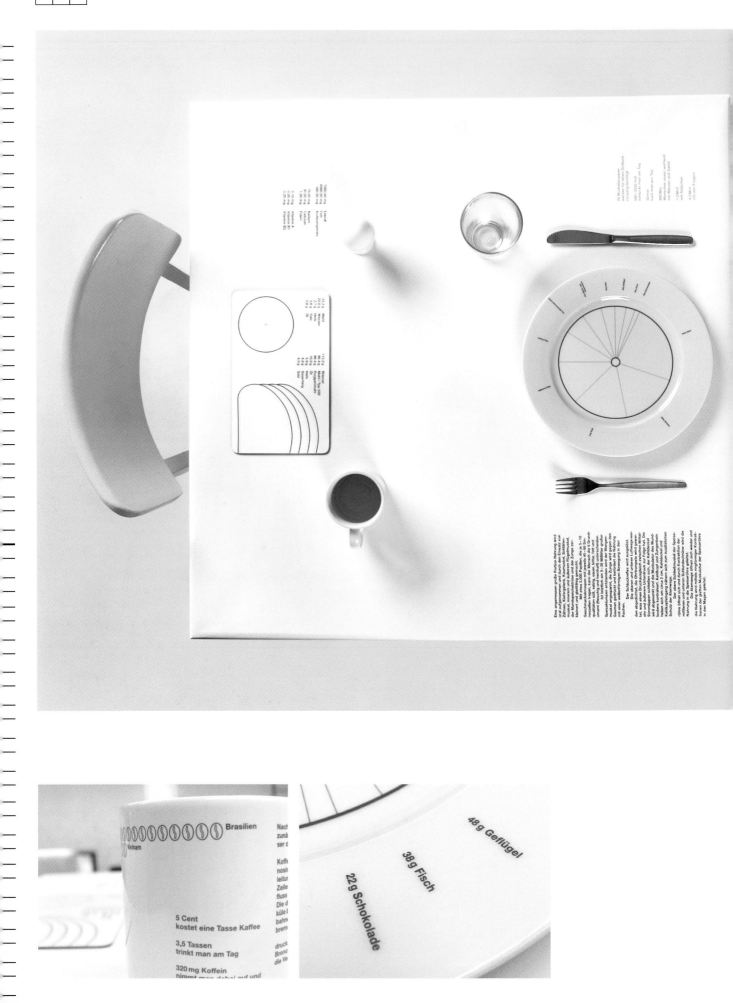

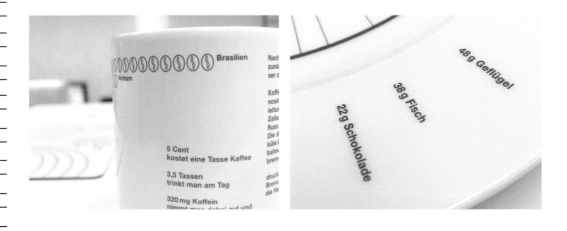

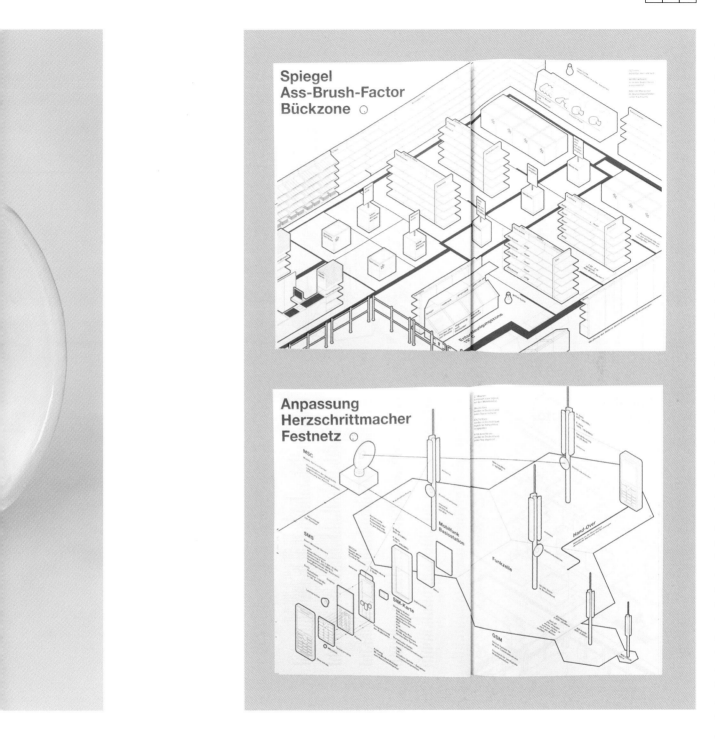

24_7

Ⓓ Designer: Benjamin Schulte

24_7 explores the things that comprise our daily routines, and inverts them. Objects from everyday life are taken, and turned into exhibits that 'speak' for themselves.

FOOD FOR THOUGHT - A LOCAL KITCHEN FOR A GLOBAL COMMUNITY

Ⓓ Designer: Niels Groeneveld

For centuries, the richest arable lands in the Netherlands have been shaped by food production. Recent developments in the global food chain have led to an uncertain existence for farmers. This infographic aims to raise awareness, by visualizing the fragile reality of modern farm life.

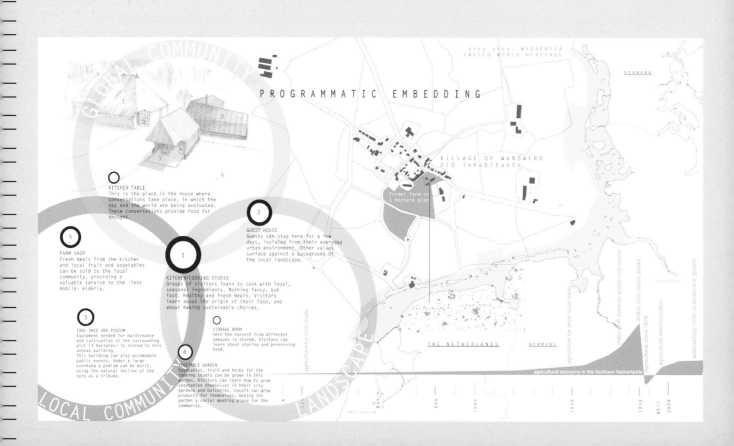

PROGRAMMATIC EMBEDDING

Grey area: WADDENSEA
UNESCO WORLD HERITAGE

DENMARK

VILLAGE OF WANSWERD
210 inhabitants

former farm on
3 hectare plot

THE NETHERLANDS   GERMANY

agricultural economy in the Northern Netherlands

KITCHEN TABLE
This is the place in the house where conversations take place, in which the day and the world are being evaluated. These conversations provide food for thought.

GUEST HOUSE
Guests can stay here for a few days, isolated from their everyday urban environment. Other values surface against a background of the local landscape.

FARM SHOP
Fresh meals from the kitchen and local fruit and vegetables can be sold to the local community, providing a valuable service to the -less mobile- elderly.

KITCHEN/COOKING STUDIO
Groups of visitors learn to cook with local, seasonal ingredients. Nothing fancy, but fast, healthy and fresh meals. Visitors learn about the origin of their food, and about making sustainable choices.

TOOL SHED AND PODIUM
Equipment needed for maintenance and cultivation of the surrounding plot (3 hectares) is stored in this annexe building.
This building can also accomodate public events. Under a large overhang a podium can be built, using the natural incline of the terp as a tribune.

STORAGE ROOM
Here the harvest from different seasons is stored. Visitors can learn about storing and preserving food.

VEGETABLE GARDEN
Vegetables, fruit and herbs for the cooking studio can be grown in this garden. Visitors can learn how to grow vegetables themselves in their city gardens and balconies. Locals can grow products for themselves, making the garden a social meeting place for the community.

GLOBAL COMMUNITY

LOCAL COMMUNITY   LANDSCAPE

DEVELOPMENT OF THE GLOBAL FOOD CHAIN

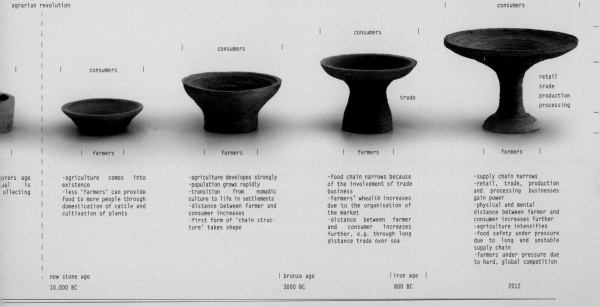

agrarian revolution

consumers

consumers

consumers

consumers

retail
trade
production
processing

distance between
farmer and consumer

...erers age
...ual is
...ollecting

| farmers |

| farmers |

| farmers |

| farmers |

-agriculture comes into existence
-less 'farmers' can provide food to more people through domestication of cattle and cultivation of plants

-agriculture developes strongly
-population grows rapidly
-transition from nomadic culture to life in settlements
-distance between farmer and consumer increases
-first form of 'chain struc-ture' takes shape

-food chain narrows because of the involvement of trade business
-farmers' whealth increases due to the organisation of the market
-distance between farmer and consumer increases further, e.g. through long distance trade over sea

-supply chain narrows
-retail, trade, production and processing businesses gain power
-physical and mental distance between farmer and consumer increases further
-agriculture intensifies
-food safety under pressure due to long and unstable supply chain
-farmers under pressure due to hard, global competition

new stone age
10.000 BC

bronze age
3000 BC

iron age
800 BC

2012

time

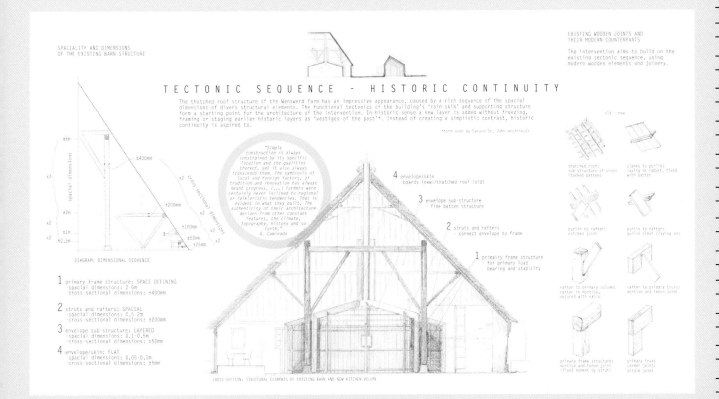

SPACIALITY AND DIMENSIONS
OF THE EXISTING BARN STRUCTURE

EXISTING WOODEN JOINTS AND
THEIR MODERN COUNTERPARTS

The intervention aims to build on the existing tectonic sequence, using modern wooden elements and joinery.

TECTONIC SEQUENCE - HISTORIC CONTINUITY

The thatched roof structure of the Wanswerd farm has an impressive appearance, caused by a rich sequence of the spacial dimensions of divers structural elements. The functional tectonics of the building's 'rain skin' and supporting structure form a starting point for the architecture of the intervention. In historic sense a new layer is added without freezing, framing or staging earlier historic layers as 'vestiges of the past'*. Instead of creating a simplistic contrast, historic continuity is aspired to.

*term used by Caruso St. John architects

"Simple construction is always constrained by its specific location and the qualities thereof, yet it is also always transcends them. The symbiosis of local and foreign factors, of tradition and innovation has always meant progress. (...) Farmers were certainly never inclined to regional or folkloristic tendencies. That is evident in what they built. The authenticity of their architecture derives from other constant features, the climate, topography, history and so forth."
G. Caminada

old - new

thatched roof:
sub structure of cross
stacked battens

planks to purlin:
laying in rabbet, fixed
with batten

4 envelope/skin
-boards (new)/thatched roof (old)

3 envelope sub-structure
- fine batten structure

2 struts and rafters
- connect envelope to frame

1 primary frame structure
for primary load
bearing and stability

purlin to rafter:
notched joint

purlin to rafter:
purlin cleat (laying on)

DIAGRAM: DIMENSIONAL SEQUENCE

rafter to primary column:
rafter in mortise,
secured with nails

rafter to primary truss:
mortise and tenon joint

1 primary frame structure: SPACE DEFINING
-spacial dimensions: 2.6m
-cross-sectional dimensions: ±400mm

2 struts and rafters: SPACIAL
-spacial dimensions: 0.5-2m
-cross-sectional dimensions: ±200mm

3 envelope sub-structure: LAYERED
-spacial dimensions: 0.1-0.5m
-cross-sectional dimensions: ±50mm

4 envelope/skin: FLAT
-spacial dimensions: 0.05-0.1m
-cross-sectional dimensions: ±5mm

primary frame structure:
mortise and tenon joint
(fixed moment by strut)

primary truss
corner joints:
bridle joint

CROSS-SECTION: STRUCTURAL ELEMENTS OF EXISTING BARN AND NEW KITCHEN VOLUME

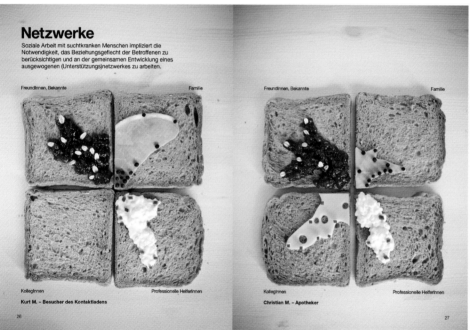

CARITAS KONTAKTLADEN ANNUAL REPORT (2010 AND 2011)

Ⓓ Designer: Marion Luttenberger (moodley)
Ⓒ Client: Caritas der Diözese Graz-Sekau

Aid organization CARITAS/Steiermark, Austria, offers help in the field of drugs, through street work and a special drop-in centre.

The designers have translated all the facts and figures into a subtle visual language, focusing on the commitment of street workers and people working within the organization.

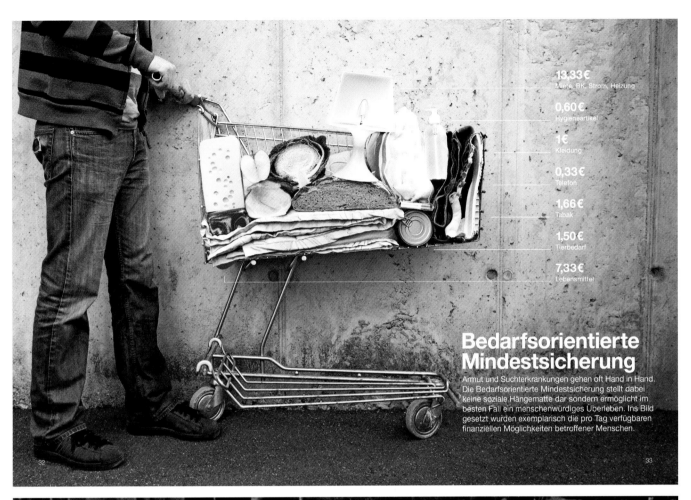

13,33 €
Miete, BK, Strom, Heizung

0,60 €
Hygieneartikel

1 €
Kleidung

0,33 €
Telefon

1,66 €
Tabak

1,50 €
Tierbedarf

7,33 €
Lebensmittel

Bedarfsorientierte Mindestsicherung

Armut und Suchterkrankungen gehen oft Hand in Hand. Die Bedarfsorientierte Mindestsicherung stellt dabei keine soziale Hängematte dar sondern ermöglicht im besten Fall ein menschenwürdiges Überleben. Ins Bild gesetzt wurden exemplarisch die pro Tag verfügbaren finanziellen Möglichkeiten betroffener Menschen.

Kontakte im Streetworkeinsatz

1.306	1.661	3.323	3.439	4.955	4.928	4.869	5.955
2004	2005	2006	2007	2008	2009	2010	2011

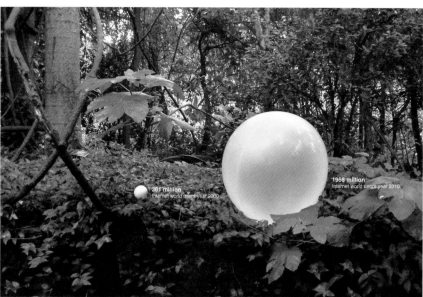

INTERNET HANDMADE VISUALIZED

Ⓓ Designer: Jose Duarte

This infographic is an extension of the designer's handmade visualization kit, which was intended to make infographics much more tactile.

@ladygaga
9062883 twitter followers

@BarackObama
7183716 followers

@katyperry
6430594 followers

@algore
2226181 followers

420 million
China Internet users

337 million
European Union

110 million
India

76 million
Brazil

32 million
Mexico

5 million
Portugal

GOLDEN AGE

ⓓ Designer: Domestic Data Streamers

Golden Age questions the meaning of a person's age. It uses two simple questions: 'What is your current age?' and 'What is your dream age?'. A physical graph is created using real tree trunks.

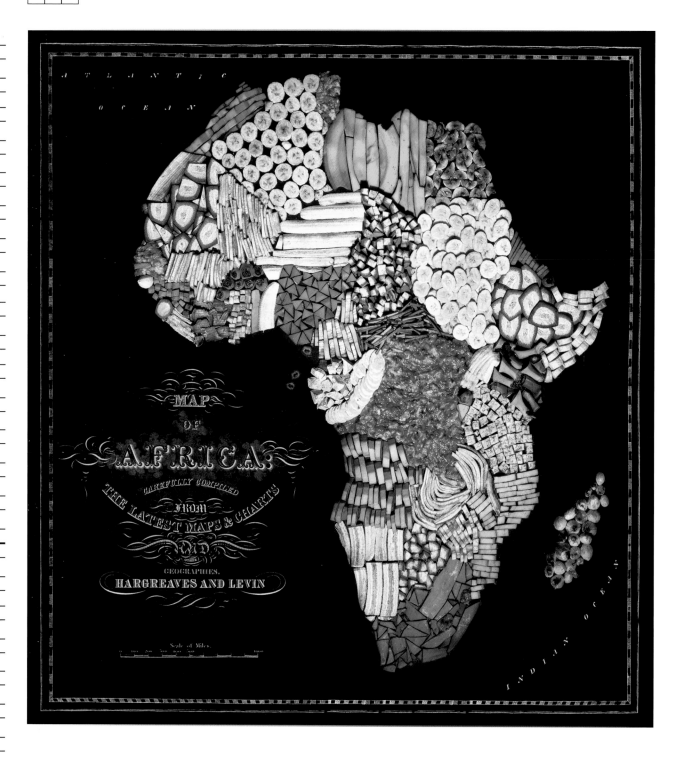

FOOD MAPS

Ⓓ Designer: Henry Hargreaves and Caitlin Levin

Inspired by a passion for travel, these maps are a playful representation of the designers' interpretation of food from around the world, painstakingly created using real, unadulterated food. This project speaks to the universality of how food unites people, bringing them together and starting conversations.

MAP OF ITALY, (CONSTRUCTED) from information in possession of Latest Authorities HARGREAVES AND LEVIN

ROMEO & JULIET

Ⓓ Designer: Ilias Pantikakis (Beetroot Design Group)

Ideas that seem impossible to get across with traditional media, including design software, often trigger concepts for self-initiated projects. Armed with this philosophy, the resulting infographic is an experiment using the text from Shakespeare's *Romeo and Juliet*.

Romeo and Juliet, finally brought together.

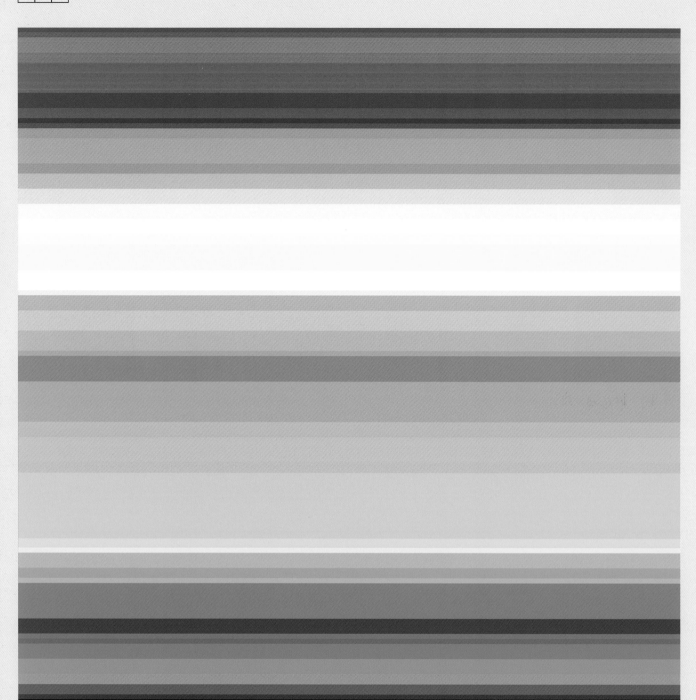

COLOUR SIGNATURES

Ⓐ Artist: Jaz Parkinson

For the core process of *Colour Signatures*, colour data is taken from works of fiction and transformed into unique graphs, which show the total colour content of a given novel. All obvious mentions of a colour (e.g. 'red'), and all inferred mentions of colour are tallied (e.g. 'blood', 'sunset'). All the colours are then grouped, put into a spectrum, and digitally constructed, to show a unique graph of a book's colour content. Despite being raw data, this is often representative of the themes and emotions behind the text.

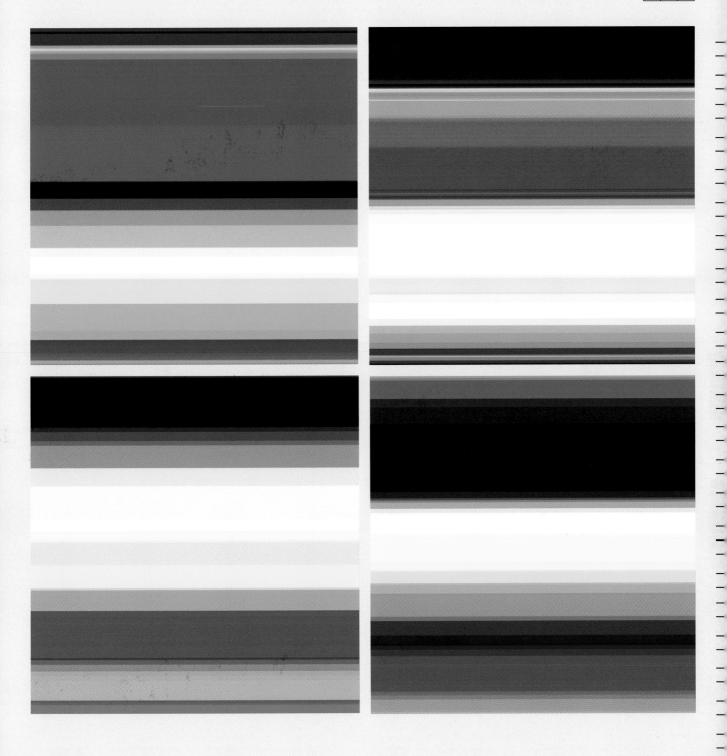

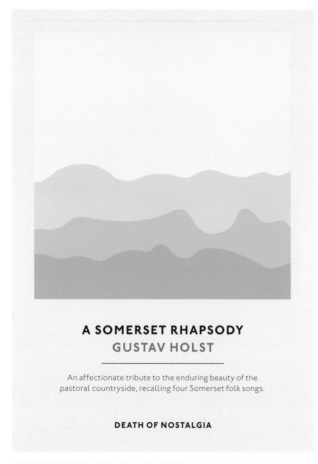

A SOMERSET RHAPSODY
GUSTAV HOLST

An affectionate tribute to the enduring beauty of the
pastoral countryside, recalling four Somerset folk songs.

DEATH OF NOSTALGIA

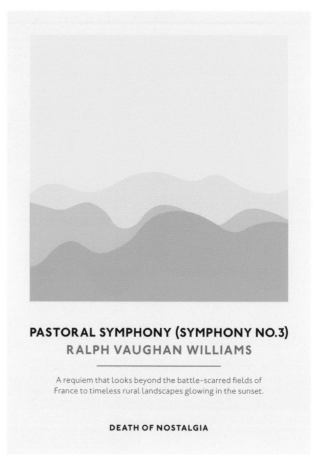

PASTORAL SYMPHONY (SYMPHONY NO.3)
RALPH VAUGHAN WILLIAMS

A requiem that looks beyond the battle-scarred fields of
France to timeless rural landscapes glowing in the sunset.

DEATH OF NOSTALGIA

WORCESTERSHIRE SUITE
JULIUS HARRISON

A golden oldie from 1918 that keeps the home
fires burning with the warm glow of reminiscence.

DEATH OF NOSTALGIA

THE REST IS NOISE

Ⓓ Designer: Studio Output

A set of postcards were designed for the
BBC Concert Orchestra, to promote a
series of events, by taking sound waves
as a graphic cue.

THE REST IS NOISE

THE SOUNDTRACK OF THE 20TH CENTURY

A cultural and musical history told through
250 events at Southbank Centre in 2013.

BBC *Concert* ORCHESTRA

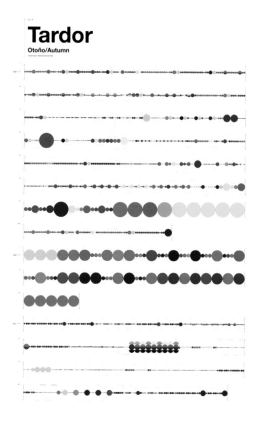

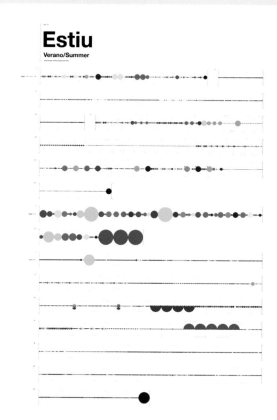

LESQUATRESTACIONS

(A) Agency: Mot Studio
(AD) Art Director: Laia Clos and Despina Kannaourou
(D) Designer: Laia Clos and Despina Kannaourou

Lesquatrestacions, otherwise known as The Four Seasons, makes reference to the music of 18th century Italian composer, Antonio Vivaldi. It is essentially a graphic interpretation of the four violin concertos that comprise this baroque masterpiece.

Part · I

Primavera

Primavera/Spring

violà principal/violìn principal/lead violìn

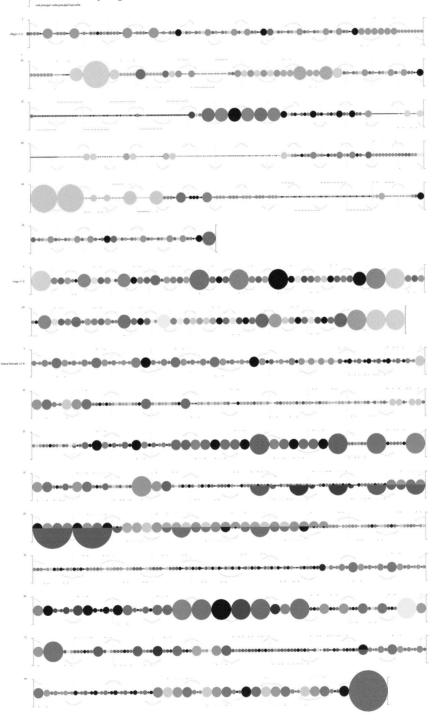

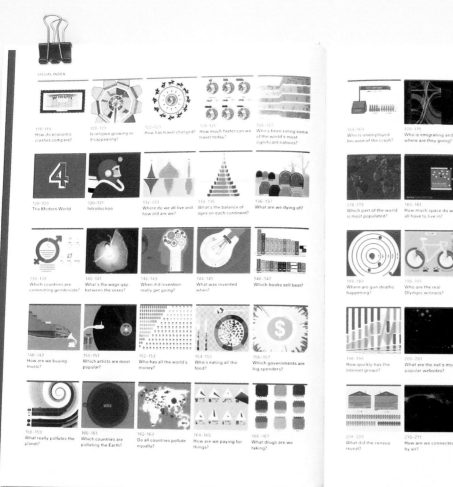

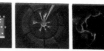

THE INFOGRAPHIC HISTORY OF THE WORLD

Ⓓ Designer: Valentina D'Efilippo
Ⓒ Co-Author: Valentina D'Efilippo and James Ball
Ⓦ Writer: James Ball
Ⓔ Editor: Craig Adams

Infographics are the storytellers in this book. Data, images and words work in a system to simplify information, reveal interesting patterns and engage readers, through an unconventional narrative. The visual grammar of the book evolves with its content. Changes in typography, colour palettes, paper stock and illustration styles give distinct identities to each of the four historical chapters. Individual spreads achieve within-context and stand-alone readability, allowing for different levels of reader engagement.

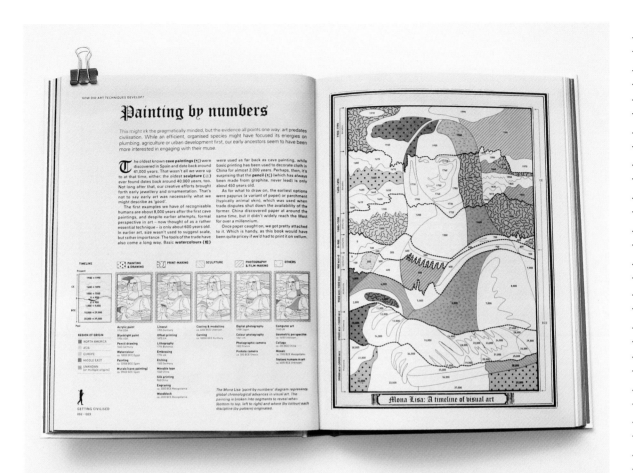

Painting by numbers

This might irk the pragmatically minded, but the evidence all points one way: art predates civilisation. While an efficient, organised species might have focused its energies on plumbing, agriculture or urban development first, our early ancestors seem to have been more interested in engaging with their muse.

The oldest known **cave paintings** (✱) were discovered in Spain and date back around 41,000 years. That wasn't all we were up to at that time, either: the oldest **sculpture** (▲) ever found dates back around 40,000 years, too. Not long after that, our creative efforts brought forth early jewellery and ornamentation. That's not to say early art was necessarily what we might describe as 'good'.

The first examples we have of recognisable humans are about 8,000 years after the first cave paintings, and despite earlier attempts, formal perspective in art – now thought of as a rather essential technique – is only about 600 years old. In earlier art, size wasn't used to suggest scale, but rather importance. The tools of the trade have also come a long way. Basic **watercolours** (▦)

were used as far back as cave painting, while basic printing has been used to decorate cloth in China for almost 2,000 years. Perhaps, then, it's surprising that the **pencil** (✱) (which has always been made from graphite, never lead) is only about 450 years old.

As for what to draw on, the earliest options were papyrus (a variant of paper) or parchment (typically animal skin, which was used when trade disputes shut down the availability of the former. China discovered paper at around the same time, but it didn't widely reach the West for over a millennium.

Once paper caught on, we got pretty attached to it. Which is handy, as this book would have been quite pricey if we'd had to print it on vellum.

TIMELINE

	PAINTING & DRAWING	PRINT-MAKING	SCULPTURE	PHOTOGRAPHY & FILM-MAKING	OTHERS

Present

1750 = 1990
1400 = 1690
1000 = 1500
0 = 600
1,000 = 4,000
10,000 = 29,000
30,000 = 39,000

Past

REGION OF ORIGIN
- NORTH AMERICA
- ASIA
- EUROPE
- MIDDLE EAST
- UNKNOWN (or multiple origins)

Acrylic paint
1934 USA

Blacklight paint
1930s USA

Pencil drawing
1560 Germany

Watercolour
ca. 3000 BCE Egypt

Painting
ca. 3200 BCE Spain

Murals (cave painting)
ca. 39,000 BCE Spain

Linocut
1905 Germany

Offset printing
1875 UK

Lithography
1796 Bohemia

Embossing
ca. 1400 China

Etching
1500 Germany

Movable type
1040 China

Silk printing
960 China

Engraving
ca. 3000 BCE Mesopotamia

Woodblock
ca. 200 BCE Mesopotamia

Casting & modelling
ca. 4000 BCE Unknown

Carving
ca. 38000 BCE Germany

Digital photography
1988 Japan

Colour photography
1861 UK

Photographic camera
1822 France

Pinhole camera
ca. 400 BCE Greece

Computer art
1960s UK

Geometric perspective
ca. 1470 Unknown

Collage
ca. 200 BCE China

Mosaic
ca. 1500 BCE Mesopotamia

Stylised humans in art
ca. 4000 BCE Unknown

The Mona Lisa 'paint by numbers' diagram represents global chronological advances in visual art. The painting is broken into segments to reveal when (bottom to top, left to right) and where (by colour each discipline (by pattern) originated.

Mona Lisa: A timeline of visual art

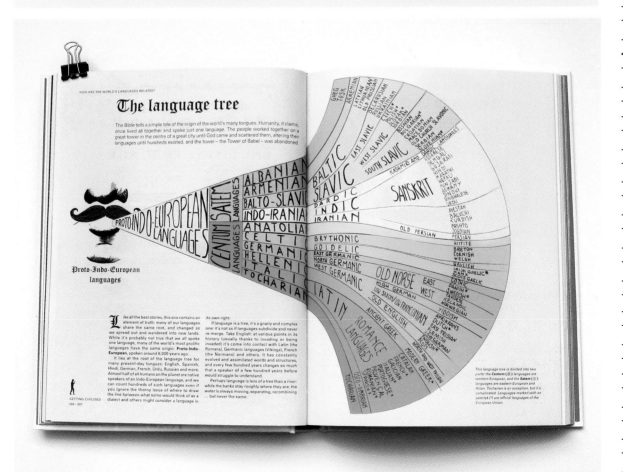

The language tree

The Bible tells a simple tale of the origin of the world's many tongues. Humanity, it claims, once lived all together and spoke just one language. The people worked together on a great tower in the centre of a great city until God came and scattered them, altering their languages until hundreds existed, and the tower – the Tower of Babel – was abandoned.

Proto-Indo-European languages

Like all the best stories, this one contains an element of truth: many of our languages share the same root, and changed as we spread out and wandered into new lands. While it's probably not true that we all spoke one language, many of the world's most prolific languages have the same origin: **Proto-Indo-European**, spoken around 6,000 years ago.

It lies at the root of the language tree for many present-day tongues: English, Spanish, Hindi, German, French, Urdu, Russian and more. Almost half of all humans on the planet are native speakers of an Indo-European language, and we can count hundreds of such languages even if you ignore the thorny issue of where to draw the line between what some would think of as a dialect and others might consider a language in

its own right.

If language is a tree, it's a gnarly and complex one: it's not as if languages subdivide and never re-merge. Take English: at various points in its history (usually thanks to invading or being invaded) it's come into contact with Latin (the Romans), Germanic languages (Vikings), French (the Normans) and others. It has constantly evolved and assimilated words and structures, and every few hundred years changes so much that a speaker of a few hundred years before would struggle to understand.

Perhaps language is less of a tree than a river: while the banks stay roughly where they are, the water is always moving, separating, recombining ... but never the same.

*This language tree is divided into two parts: the **Centum** (▦) languages are western European, and the **Satem** (▦) languages are eastern European and Asian. Tocharian is an exception, but it's complicated. Languages marked with an asterisk (*) are official languages of the European Union.*

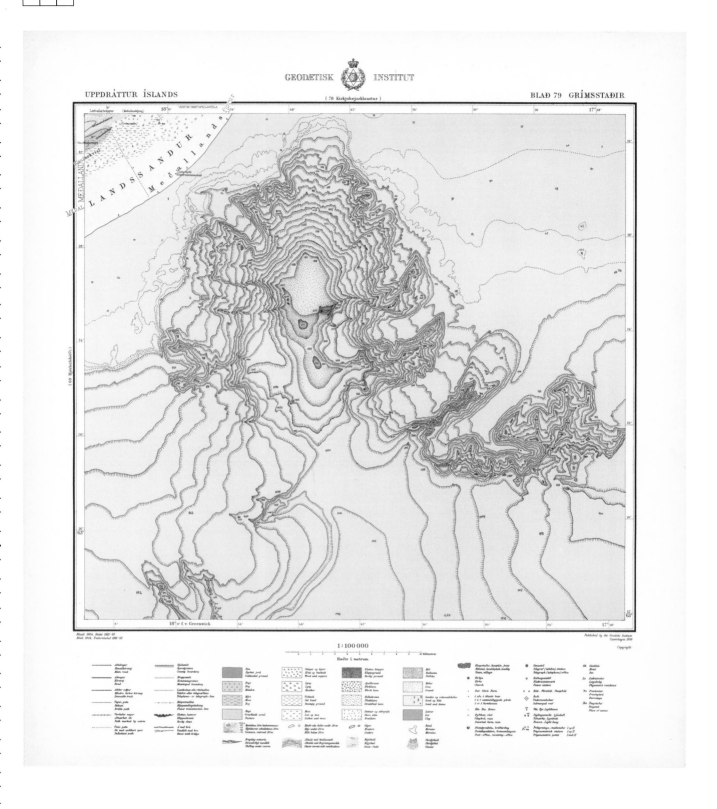

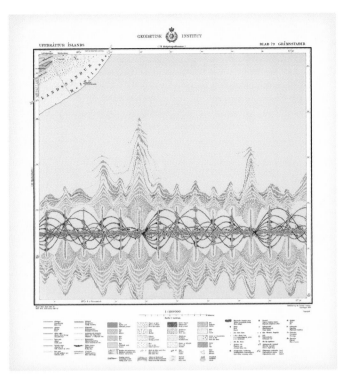

MEDALLANDSSANDUR

Ⓓ Designer: Torgeir Husevaag
Ⓟ Photographer: Vegard Kleven

Intended as a work of art, the designer created this series by drawing on some old maps bought from a second-hand bookstore in Reykjavik, Iceland.

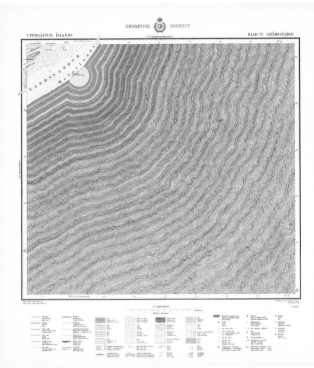

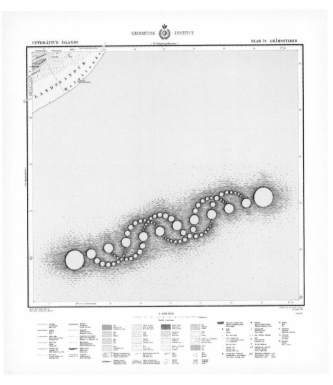

Anger   Joy   Fear   Sadness   Love

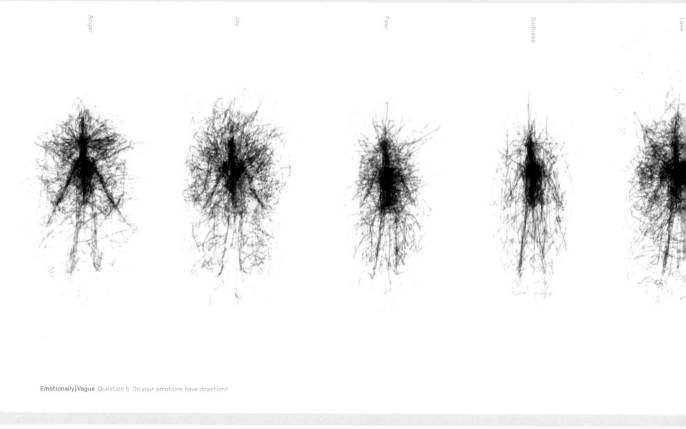

Emotionally}Vague Question 5: Do your emotions have direction?

Anger   Joy   Fear   Sadness   Love

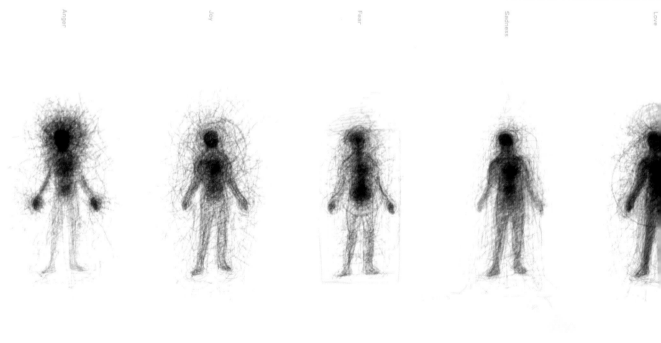

Emotionally}Vague Question 2: How do you feel these emotions in your body?

EMOTIONALLY]VAGUE SOMATIC RESEARCH

Ⓓ Designer: Orlagh O'Brien

250 people of various ages and from different cultures were asked to draw how they feel anger, joy, fear, sadness and love in their bodies. Each drawing was then scanned, registered and layered in Photoshop. The results describe the experience of emotion as a process of changes, and reflect a distinct difference from one emotion to another.

How much area of your body is involved in these emotions?
Please indicate simply with the marker

Anger	Joy	Fear	Sadness	Love

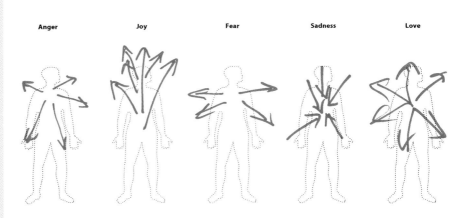

What direction are these emotions?
Please indicate simply with the marker

Anger	Joy	Fear	Sadness	Love

R18 ULTRA CHAIR PUBLIC BETA

Ⓓ Designer: Kram Weisshaar

Exhibited at the *Salon Internazionale del Mobile Milan*, 2012, visitors to the installation were invited to use the R18 chair and view their unique physical impact on it, displayed using a video wall inside the testing booth. Hundreds of industrial sensors integrated into the prototype captured every movement, and simultaneously displayed them through real-time, false colour-force simulation. This exposed and visualized the flow of forces normally hidden from the human eye.

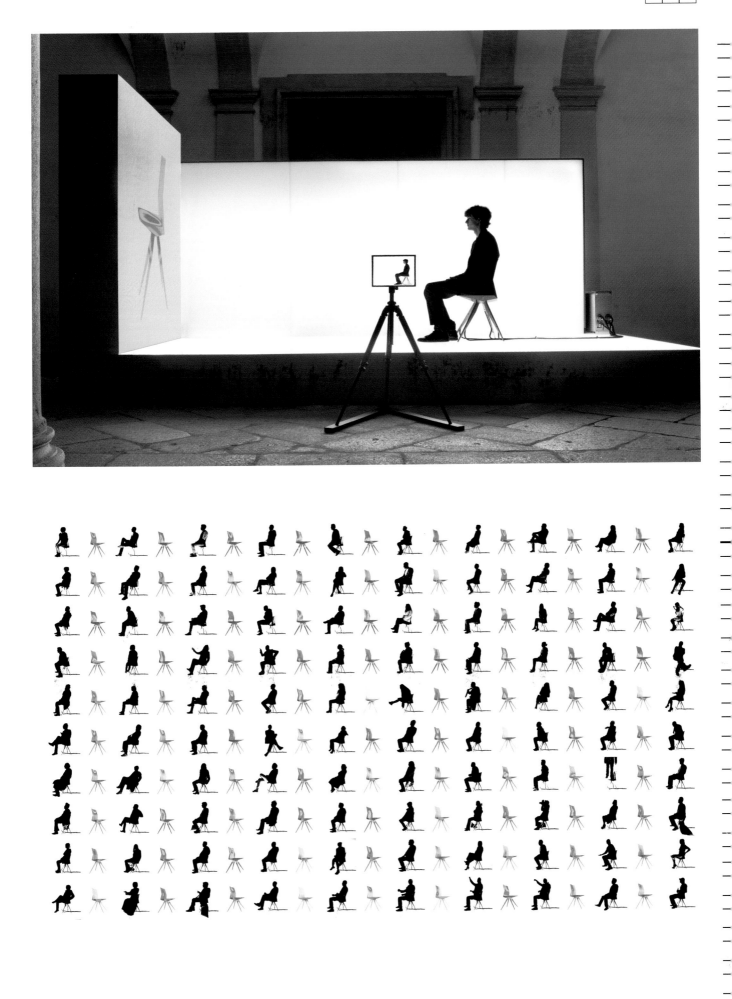

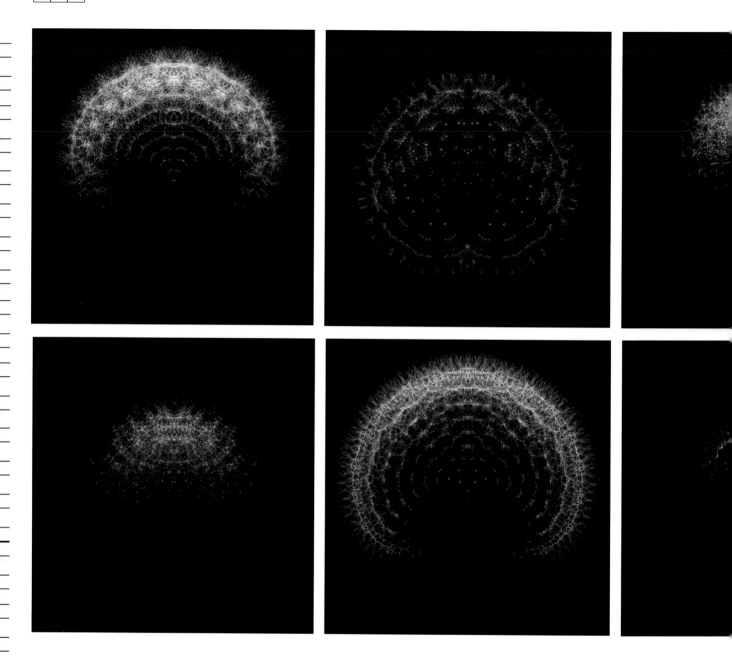

DANDELION MIRROR

Ⓓ Designer: Scottie Chih-Chieh Huang and team
Ⓢ Sponsor: National Science Council

The *Dandelion Mirror* is a physiological measurement device featuring non-contact sensor technology. The biosensor-based unit is able to measure a person's temperature, pulse, respiration and blood pressure, through a webcam, and thereby check their current state of health. The data measured are then visualized, in the shape of a 'growing' virtual plant, which mirrors each user's health.

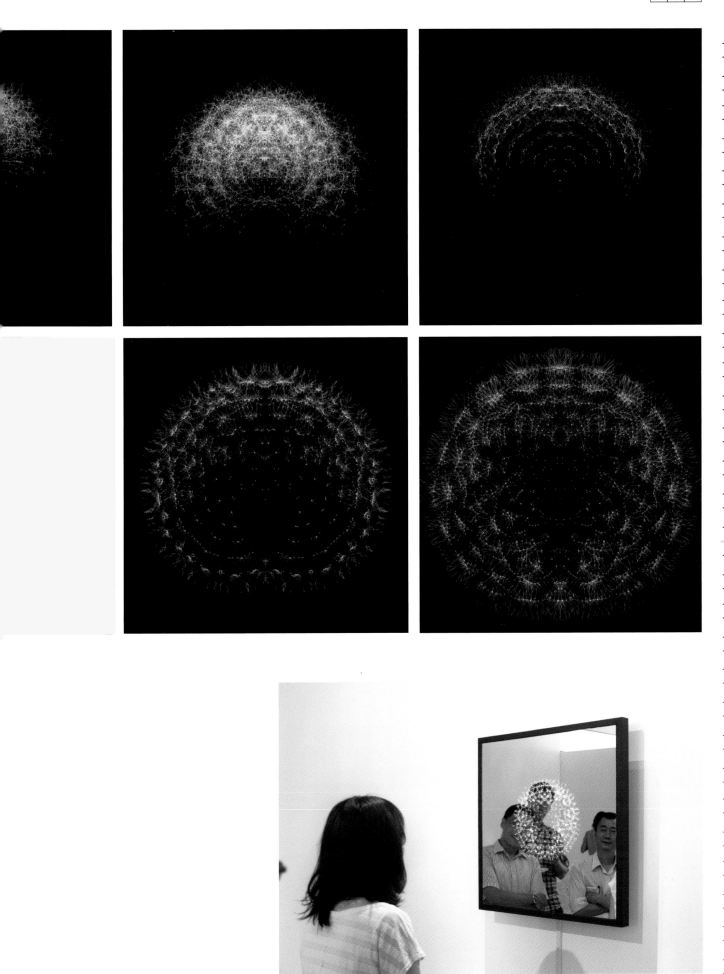

THE CURTAIN I, II AND III

Ⓓ Designer: Namwoo Bae

This was an experiment using raw data. Images were edited with Audacity and the end result was a series of digital still-data images, which, when processed, sound like heartbeats.

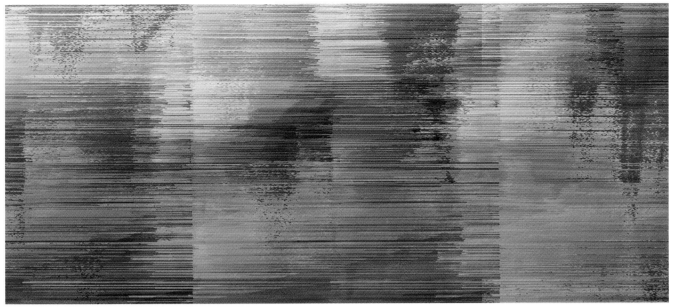

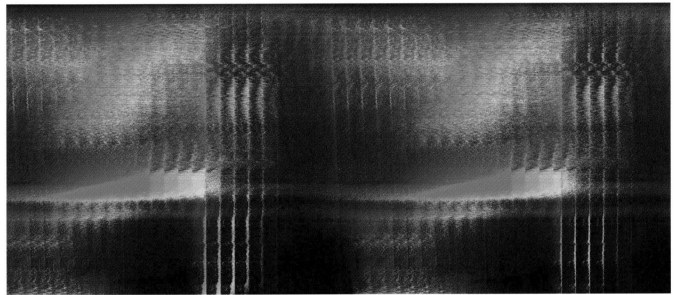

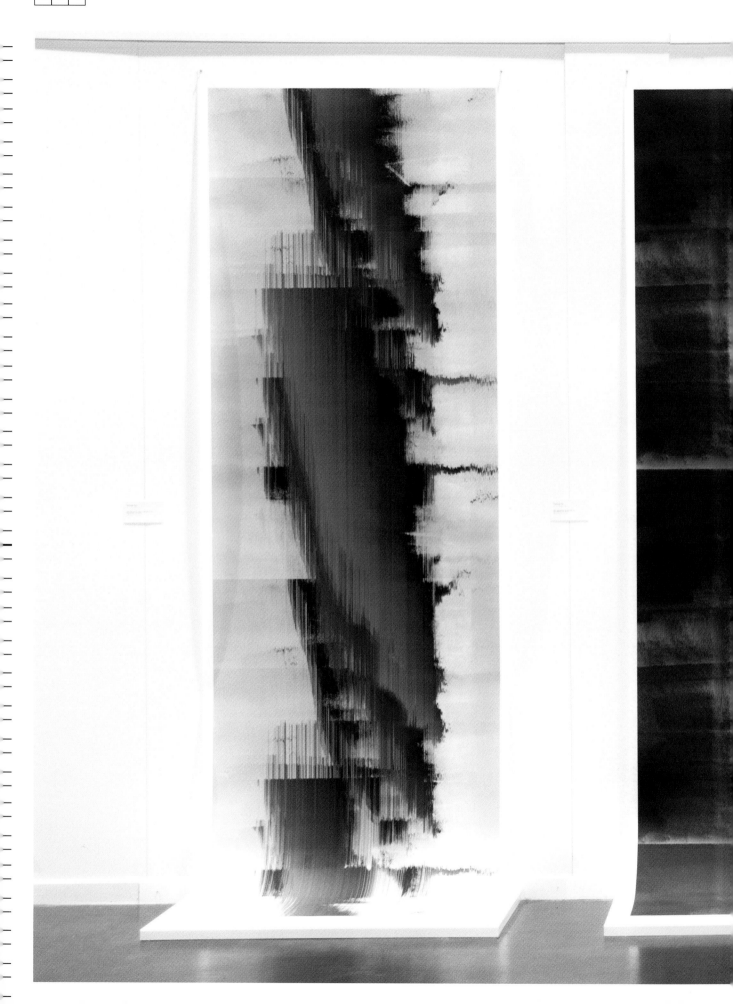

NATIONAL EXCITEMENT

Ⓓ Designer: Raphael Volkmer and Marco Rizzo

More than 50 nations were asked to respond to the following statement: 'Adventure and taking risks are important to have an exciting life'.

As a series of translating objects, *National Excitement* attempts to visualize this worldwide survey about the attitude of different cultures towards risk-taking. To have expressed values and emotions through numbers and graphs would have seemed insincere, overly objective and infeasible. The German tradition of lead pouring was therefore used, to generate physical forms translated from the results of the survey. Pewter is poured into water. Depending on the pouring temperature of the pewter, the resultant form comes out as more extreme or calmer. This visualizes the attitude of the particular country towards the given statement.

GHANA 147g

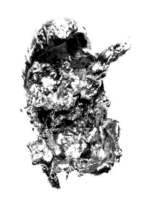

AUSTRALIA 58g

✳
650°C NATIONAL EXCITEMENT 250°C

TRANSLATING OBJECTS

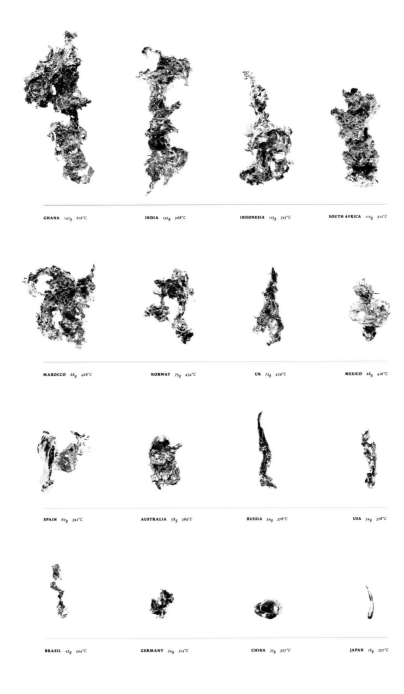

GHANA 147g 616°C   INDIA 132g 568°C   INDONESIA 115g 525°C   SOUTH AFRICA 110g 512°C

MAROCCO 88g 468°C   NORWAY 75g 434°C   UK 73g 429°C   MEXICO 68g 416°C

SPAIN 60g 392°C   AUSTRALIA 58g 389°C   RUSSIA 54g 378°C   USA 54g 378°C

BRASIL 45g 344°C   GERMANY 34g 314°C   CHINA 33g 307°C   JAPAN 16g 257°C

FORM FOLLOWS EXCITEMENT

✳

ADVENTURE AND TAKING RISKS ARE IMPORTANT / TO HAVE AN EXCITING LIFE

WWW.WORLDVALUESSURVEY.ORG

LIFELINE

Ⓓ Designer: Domestic Data Streamers

A volatile and ephemeral piece, which questions our desire to live. It considers the irrefutable end of a journey, what we call our lifeline. The installation comprises a grid of 800 balloons, which mark the point between a person's real age and the age at which they would like to die, contrasting the information against their gender. The coordinates where no one wants to die are represented in white, whereas the ones that represent death are in black.

INDEX
|DESIGNERS|

| A |

ACCURAT

Ⓦ www.accurat.it

Ⓑ *Accurat* is an information design agency. They analyze data and contexts and design analytical tools and visual narratives, which provide awareness, comprehension and engagement. They envision and identify new ways to structure information, revealing and addressing latent needs, desires and opportunities. Basing their methods on the design thinking approach, they specialize in providing their clients with consultation, services and products.

Ⓟ 066-069

ADAM GRIFFITHS

Ⓦ www.ra-bear.com

Ⓑ *Ra Bear* is the brainchild of Adam Griffiths, a designer, graphic artist and art director based in Manchester, UK.

Ⓟ 046-047

ANNA REINBOLD

Ⓦ www.annareinbold.com

Ⓑ Anna Katharina Reinbold is a German designer, based in London. Since completing her degree in information design, at the London College of Communication, in 2013, her work has been short-listed for the *Information is Beautiful* awards.

Her work is about explaining one little piece of the world at a time.

Ⓟ 092-093, 168-169, 173

ANDREAS SCHLEGEL

Ⓦ www.sojamo.de

Ⓑ Andreas Schlegel (b. 1975, Germany) currently lives and works in Singapore. He is interested in creating artefacts, tools and interfaces where technology meets every day life situations, in a playful way. His work is concerned with emerging and open-source technologies for creating audio, visual and physical output, using computational and generative processes. Andreas is currently coordinating the Media Lab at Lasalle College of the Arts, Singapore, where he also lectures in the Media Arts Department.

Ⓟ 150-151

ARCHIE'S PRESS

Ⓦ www.archiespress.com

Ⓑ Archie Archambault is a designer and entrepreneur from Portland, Oregon. He uses urban design (from the Lynchian perspective), philosophy (in the continental tradition), and advertising problem-solving (with the Wieden+Kennedy ethos), to create truthful and compelling ideas about places and cultures. His maps are thoroughly researched, through on-the-ground exploration and discourse with native city-dwellers. His work has been featured on slate.com, *Lonny, Paste*, and in many other places. He is currently touring the United States, making new maps.

Ⓟ 148-149

ART+COM

Ⓦ www.artcom.de

Ⓑ *ART+COM* creates interactive installations, media spaces and architectures. The studio translates themes and content into media formats, staged exhibits, full exhibitions, showrooms, and installations for public spaces. For each respective context, an interdisciplinary team of designers, developers and media technicians devises an original project. Content is always in the foreground, never technology.

The studio has worked at the forefront of the development of new forms of communication based on new media since 1988.

Ⓟ 048-049

| B |

BEETROOT DESIGN GROUP

Ⓦ www.beetroot.gr

Ⓑ *Beetroot Design Group* is a Thessaloniki-based, multi-award-winning communication design office and think tank, which provides design services and solutions for a worldwide clientèle. Their team consists of experts with a wide and diverse range of skills in the creative field. *Beetroot's creative* mission is to discover, develop and utilize the true essence of a brand, product or service, and then grow and expand it, so it can be recognised, appreciated and praised worldwide.

Ⓟ 204-205

BEN WILLERS

Ⓦ lifeindata.site50.net

Ⓑ Ben Willers's background in graphic design and his fascination with statistics lead to his desire to develop his skills as a data visualization and infographic designer. His *Life in Data* website was originally created to share the outcomes of his MA degree, but he has expanded it to include a series of personal projects and freelance work, produced since graduation.

Ⓟ 055, 063

BENJAMIN SCHULTE

Ⓦ www.benjaminschulte.com

Ⓑ Benjamin Schulte is a designer based in Düsseldorf, Germany. He works in different fields of design and specializes in infographics, corporate design, websites and posters. His work has received numerous national and international design awards.

Ⓟ 134-135, 138-139, 192-193

BOWLGRAPHICS

Ⓦ www.bowlgraphics.net

Ⓑ TOKUMA (b. 1973) is founder of the bowlgraphics design studio. Since 2002, bowlgraphics has worked primarily with infographics, but it is also a specialist in graphic design and illustration.

Ⓟ 040, 170-171

BRENDAN DAWES

Ⓦ brendandawes.com

Ⓑ Brendan Dawes is a designer and artist who explores the interaction of objects, people, technology and art. He uses an eclectic mix of digital and analogue materials, for himself and for clients around the globe. While his output takes on many forms, consistent themes of playfulness, curiosity and experimentation run through all his work.

Ⓟ 110-111

BRETT O'MAHONY

Ⓦ www.brettomahony.com

Ⓑ Brett O'Mahony is an Irish designer, currently living and working in London. Her focus is taking clean, minimal approaches to complex communication problems, using typography, photography and illustration as visual tools for branding, editorial, digital and video projects. Brett also uses infographics as a means of taking large volumes of information and putting it into a system that allows the viewer to dip in and out of the information itself, to make the communication of vast information systems clear. In 2013, she was selected for the *Visual Futures – A Design Industry Initiative* award, and her project Disparate Connections was awarded the LIT Collection award.

Ⓟ 086-087, 121

| C |

C2F

Ⓦ www.c2f.ch

Ⓑ C2F is a Swiss communication design studio lead by three partners: Cybu Richli, Fabienne Burri, both founders in 2006, and Dani Klauser. They provide visual communication solutions for clients from the fields of culture and commerce. Their focus is on editorial design, identity and information design. They have received several awards and grants for their projects, for instance, the *Certificate of Typographic Excellence*, awarded by the Type Directors Club, New York; and the ADC Young Guns, from the Art Directors Club, New York.

Ⓟ 036-037

CAREY SPIES

Ⓦ www.careyspies.com

Ⓑ Carey is a graduate of the University of Cincinnati, having studied graphic design. Her passions are information design and gathering data, while teaching herself programming. She has worked in industries ranging from environment and branding, to user interface design, but her true passion is data visualization.

Ⓟ 126-127, 129

CLEVER°FRANKE

Ⓦ www.cleverfranke.com

Ⓑ CLEVER°FRANKE is a multidisciplinary design agency. It works on diverse projects for a range of clients. Its work focuses on visual identities, websites, books, campaigns and data visualization.

Ⓟ 060-061

COLUMN FIVE

Ⓦ columnfivemedia.com

Ⓑ *Column Five* is a creative agency with offices in California and New York City. It builds and distributes powerful visual content, to educate, engage and inspire.

Ⓟ 188-189

| D |

D3

Ⓦ d3.do

Ⓑ *D3* is a digital production company and the home of enthusiasts. It works alongside advertising agencies, seeking contemporary processes to create interactive experiences.

Ⓟ 084-085

DATAVEYES

Ⓦ dataveyes.com

Ⓑ *Dataveyes* translates data into experiences, to share narratives, support new uses, and make sense of a world that is increasingly shaped by algorithms. Its team designs useful, relevant interfaces, through its workflow, which revolves around data and user needs. The members of *Dataveyes*, share

the firm conviction that the upcoming era of rich data and smart objects will disrupt the way data is conventionally used.

Ⓟ 140

DAVIDE MOTTES

Ⓦ www.behance.net/davidemottes

Ⓑ Davide Mottes (b. 1986) is an Italian graphic designer. He studied graphic arts at secondary school and is a communication design graduate from the Polytechnic University of Milan. Since 2009, he has worked for *IL (Intelligence in Lifestyle)*, the monthly news magazine issued by *Il Sole 24 ORE*, the leading finance and economic newspaper in Italy. In 2009 he designed a typeface called *Whale*, a fat italic font. He loves magazines, typography, lettering and pictograms.

Ⓟ 176–177

DEREK KIM

Ⓦ www.networkosaka.com

Ⓑ *Network Osaka* is the design moniker for Derek Kim, an artist and designer living and working in San Francisco, CA. His design experience includes work for world-class brands, such as Nike, Wieden+Kennedy, Target, Dodge, Nokia, Stanford University, Google and Microsoft, among others.

Ⓟ 008-011, 095

DOMESTIC DATA STREAMERS

Ⓦ domesticstreamers.com

Ⓑ *Domestic Data Streamers* is a team of designers and researchers from Barcelona. They create real-time data installations, and interact with people and their surroundings.

Ⓟ 052-053, 98-99, 104-107, 142-145, 200-201, 228-231

DOROTA GRABKOWSKA

Ⓦ www.fanatic-house.com

Ⓑ Fanatic House was founded by a design and architecture duo, Dorota Grabkowska and Kuba Kolec. With previous experience in furniture, lighting and spatial design, the studio is dedicated to creating everyday objects with a strong, iconic character.

Ⓟ 100-103

| F |

FABRIZIO TARUSSIO

Ⓦ www.behance.net/tarumbo

Ⓑ Fabrizio Tarussio is an Italian senior copywriter.

Ⓟ 042–043

FRANCESCO FRANCHI

Ⓦ www.francescofranchi.com

Ⓑ A professional journalist since 2010, Francesco Franchi wears multiple hats, as a designer, art director, lecturer and author.

Ⓟ 016-021, 070-071

| G |

GRUNDINI

Ⓦ www.grundini.com

Ⓑ Peter Grundy and Tilly Northedge met at the Royal College of Art, in the late 70s, where they became interested in a visual communication that explained things, rather than selling them. In 1980 they started a studio, to offer a new, creative type of information design, calling it *Grundy & Northedge*.

Ⓟ 141

| H |

HARGREAVES AND LEVIN

Ⓦ www.hargreavesandlevin.com

Ⓑ Henry Hargreaves and Caitlin Levin met over several glasses of rosé, and quickly recognized their shared passion for all things food, photography, travel and art. Their collaborations have spanned a decade, and they continue to push boundaries, always attempting to find a balance between beauty and far-fetchedness. With food as their preferred medium, they always manage to turn the mundane into works of art.

Ⓟ 202–203

HEY

Ⓦ heystudio.es

Ⓑ A small design studio based in Barcelona, which works mostly in brand identity, illustration and editorial design.

Ⓟ 132, 167

| J |

JAN FRANCISZEK CIEŚLAK

(W) www.behance.net/polkolor

(B) Jan designs websites, interfaces and identities. He also runs a small NGO and a co-op called *Miastodwa*, which brings together designers, architects and sociologists, in common projects that benefit the city.

(P) 038

JAZ PARKINSON

(W) www.jazparkinson.com

(B) Originally from Preston, UK, Jaz Parkinson is currently studying and working as an artist in Sheffield. Motivated by raw data, colour and curiosity, it was out of mere interest that she began extracting raw information from text, a practice she has obsessively expanded, over a wealth of subjects. Her *Colour Signatures* explore notions of objective data visualization, alongside poetic literature and abstract field painting. She believes in the importance of sharing information and of happenstance in art practice. In the future, her ultimate aim is to teach fine art.

(P) 206–207

JOSE DUARTE

(W) www.handmadevisuals.com

(B) Jose Duarte is a Colombian designer, communication teacher and co-founder of Ledfish, an information design company. His work has been published by Gestalten, in *Visual Storytelling*, and has appeared worldwide, in specialist magazines and blogs, including *Owni, Marie Claire, infoaesthetics*, brainpickings and *Co.Design*, among others.

(P) 198-199

JOSH GOWEN

(W) www.joshgowen.co.uk

(B) Josh Gowen is a multidisciplinary, ideas driven, designer, with special interest in editorial design, typography and data visualization. Originally from Great Yarmouth, Norfolk, he is now based in London.

(P) 082-083

JULIAN HRANKOV

(W) www.julianhrankov.com

(B) Julian Hrankov is a Berlin-based designer, specializing in corporate design.

(P) 072-073

| K |

KELLI ANDERSON

(W) www.kellianderson.com

(B) Kelli Anderson is an artist, designer, and tinkerer, who pushes the limits of ordinary materials and formats, by seeking out hidden possibilities in the physical and digital world. Her living/working space houses a 1919 letterpress and 'an assortment of other benevolent contraptions'.

(P) 118-119, 182-183

KIM ALBRECHT

(W) kimalbrecht.com

(B) Kim Albrecht is interested in visualizing complexity.

(P) 88-89, 114, 124-125

KOMBOH

(W) komboh.com

(B) *KOMBOH* is a Canadian design and illustration practice, run by Michael Mateyko and Hans Thiessen. They produce work that stems from a deeply rooted desire for order, conformity and the absurd.

(P) 164-165

KRAM WEISSHAAR

(W) www.kramweisshaar.com

(B) Reed Kram and Clemens Weisshaar are rising stars in the field of design. They have been referred to as being in 'the vanguard of the next generation of digital designers' *(FORM Magazine)* and 'the poster boys of a new breed of designers' (International Herald Tribune). Their office engages in designing spaces, products and media. Key projects include the technology for Prada's Epicenter stores (2001–2004), the seminal *Breeding Tables* (2003); *Hypersky* (2006); and *Outrace* (2010).

(P) 96-97, 218-219

| L |

LETIZIA BOZZOLINI

(W) www.behance.net/letiziabozzolini

(B) Letizia Bozzolini is an Italian art director and graphic designer.

(P) 042-043

LUKE JERRAM

(W) www.lukejerram.com/

(B) Luke Jerram's multidisciplinary practice involves the creation of sculptures, installations, live arts projects and gifts.

Based in the UK, but working internationally, for 17 years, Jerram has created a number of extraordinary art projects, which have excited and inspired people around the globe. He is also visiting senior research fellow at CFPR, University of West of England.

(P) 076-077

L'ESSTUDI STUDIO

(W) www.lesstudi.com

(B) Based in Barcelona, L'esstudi loves design in any of its variations. The team loves colours, vectors and typography.

(P) 178-179

| M |

MARCELO DUHALDE

(W) www.behance.net/marcelodc

(B) Marcelo Duhalde is a Chilean infographic designer, illustrator and visual journalist. With vast experience in newspapers and magazines, since 1996, he has collaborated with several publications in France, Chile, England, Australia, Poland and the US.

(P) 041, 045, 058, 094, 136-137, 172

MARSELIN ACEL WIDJAJA

(W) www.behance.net/acel

(B) Acel Marselin Widjaja is a graphic designer based in Indonesia. A graduate from LASALLE College of the Arts, Singapore, she loves exploring different branches of design, including editorial design, branding, illustration, experimental typography and stop-motion video. Many of her works are underpinned by her deep interest in hands-on crafts and tactile mediums, and every project is treated as a process and unique experience.

(P) 112-113

MAXWELL ROBERTS

(W) www.tubemapcentral.com

(B) Dr Maxwell Roberts is a lecturer in psychology at the University of Essex. He has been researching schematic map design for over ten years, creating original designs that challenge preconceptions, and submitting them to objective usability studies. He has published numerous papers on the psychology of reasoning and intelligence, and his latest book, *Underground Maps Unravelled: Explorations in Information Design*, is available from his website.

(P) 152-153

MGMT. DESIGN

Ⓦ www.mgmtdesign.com

Ⓑ *MGMT* is a graphic design studio based in Brooklyn, New York, whose clients include Al Gore, *The New York Times*, and the Thai royal family. Their data visualization projects have been inspired by their own ideas but have also covered the death toll in Iraq, different methods of time travel, and how to kill a wild pig. They design a lot of books about art and architecture, and a magazine about farming.

Ⓟ 026-031, 039, 166

MICHELE MAURI

Ⓦ www.densitydesign.org

Ⓑ Michele Mauri is a PhD design student, at the Polytechnic University of Milan. He is part of *Density Design Lab*. His main challenge is to make intuitions possible, by using any available visualization tool or coding language. Outside work, he likes climbing, joining any *collaborative projects*, like *Wikipedia* and *OpenStreetMap*, and trying to visualize disparate data sources. He gets excited when he discovers a new visualization method. In 2012, he won the Gold Award in Information Design, at the *Information is Beautiful* Awards.

Ⓟ 059, 062, 064, 090-091

MIGUEL COELHO

Ⓦ www.behance.net/MiguelCoelho

Ⓑ Miguel Coelho has a degree in communication and multimedia design, and has worked in a communication and design office in a theatre. He has been a freelance designer for the past three years, and is now working at an advertising company. His animated short film, which was completed along with three other friends in the last year of his bachelor's degree, has received two awards at two Portuguese film festivals.

Ⓟ 131

MIKELL FINE ILES

Ⓦ cornedbeefandgrits.com

Ⓑ Mikell is a designer based in Brooklyn, NY. While growing up in the culturally diverse Mission district, San Francisco, Mikell became fascinated with the music, murals, and graffiti that engulfed the world surrounding him. Mikell went attended Clark Atlanta University as an undergraduate, and majored in graphic design, because it seemed to merge many of his interests into one industry. Mikell has been working professionally since 2002, beginning with print design. His current position is Director of Design at a digital agency, called Noise. Mikell is excited by new technologies

and is influenced by the graphic design of earlier generations. With each of his projects, Mikell's goal is to create work that is vivid, bold, iconic, daring, and fervent.

Ⓟ 174-175

MINSUN MINI KIM

Ⓦ minsunmini.com

Ⓑ Mini is an interaction designer whose eyes sparkle when she talks about system maps, process maps and data visualization. She is a lead interaction designer at UNICEF Innovation Unit, and works on various projects related to systems, processes and data.

Ⓟ 065

MOÉ TAKEMURA

Ⓦ www.moe-takemura.com

Ⓑ Moé Takemura is an industrial designer. Originally from Japan, she was educated in Sweden.

Ⓟ 184-185

MOODLEY

Ⓦ www.moodley.at

Ⓑ *Moodley* is an owner-led, award-winning strategic design agency, with offices in Vienna and Graz. Since 1999, *Moodley* has worked with its customers to develop corporate and product brands that live, breathe and grow. *Moodley* believes their key contribution is to analyze complex requirements and develop simple, smart solutions, with emotional appeal, whether this be for a corporate startup, product launch or brand positioning. The team currently consists of about 60 employees, from seven different countries.

Ⓟ 196-197

MOT

Ⓦ motstudio.com

Ⓑ *Mot*, a multi-disciplinary design studio based in Barcelona, was founded by Laia Clos, in 2006. Working with a variety of clients, its projects range from small private commissions to public corporate identities and large publications. The studio's mission is to treat each project with the same care and attentiveness, in order to produce sensitively finished and functional design. They take pleasure in developing concept-driven work and pay great attention to detail and craft.

Ⓟ 210-211

| N |

NAMWOO BAE

Ⓦ www.namwoobae.com

Ⓑ Namwoo Bae, who lives and works in Seoul, South Korea, is an interdisciplinary artist. He earned his MFA in digital and media design at the Rhode Island School of Design. New media and technology are important in his work because they often give him chances to go beyond digital media. As an artist and educator, his goal is to build a foundation that involves processing and customizing digital media, as an art medium for studio practice and artistic expression.

Ⓟ 222-225

NICEWORK

Ⓦ www.iamalexandra.com

Ⓑ NICEWORK is a graphic and information design studio. Run by *iamalexandra*, the studio specializes in creating communication materials for charities and non-profit organizations.

Ⓟ 133

NICOLE LYNDAL SMITH

Ⓦ www.nicolyn.com.au

Ⓑ Nicole Lyndal Smith is a graphic designer from Canberra, Australia, currently based in Amsterdam. She has a bachelor of graphic design degree from the University of Canberra, where she first became interested in data visualization. Since then, she has worked as an event production coordinator, at Canberra Stadium, and as a freelance graphic designer, throughout Australia and Europe.

Ⓟ 054

NIELS GROENEVELD

Ⓦ www.nielsgroeneveld.nl

Ⓑ Dutch architect Niels Groeneveld likes to design from a carpenter's perspective. By building some of his designs with his own hands, he wants to stay close to material and detail. Creating healthy environments using ecological materials is one of his priorities.

Ⓟ 194-195

NOBUTAKA AOZAKI

Ⓦ www.nobutakaaozaki.com

Ⓑ Nobutaka Aozaki is a New York-based artist, born in Japan. His work plays with everyday interactions, to explore the relationships between artistic and non-artistic labour, public space and subjective experience, and art and commodity. He holds an MFA, from Hunter College, NY. His recent exhibitions include *Queens International,*

2013; Queens Museum of Art, New York, 2013; *C12 Emerging Artist Fellowship Exhibition*, Marianne Boesky Gallery, New York, 2013; *New Wight Biennale, 2012*; University of California, Los Angeles, 2012; and *Japanese Artists In New York*, Marunouchi House, Tokyo, Japan, 2013. He was awarded the *Artist Files* grant, by *A Blade of Grass*, 2013; and received the *C12 Emerging Artist Award*, from Hunter College, 2012.

Ⓟ 154-155

| O |

ORLAGH O'BRIEN

Ⓦ www.orlaghobrien.com

Ⓑ Orlagh O'Brien is a graphic designer with over thirteen years' experience in branding, corporate presentations, annual reports and promotion, for multinational and individual clients, such as Vodafone, Safefood, Tourism Ireland, Diageo, Brown Thomas, Áras an Úachtaráin, Bulmers and Toyota. Orlagh has worked for established agencies in Dublin, London and Sydney (Designworks, Language, Landor, Maxwell Rogers, and Heywood Innovation), and was part of the team that won the top Irish design award in 2002: the *ICAD Gold Bell*.

Ⓟ 032-033, 216-217

| P |

PATRICK KOCHLIK

Ⓦ www.patrickkochlik.de

Ⓑ Patrick Kochlik (b. 1977, Germany) is a Berlin-based designer with a profound interest in the aesthetics of natural, social and technological systems and processes.

He oscillates between freelance collaborations, his interaction design studio, *Syntop*, and a position as a visiting professor at Berlin University of the Arts.

Ⓟ 150-151

PETER ØRNTOFT

Ⓦ www.peterorntoft.com/

Ⓑ Peter Ørntoft is a designer in the field of visual communication. He has a BA from the University of the Arts London, and an MA from the Danish Design School. Peter usually takes a contextual and research-based approach to traditional fields of visual communication. By using this approach, his projects are able to contain multiple layers, and tell more stories about the subject or client in question.

Ⓟ 022-025

| R |

RAPHAEL VOLKMER

Ⓦ www.raphaelvolkmer.com

Ⓑ Raphael Volkmer is a hybrid designer, currently studying visual communication and product design at the Free University of Bozen-Bolzano, Italy. Besides working for a graphic design agency in Munich and studying in Bolzano, he is continuously involved in self-initiated and collaborative projects, within the field of conceptual communication design. He has previously worked in Amsterdam, with Jolan van der Weil, on a range of projects, and studied in Jerusalem, at the Bezalel Academy of Arts and Design.

Ⓟ 226-227

REINHARDT MATTHYSEN

Ⓦ www.behance.net/reinhardtmatthysen

Ⓑ Reinhardt Matthysen is currently studying information design, at the University of Pretoria. Without a background in art or design, he considers himself lucky to have had the opportunity to do what he loves.

Ⓟ 116-117

RELAJAELCOCO

Ⓦ www.relajaelcoco.com

Ⓑ Relajaelcoco is a laid-back graphic design studio, based in Madrid. Their purpose is to spread graphic design all over the world, and improve talent and knowledge.

Ⓟ 012-015, 162-163, 190-191

ROMUALDO FAURA

Ⓦ www.romualdofaura.com

Ⓑ Romualdo currently works as a freelance graphic designer in Murcia, Spain, doing projects for his clients as well as for other design studios in Spain, France, Lebanon and the USA. His background is focused on corporate branding, icon design, illustration and editorial projects. He has taught graphic design at various universities and design schools in Mexico, Guatemala and Spain. He tries to use limited colours, flat shapes, and minimal information, claiming simplicity as an approach to responsible and sustainable design.

Ⓟ 158-161

RUSLAN ENIKEEV

Ⓦ internet-map.net, disease-map.net

Ⓑ Creator of *The Internet Map* (visited by more that half a million people without any advertising), Ruslan has worked at The Central R&D Institute of Robotics and Technical Cybernetics, and for the Apac Sale

Group, which has branches in Russia and Singapore. He is currently head of the Singapore IT Team.

Ⓟ 146-147

RYAN MACEACHERN

Ⓦ www.be.net/ryanmac

Ⓑ Ryan MacEachern is a Bristol-based designer, currently in his 3rd year of university, studying BA (Hons) in graphic design, at the University of the West of England (UWE). He specializes primarily in print- and type-based design, but is also known for his motion and poster design work.

Ⓟ 180-181

| S |

SARA PICCOLOMINI

Ⓦ sarapiccolomini.com

Ⓑ Sara Piccolomini is a communication designer, based in Milan, Italy, with a focus on information design and data visualization. She graduated in communication design at the Polytechnic University of Milan, 2012.

She is currently interning at Visual Agency, and freelances on multidisciplinary projects concerning graphic and web design.

Ⓟ 115

SCOTTIE HUANG

Ⓦ www.shkinetic.com

Ⓑ Scottie Chih-Chieh Huang is a media artist, and assistant professor at the Chung Hua University (CHU) School of Architecture and Design (Hsinchu, TW). He has taught computer graphics, interactive techniques and multimedia tools for design applications, in the Department of Industrial Design, since it was founded, in 2012. He founded and directs the Biologically Inspired Objects (BIO) research laboratory and the SDAID (Studio of Digital Art and Innovative Design). He has served as Director of the Innovation and Creativity Center (ICC), at the Office of Research and Development (ORD), at CHU since 2014.

His works have been showcased at ISEA, 2014; IF *Design Award*, 2014; *Red Dot Award*, 2013; *Avignon Off Festival*, 2013; *Holland Animation Film Festival*, 2013; SIGGRAPH Asia art gallery, 2012; and LEONARDO/ SIGGRAPH art gallery, 2009.

Ⓟ 220-221

SEVERINO RIBECCA

Ⓦ www.rinodesign.co.uk

Ⓑ Severino Ribecca is a graphic designer, whose main interest lies in information design and data visualization. He enjoys making difficult systems easier to read and

ACKNOWLEDGEMENTS

We would like to extend our gratitude to the artists and designers who have contributed generously to this publication. We are also grateful to those whose names are not mentioned in the credits, but who have provided their assistance and support. Last but not least, thanks goes to the people who put this book together. It would not have been possible without your innovation and creativity.

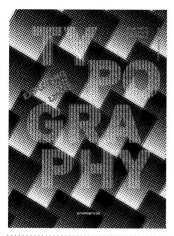

TYPOGRAPHY
Graphic Design Elements
Exploring the limits

Editor: Wang Shaoqiang

ISBN: 978-84-16504-48-0

This book brings together the most creative typography projects from all over the world. Whether they are used in branding, advertising, packaging or other creative designs, the typefaces featured here have the power to catch the eye and inspire the mind.

DESIGN FOR SCREEN
Graphic Design Solutions for Great User Experiences

Editor: Wang Shaoqiang

ISBN: 978-84-16504-56-5

This title explores from the designer's perspective how essential elements produce functionality and elegance for websites and mobile applications. This selection encompasses over one hundred refreshing cases, and it includes insider insights from practicing designers.

OPTICAL ILLUSIONS
Graphic Design Elements

Editor: Wang Shaoqiang

ISBN: 978-84-16504-50-3

This showcase of the most intriguing and eye-deceiving graphic designs includes waves and mazes formed by simple lines, overlapping images, 3D effects, and anamorphic spatial experiences. The techniques featured reveal how basic elements can have an impressive visual impact.

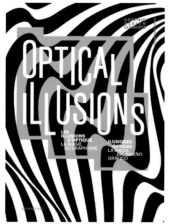

PLAYFUL GRAPHICS
Graphic Design That Surprises

Editor: Wang Shaoqiang

ISBN: 978-84-15967-74-3

Interactivity and enjoyment allow graphic designers to encourage audiences to connect with their works. By triggering all five of our senses through a diverse range of interactive and playful ideas, designers can turn the task of communicating into a fun and surprising experience.

SHAPES
Graphic Design Elements
Geometric Forms in Graphic Design

Editor: Wang Shaoqiang

ISBN: 978-84-16504-54-1

This book reveals how the world's most innovative design agencies continually reinvent geometric forms to create new design philosophies and trends. It is an essential resource for designers who are eager to incorporate new approaches to shapes into their creative repertoire.

SIMPLICITY
Graphic Design Elements
The Charm of Minimalism

Editor: Wang Shaoqiang

ISBN: 978-84-16504-52-7

Simplicity collects over one hundred works completed with limited elements—mainly pictographs, numbers, and letters—by globally renowned graphic designers. It aims to serve as an indispensable guide for designers who want to achieve a sophisticated yet simple style.

DESIGNING YOUR IDENTITY
Stationery Design

Editor: Wang Shaoqiang

ISBN: 978-84-15967-44-6

How can stationery sets communicate an organization's core values, philosophy and concept as well as stand out from the competition? With its abundant creative stationery designs, this title guides you through how to select the perfect color, typography and other design elements.

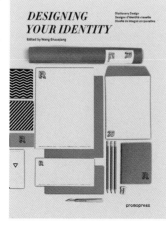

500 GREETINGS
Invitations, Greetings Cards, Postcards, & Self-promotion Material

Editor: David Lorente / Claudia Parra

ISBN: 978-84-15967-71-2

This book offers a look into the universe of visual personal communication and identity. Through the works of a selection of artists, designers and illustrators, this book explores styles and techniques. *500 Greetings* is a compendium of projects by some of the most talented minds.

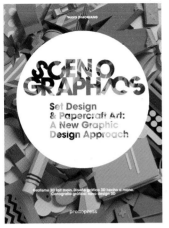

SCENOGRAPHICS
Set Design & Papercraft Art: A New Graphic Design Approach

Editor: Wang Shaoqiang

ISBN: 978-84-15967-31-6

Set design is more than prop building. It is a form of reimagining and recreating that allow us to visualize our ideas and transforms the ordinary into the extraordinary. This volume features a variety of playful projects that will inspire designers and artists to create innovative works.

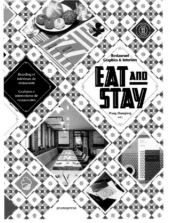

EAT & STAY
Restaurant Graphics & Interiors

Editor: Wang Shaoqiang

ISBN: 978-84-16504-09-1

From menu design and branding to signage design and interiors, *Eat & Stay* features remarkable branding solutions used by restaurants, cafés, bars, sweet shops and groceries from all over the world. It is an innovative and powerful source of inspiration.

NEW SIGNAGE DESIGN
Connecting People & Spaces

Editor: Wang Shaoqiang

ISBN: 978-84-15967-27-9

This book collects the latest and freshest signage and wayfinding designs from all over the world. These unique designs are all tailor-made for specific spaces, including schools, hotels, shopping malls, libraries, parking garages and medical facilities.

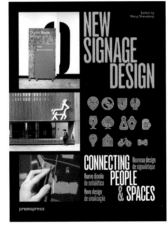

EXHIBITION ART
Graphics and Space Design

Editor: Wang Shaoqiang

ISBN: 978-84-16504-49-7

Exhibition Art collects almost one hundred of the most creative exhibition designs, including fascinating space designs and sophisticated graphic designs. It will surely serve as a significant guide for exhibition designers, graphic designers, curators and event organizers.

UNPACK ME AGAIN!
Packaging meets creativity

Editor: Wang Shaoqiang

ISBN: 978-84-16504-53-4

This book examines fabulous packaging designs made from a variety of materials such as paper, plastic, wood, steel, and glass. This book reveals how designers bring a package to life through creative graphic and structural design.

NEW STRUCTURAL PACKAGING /GOLD/

Author: Josep M. Garrofé

ISBN: 978-84-15967-07-1

The 125 stunning and innovative designs contained in this book reveal the possibilities this area of design offers. This book reveals the talent and ingenuity that go hand-in-hand with a strict work ethic and zeal for perfection. All the projects are available online for free.

MONOCHROME GRAPHICS
Maximum creativity within a minimum budget

Editor: Ling Shijian

ISBN: 978-84-15967-30-9

The use of black, white, and gray in the design process helps to narrow the focus of the design itself, enabling viewers to grasp its essence. This title showcases graphic designs that are based on these three colors, and additionally provides designers' perspectives on the optimum use of monochrome.

ANIMALS HANDMADE ILLUSTRATION
850 Vintage Drawings

Author: Joan Escandell

ISBN: 978-84-16504-19-0

This volume contains more than 850 illustrations of many different species of animals, from insects and sea creatures to the largest and most unusual mammals. All the illustrations can be downloaded for free.